W9-ASC-313

GREY EMINENCE

FATHER JOSEPH OF PARIS

Engraving by Michel Lasne

GREY EMINENCE

A Study in Religion and Politics

by

Aldous Huxley

Aldous Leonard Huxley

GREENWOOD PRESS, PUBLISHERS
WESTPORT, CONNECTICUT

Library of Congress Cataloging in Publication Data

Huxley, Aldous Leonard, 1894-1963.
Grey eminence.

Reprint of the ed. published by Harper, New York.
Bibliography: p.
Includes index.
1. Le Clerc du Tremblay, François, 1577-1638. I. Title.
DC123.9.L5H8 1975 944'.032'0924 [B] 74-5555
ISBN 0-8371-7508-9

Originally published in 1941 by Harper & Brothers Publishers, New York

Reprinted in 1975 by Greenwood Press,
a division of Williamhouse-Regency Inc.

Library of Congress Catalog Card Number 74-5555

ISBN 0-8371-7508-9

Printed in the United States of America

Contents

List of Illustrations

GREY EMINENCE

I

On the Road to Rome

THE friar had kilted up his habit, and his bare legs were muddy to the knees. After the spring rains, the road was like a swamp. It had been like a lime kiln, he reflected, last time he walked this way. He recalled the poem he had written on another of his journeys.

Quand au plus chaud du jour l'ardente canicule
Fait de l'air un fourneau,
Des climats basanés mon pied franc ne recule,
Quoy que je coule en eau.[1]

That summer of 1618, when the three of them had taken the road for Spain! Poor Brother Zeno of Guingamp had died of sunstroke at Toulouse. And a week later, near Burgos, Father Romanus had fallen sick with dysentery. In three days it was all over. He had limped into Madrid alone. And alone he was now to limp into Rome. For Father Angelus had had to be left behind with the Capuchins of Viterbo, too sick of the ague to walk another step. God bring him soon to health again!

Ni des Alpes neigeux, ni des hauts Pirénées
Le front audacieux
N'a pu borner le cours de mes grandes journées,
Qui tendent jusqu'aux cieux.[2]

[1] When, at day's hottest hour, the burning Dog Star makes a furnace of the air, my roving feet affront the swarthy regions of the earth, though I be streaming with sweat.

[2] The aspiring crests of the snowy Alps and Pyrenees have not sufficed to limit my long marches that aim at the very heavens.

Cher Seigneur, si ta main m'enfonça la blessure
De ce perçant dessein,
J'ay droit de te montrer ma tendre meurtrissure
Et descouvrir mon sein.[3]

"La blessure de ce perçant dessein," he repeated to himself. The phrase was particularly felicitous. Almost Latin in its pregnancy—like one of those phrases of Prudentius. . . .

The Capuchin sighed profoundly. That wound, he reflected, was still open, and, goaded by the barb of God's piercing design, he was still hurrying, at the rate of fifteen leagues a day, across the face of Europe. When would that design be carried into execution? When would it be granted to another Godefroy of Bouillon to storm Jerusalem? Not yet awhile, to all appearances—not till the wars were over, not till the House of Austria should be humbled and France grow strong enough to lead the nations on the new Crusade. How long, Oh Lord, how long?

He sighed again, and the sadness of his thoughts was reflected upon his face. It was the face of a man in middle life, weathered, gaunt with self-inflicted hardship, lined and worn with the incessant labour of the mind. Beneath the broad, intellectual forehead, the prominent blue eyes were widely opened, almost staring. The nose was powerfully aquiline. Long and unkempt, a reddish beard already grizzled, covered his cheeks and chin; but the full-lipped, resolute mouth suggested a corresponding firmness of the jaw beneath. It was the face of a strong man,

[3] Dear Lord, if it is Thy hand which has penetrated me with the wound of this piercing design, I have the right to show Thee my tender hurt and to unveil my breast.

a man of firm will and powerful intelligence; a man also, under the second nature imposed by a quarter-century of the religious life, of powerful passions and a fierce intensity of feeling.

Barefooted—for he had taken off his sandals and was carrying them in his hand—he walked on through the mud, engrossed in his melancholy thoughts. Then, recollecting himself, he suddenly realized what he was doing. Who was *he* to criticize God's ways? His sadness was a recrimination against Providence, a flying in the face of that divine will, to obey which was the only purpose of his life. And it must be obeyed without reluctance, wholeheartedly, joyfully. To be sad was a sin and, as such, an obstacle between his soul and God. He halted and for more than a minute stood there in the road, covering his face with his hands. His lips moved; he was praying to be forgiven.

When he walked on, it was in a contrite mood. The natural man, he was thinking, the old Adam—what a sleepless hostility to God one carried about in the depths of one's own mind and body! What a fixed resolve to sin! And what resourcefulness in the art of sinning, what skill, when one temptation had been overcome, in discovering another and more subtle evil to surrender to! There was no remedy but in perpetual vigilance. Sentinels for ever on guard against the stratagems of the enemy. *Timeo Danaos et dona ferentes.* But there was also the great ally—the Divine friend, without whose aid the garrison must infallibly be destroyed. Oh, ask him in! Open the gates! Sweep clean the streets and garnish the town with flowers!

The sun came out from behind the clouds. The Capuchin looked up and, from its position in the sky, calculated that the time must be a little after two o'clock. Rome was still three leagues away. There was no time to stop. He would have to practise his annihilation in the Essential Will as he walked. Well, it would not be the first time.

He repeated the Lord's Prayer slowly and aloud; then addressed himself to the opening phase of his exercise, the act of pure intention. To do the will of God, the exterior will, the interior will, the essential will. To do it for the sake of God alone, and without reference to what he himself desired, or hoped, or might gain in this world or the next. . . . To annihilate himself in all he thought and felt and did, so that there should be nothing left but the instrument of God's will and a soul united by God's grace with that divine substance, which was identical with the divine, essential will. He held his mind unwaveringly upon that resolution, while he walked a furlong or more. Then words came once again. "To expose myself to God, to prepare my soul for his coming, watchfully and with reverence. To turn myself, naked of every other design, every other feeling and thought and memory, towards such radiance of divine love and knowledge as God may vouchsafe to give. And even if he should vouchsafe to give me nothing, even if it should be his will to leave me without light or consolation, to turn towards him none the less with thankfulness and in perfect faith. *Qui adhaeret Deo, unus spiritus est.*"[4]

To adhere, he repeated, to adhere. . . .

[4] He who cleaves to God, is one spirit with God.

From the act of pure intention he passed to that of adoration and humility. "God for his own sake and not with any thought of myself." For what was this self of his? A nothing—but an active nothing, capable of sin and therefore capable of cutting itself off from the All. An active nothing that had to be annihilated into passive nothingness, if God's will was to be done.

He had worked hard to annihilate that active nothing, and God in his great mercy had granted him many favours—strength to control at least the grosser impulses of nature, sensible consolations, visions and revelations, access at moments to the outskirts of the divine presence. But for all that his active nothingness still persisted; he was still capable of negligence and imperfection, even of such downright wickedness as complacency in the recollection of his own work and God's past favours. The Old Adam knew how to make use even of the soul's efforts to annihilate the Old Adam and, by taking pride in those efforts, was able to undo their results and strengthen his own resistance to God. Nay, the very graces of God could be turned, unless the soul was unremittingly on guard, into a stumbling block and a source of grievous sins and imperfection. The Son of God, the incarnate source of all grace—how had *he* proclaimed his divinity? By humility, by adoration and love of God.

"Love, love, love," the Capuchin repeated, "humility and love, humility of the nothing before the all, love and adoration of the all by the nothing, love . . ."

Horny like a savage's from their incessant marching and counter-marching across the face of Europe, his bare feet splashed through the puddles, stepped unflinching on the stones, treading the beat of the reiterated words. "Love, Christ's love, love . . ." It was said that the Cardinal Nephew had been offended by the behavior of His Catholic Majesty's ambassador. "Christ's love, Christ's love . . ." These Spaniards were forever undoing themselves by their stupid arrogance. "Love, love, love . . ." Well, so much the better for France. All at once he perceived that the words he was still repeating to himself had become separated from his thoughts, that the flame he had been cherishing was extinguished.

"Martha, Martha, thou art careful and troubled about many things; but one thing is needful." He excluded the Cardinal Nephew and the Spanish ambassador, and re-established the connection between his thoughts and his words. "Love, love, love, Christ's love . . ." The little flame was alight again. He kept it burning unwaveringly while he walked a quarter of a mile. Then it was time to pass on to operation—the repudiation of distracting thoughts and the resolve to banish them from the mind.

The Cardinal Nephew and the Spanish ambassador . . . . More than five and twenty years had passed since Father Benet of Canfield had taught him how to pray. More than five and twenty years—and his mind was not yet completely under control, the devils of distraction still had power, sometimes, to intrude even into the sanctuary of orison. There was no final remedy but the grace of God. Meanwhile, one could only resolve to banish the distracting thoughts each time they found their way past the defences. If one persisted in the struggle, if one worked hard and patiently, it would be counted, no doubt, as a merit. God knew one's weaknesses and the efforts one made to overcome them.

Headed in the opposite direction, a train of pack animals from the City jingled slowly past him. The muleteers interrupted their talk for a moment and respectfully doffed their hats. Half blind, as he was, with too much straining over books and documents, the friar saw their gesture as a blur of movement against the sky. Recognizing its intention, he raised a hand in blessing; then went back once again to his orison.

In the form of prayer he was accustomed to use, an act of discursive meditation succeeded the preparatory exercises. Today the perfection he had chosen as his theme was love. Following the established order of his discourse, he addressed himself first of all to the consideration of God as the source of love. *Pater noster, qui es in coelo. Qui* ES *in coelo.* God, the eternal and Infinite Being. But when a finite being abandoned itself to the Infinite Being, Infinite Being was apprehended as Love. Thus, Infinite Being was at the same time a loving Father—but of children so rebellious and ungrateful that they were for ever doing all in their power to shut themselves out from his love. They shut themselves out from his love and, by that act, cut themselves off from their own happiness and salvation.

"All manner of virtue and goodness," the Capuchin repeated in a whisper, "and even that Eternal Good which is God Himself, can never make a man virtuous, good, or happy, so long as it is outside the soul."

He raised his head for a moment. In the blue gap of rain-washed sky between the clouds, the sun was gloriously bright. But if one chose to drop one's eyelids against the light, so—why, then one was blind, one walked in darkness. God was love; but the fact could be fully known only to one who himself loved God.

This thought served as a bridge between the first stage of his meditation and the second, between God as the source of love and his own shortcomings as a lover of God.

He loved God insufficiently because he was insufficiently detached from the world of creatures in which he had to do his work. *Factus est in pace locus ejus.*[5] God can be perfectly loved only by a heart that has been sanctified by the divine presence; and God is present only in a heart at peace. He is excluded by anxiety, even when that anxiety is a concern about the works of God. God's work must be done; but if it is not done in the peace of perfect detachment, it will take the soul away from God. He himself had come nearest to that perfect detachment in the days when he had worked at preaching and spiritual instruction. But now God had called him to these more difficult tasks in the world of great events, and the peace of detachment had become increasingly difficult of achievement. To dwell in the essential will of God while one was negotiating with the Duke of Lerma, say, or the Prince of Condé—that was hard indeed. And yet those negotiations had to be undertaken; they were a duty, and to do them was God's exterior will. There could be no shrinking from such tasks. If peace eluded him while he undertook them, it was because of his own weakness and imperfection. That highest degree of orison—the active annihilation of self and all creatures in the essential will of God—was still beyond him. There was no remedy but God's grace, and no way to earn God's grace but through constant prayer, constant humility, con-

[5] In peace is his place established.

stant love. Only so could God's kingdom come in him, God's will be done.

It was time to pass to the third phase of his meditation—reflection on the Saviour's acts and sufferings as related to the love of God. *Fiat voluntas tua.*[6] Once in the world's history God's will had been done, fully and completely; for God had been loved and worshipped by one who, being himself divine, was able to give a devotion commensurate with its object.

The image of Calvary rose up before the friar's mind—the image that had haunted him ever since, as a tiny child, he had first been told of what wicked men had done to Jesus. He held the picture in his imagination, and it was more real, more vivid than what he actually saw of the road at his feet. "Father forgive them, for they know not what they do." Pity and love and adoration suffused his whole being, as with a sensible warmth that was at the same time a kind of pain. Deliberately, he averted the eyes of his mind. The time had not yet come for such an act of affection and will. He had still to consider, discursively, the ends for which the Saviour had thus suffered. He thought of the world's sins, his own among them, and how he had helped to hew the cross and forge the nails, to plait the scourge and the crown of thorns, to whet the spear and dig the sepulchre. And yet, in spite of it, the Saviour loved him and, loving, had suffered, suffered, suffered. Had suffered that the price of Adam's sin might be paid. Had suffered that, through his example, Adam's children might learn how to conquer evil in themselves. "Her sins, which are many, are forgiven; for she loved much." Loving, one was forgiven; forgiven, one became

[6] Thy will be done.

capable of forgiving; forgiving, one could open one's soul to God; opening one's soul to God, one could love yet more intensely; and so the soul could climb a little higher on the ascending spiral that led towards perfect union. *Ama, et fac quod vis.*[7]

"Let there be love," he repeated, modulating his orison out of Meditation into Affection, transforming it from an act of the discursive intellect into an act of loving, self-renouncing will. "Let there be love." And taking his own lovelessness, taking the malignantly active nothing that was himself, he offered it up as a sacrifice, as a burnt offering to be consumed in the fire of God's love.

Lose life to save it. Die, that life may be hid with Christ in God. Die, die, die. Die on the cross of mortification, die in the continuous and voluntary self-noughting of passive and active annihilation.

Die, die, die, die . . . In an act of pure contrition he begged God's forgiveness for being still himself, Joseph of Paris, and not yet wholly the instrument of the divine will, at peace even in action, detached even in the turmoil of business.

Die, help me to die, help me to love so that I may be helped to die. He laid lovelessness upon an inward altar and prayed that it might be consumed, prayed that from its ashes might arise a new birth of love.

Trotting up from behind, came a young horseman, gaily plumed, with a silver-studded saddle and the damascened butts of two fine pistols in his holsters. He interrupted his whistling to shout a friendly good day. The other did not answer, did not even raise his bowed head.

"What, is he deaf?" cried the horseman, as he drew up

[7] Love, and do what thou wilt.

level with the friar. Then, for the first time, he saw the face under the grey hood. The spectacle of those lowered lids, those lips almost imperceptibly moving in prayer, that expression of intense and focussed calm, abashed the young man into silence. He mumbled a word of apology, raised his hat, as though to the image in a wayside shrine, and crossed himself; then set spurs to his horse and cantered away, leaving the friar to perfect his act of self-immolation undisturbed.

How delicately the sacrifice had to be performed! How subtly, effortlessly, unabruptly! There were occasions when violence might be used to take the kingdom of heaven; but this was not one of them. Violent annihilation of the self would defeat its own purpose; for such violence belonged to the merely human will, and to make use of it would only strengthen that will against the will of God. In this act of self-abnegation, a man must somehow operate without effort; or rather he must permit self to be operated, passively, by the divine will. . . .

In the matter of the Valtelline, of course, His Holiness had more reason to fear the closer union between Spain and Austria than to be angry with the French for ousting a papal garrison. The Cardinal Nephew would probably. . . .

The friar became aware, once again, that concern with God's work had drifted like a dark eclipsing cloud between himself and God. Checking his first movement towards a passionate self-reproach that would only have made the eclipse completer, he gently changed the focus of his inner vision, looking past the Cardinal Nephew, past the Valtelline and Spain and France towards the pure will of God beyond and above and within them. The cloud drifted away; he was exposed once more to the light. Patiently, delicately, he opened himself to its purifying and transforming radiance.

Time passed, and a moment came at length when it seemed to him that he was fit to go on to the next stage of contemplation. The mirror of his soul was cleansed; the dust and vapours that ordinarily intervened between the mirror and that which it was to reflect had been laid to rest or dissolved. If he now turned his soul to Christ, the divine form would be reflected clearly and without blasphemous distortion; the image of the crucified Saviour would be within him, imprinting itself upon his will, his heart, his understanding, a divine model to be imitated, a spirit to inform and quicken.

Tenaciously he held the beloved image behind his half-closed eyelids; and this time he permitted himself the happiness of that adoration, intense to the point of physical pain, that boundless bliss and agony of compassion, from which he had had to turn in the earlier, discursive part of his exercise. Suffering, suffering. . . . Tears filled his eyes. Suffering of the Son of God, of God himself incarnate as man. Suffering endured by the loving Saviour of all sinners, this darkest sinner among them. *Recede a me, quia homo peccator sum.*[8] And yet the Saviour came, and took this leper in his arms, and knelt before him, and washed his feet. *Tu mihi lavas pedes?*[9] These feet that have walked in wickedness, that are all caked with the filth of sin and ignorance? Yes, and not only washes his feet, but, for the sinner's sake, permits himself to be taken, judged, mocked, scourged and crucified. He came back to

[8] Depart from me, for I am a sinful man.

[9] Dost Thou wash my feet?

the Calvary in his heart, to the suffering, the suffering of his God. And the annihilation for which he had striven seemed now to be consummated in a kind of rapture of devotion and compassion, love and pain. He was absorbed into a blissful participation in the sufferings of God incarnate—of God incarnate and therefore at the same time of the pure essential godhead out of which the God-Man had proceeded. That body upon the cross was the invisible made visible. Calvary was bathed in the uncreated light, irradiated by it, consubstantial with it. Absorbed into his source and ground, the crucified Christ was annihilated in the light, and there was nothing but the shining rapture of love and suffering. Then, as it were, re-condensing, the light took form again in Jesus crucified, until a new transfiguration once more assimilated Calvary with the glory that surrounded it.

Striding along, the friar's body measured out with its bare feet the furlongs and the minutes, the hours and the miles. Within, his soul had reached the fringes of eternity and, in an ecstasy of adoration and anguish, contemplated the mystery of the incarnation.

A donkey brayed; the outriders in front of a coach sounded their bugles; someone shouted and there was a sudden outburst of women's laughter.

Under the Capuchin's hood, there was a distant consciousness of these things. Eternity receded. Time and self came gliding in again to take its place. Reluctantly, the friar raised his head and looked about him. His myopic eyes discerned a house or two and the movement of men and animals on the road before him. He looked down again and, to cushion the shock of this abrupt return from one world to another, reverted to a discursive meditation on the Word made Flesh.

At the Milvian Bridge a group of soldiers had been posted to keep check on all incoming travellers from the North. The Capuchin answered their questions fluently, but with a foreign accent that automatically aroused suspicion. He was taken to the guard room to give an account of himself. The officer in charge touched his hat as the friar entered, but did not rise or remove his booted feet from the table on which he had propped them. Standing before him his hands crossed over his breast, the traveller explained that his name was Father Joseph, that his convent was in Paris, that he had been sent by his superiors to attend a meeting of the Chapter General of his order. The officer listened, picking his teeth, as he did so, with a silver-gilt toothpick. When the Capuchin had finished, he touched his hat again, belched and said that, while of course he had no reason whatever to doubt the truth of the Reverend Father's words, the existence of certain malefactors, certain brigands, certain (he made an emphatic flourish with the toothpick) certain enemies of God and man, who did not scruple to hide their wickedness under the Franciscan habit, made it necessary for him to ask for the Reverend Father's papers. The Capuchin hesitated for a moment, then inclined his head in acquiescence. Opening his habit at the neck, he reached into an inner pocket. The packet which he brought out was wrapped in blue damask and tied with a white silk ribbon. The officer raised his eyebrows as he took it, then smiled. Undoing the ribbon, he remarked facetiously that there had been a time when he carried his mistresses' love letters in just such a packet as this. Now, with a jealous wife in his bed and his mother-in-law actually living in the house . . . Suddenly the smile on his fat face was replaced by a look of astonishment that gave place to one positively of alarm. The object he had extracted from the packet was a letter sealed with the royal arms of France and addressed, with the most magnificent flourishes, to His Holiness, Urban VIII. He glanced apprehensively at the friar, then back again at that formidable superscription, that portentous seal; then with a great jingling and clatter he took his feet off the table, sprang out of his chair and, removing his hat, made a deep bow.

"Forgive me, Reverend Father," he said. "If I had only known . . . If only you had made it clear from the outset. . . ."

"There is also a letter to His Eminence, the Cardinal Nephew," said the Capuchin. "And another, if you will give yourself the trouble of looking, to His Most Christian Majesty's ambassador. And finally a passport delivered to myself and signed by His Eminence, the Cardinal Minister . . ."

At each name the officer made another obeisance.

"If I had known," he kept on repeating, while the friar gathered up the letters, "if I had only known . . ."

Breaking off, he rushed to the door and began shouting furiously at his men.

When the Capuchin left the guard room, he found his way across the bridge lined on either side by a company of papal musketeers. He halted for a moment, humbly acknowledged the officer's salute, raised a hand in blessing and then crossing his arms on his breast, he bowed his head and, without looking to right or left, hurried forward noiselessly on his bare feet between the double row of pikes.

II

Childhood and Youth

ANY given event in any part of the universe has as its determining conditions all previous and contemporary events in all parts of the universe. Those, however, who make it their business to investigate the causes of what goes on around them habitually ignore the overwhelming majority of contemporary and antecedent happenings. In each particular case, they insist, only a very few of the determining conditions are of practical significance. Where simple events are concerned this is true enough. Here, for example, is a boiling kettle. We want to find out why it boils. We investigate, discover a lighted gas ring, make experiments which seem to prove that there is an invariable connection between boiling and a rise of temperature. After which we affirm that the "cause" of ebullition in kettles is a neighbouring source of heat. The statement is crude, but adequate for most practical purposes. In the case of simple events, we can ignore all but one or at most a very few of their determining conditions, and still have sufficient understanding of them to enable us to control them for our practical purposes.

This is not true, however, in the case of complex events. Here, the determining conditions which have a practical significance are much more numerous. The most complex events with which we have to deal are events of human history. If we wish to establish the determining conditions of, say, the war of 1914-1918, we are compelled, even for such purely practical purposes as the framing of future policies, to consider a great variety of "causes," past and contemporary, local and remote, psychological, sociological, political, economic. To determine the full list of these practically significant "causes," their relative impor tance, their mode of interaction—this is an exceedingly difficult task. So difficult, indeed, as to be quite beyond the capacity of the human mind in its present state of development. But, alas, the insolubility of a problem has never deterred men and women from confidently propounding solutions. The method adopted is always the same—that of over-simplification. Thus, all but the immediate antecedents of the event under consideration are ignored, and history is treated as though it began only yesterday. At the same time, all embarrassing complexities are mentally abolished. Men are reduced to convenient abstractions. The varieties of temperament, talent and motivation are flattened into uniformity. The event is thus made to seem simple enough to admit of explanation in terms of a very few "causes," and perhaps even of only one. This theoretical conclusion is then used as a guide for future action. Not unnaturally the results are disappointing.

To over-simplify is fatal, and it is impossible to determine fully and correctly all the practically significant causes of complex events. Are we then doomed never to understand our history and therefore never to profit by the experiences of the past? The answer is that, although understanding will probably never be complete we can yet understand enough for some at least of our practical purposes. For example, we can probably find out enough about the causes of our recent catastrophes to be able (if we so desire) to frame policies at least a little less suicidal than those we have pursued in the past.

No episode in history can be entirely irrelevant to any other subsequent episode. But some events are related, for our practical purposes, more significantly than others. This friar, for example, whom we have just left on the Milvian Bridge—he seems, heaven knows, sufficiently remote from our contemporary preoccupations. But in truth, as we shall find if we look into his biography a little closely, his thoughts and feelings and desires were among the significantly determining conditions of the world in which we live today. The road trodden by those bare horny feet of his led immediately to the Rome of Urban VIII. More remotely, it led to August 1914 and September 1939. In the long chain of crime and madness which binds the present world to its past, one of the most fatally important links was the Thirty Years' War. Many there were who worked to forge this link; none worked harder than Richelieu's collaborator, François Leclerc du Tremblay, known in religion as Father Joseph of Paris and to anecdotal history as l'Eminence Grise. But this is by no means his only claim to our attention. If Father Joseph had been nothing more than an adept at the game of power politics, there would be no compelling reason for singling him out from among a number of concurrents. But the friar's kingdom was not, like the kingdoms of ordinary power politicians, exclusively of this world. Not merely intellectually, but by actual, direct acquaintance, he knew something of the other world, the world of eternity. He passionately aspired to become, and in some measure, with a part of his being, he actually was, a citizen of the Kingdom of

Heaven. Alone of power politicians, Father Joseph was able to provide, out of the depths of his proper experience, the final, objective criterion, in relation to which his policies could be judged. He was one of the forgers of one of the most important links in the chain of our disastrous destiny; and at the same time he was one of those to whom it has been given to know how the forging of such links may be avoided. Doubly instructive in the fields of politics and religion, his life is further interesting as the strangest of psychological riddles—the riddle of a man passionately concerned to know God, acquainted with the highest forms of Christian gnosis, having experienced at least the preliminary states of mystical union, and at the same time involved in court intrigue and international diplomacy, busy with political propaganda, and committed wholeheartedly to a policy whose immediate results in death, in misery, in moral degradation were plainly to be seen in every part of seventeenth-century Europe, and from whose remoter consequences the world is still suffering today.

It was in the spring of 1625 that Father Joseph plodded southward on his third visit to Rome. His business there was diplomatic and religious. On behalf of the French government he had come to talk about the Valtelline and the passes connecting Spanish-controlled Italy with the Hapsburg empire beyond the Alps. On behalf of his order he had come to get leave to found some missions. On his own account, he had come to talk with the Pope and the Cardinal Nephew about his own favourite scheme of a crusade against the Turks. Wherever he went in Rome, he would speak with authority, would be heard with deference and attention. This bare-footed monk was the confidential adviser and right-hand man of Cardinal Richelieu.

Moreover, long before Richelieu came to power, he had been the confidant and agent of Marie de Médicis and a number of other great personages of almost equal importance. Richelieu had been President of the Council of State for only a year; but Father Joseph of Paris had been known and appreciated at the Roman Curia for more than ten. Now in 1625, he was forty-eight, and he still had thirteen years of life before him—thirteen years of life that were also to be years of steadily increasing political power. Before half that time had passed, he was destined to take his place among the five or six most important men in Europe—among the two or three most generally and cordially detested. But before we trace the later stages of this strange career, let us go back to the beginnings.

François Leclerc du Tremblay was born on the fourth of November 1577, the eldest son of Jean Leclerc, Chancellor of the Duc d'Alençon and *Premier Président des Requêtes du Palais,* and of Marie de La Fayette, his wife. On his father's side he came from a distinguished line of lawyers and administrators. His mother's family belonged, not to the *noblesse de robe,* but to the landed nobility. Claude de La Fayette, her father, was the possessor of four baronies, one of which was bequeathed to his grandson, François, who was known, during his brief sojourn at Court, as the Baron de Maffliers. Claude de La Fayette and his wife, Marie de Suze, were Calvinists; but having been blessed with six daughters and, despite the four baronies, little money, they had had Marie brought up in the Catholic religion, so that she might enter a convent and so spare them the expense of a dowry. It may be remarked in passing that such transactions were not uncommon in the France of this period. Civil wars of religion might be fought, Huguenots alternately massacred and tolerated. But all the time French families continued to keep their eyes unflinchingly on the main chance. Thus in parts of the country where Catholics and Protestants were pretty evenly divided, parents would bring up their daughters without any definite religion. When a satisfactory suitor presented himself, a girl could be hurriedly trained and confirmed in whichever faith her future husband happened to profess. Not a very "heroic" way of settling denominational differences in a mixed community; but at any rate it worked, it made for peace and quiet. It has been fashionable for some time past to believe that the causes of strife are generally, even invariably, economic. This is far from true. Many disputes are purely ideological in origin. In these cases considerations of economic advantage will often intervene in the happiest manner to mitigate the furies of theological hatred.

Marie de La Fayette was saved from the convent by a distant cousin of her mother's, no less a person than the one-time favourite of François I, Anne, Duchess of Etampes. This superannuated royal concubine was now a benevolent old lady of nearly seventy and a good friend of the Leclercs. It was she who arranged the match between her young cousin and Jean Leclerc, she who supplemented Marie's meagre dowry by a considerable settlement from her own purse. The marriage, which turned out to be a happy one, was celebrated in 1574, and the first child was born, as we have seen, in 1577 and christened François. (Was the choice of that particular name intended as a delicate compliment to the old Duchess? Who knows?) A sister, Marie entered the world in the following year.

Charles, the youngest of the Leclercs' three children was not born until 1584.

François, as he emerged from babyhood, revealed himself as a strange and very remarkable little boy. At once active and introverted, he loved to be up and doing, but he loved at the same time to be left alone, so that he could think his own thoughts. Isolated even in company, he lived in nobody could discover what private world of his own. This secretiveness was not, however, incompatible with powerful emotions. He passionately loved his father and mother; he was deeply attached to his home, to the family servants, to the dogs and horses, the pigeons and the tame ducks, the falcons. Violent impulses, gusts of consuming passions not only of love, but of hatred and anger too, were an important element of that private world of his; but they existed, even in childhood, behind an iron wall of self-control, of voluntary reserve, unexpressed in words or those countless little actions by means of which the outward-turning nature gives vent so easily to its emotions. François only "let himself go" in situations where other people were not immediately and personally involved. He could be ardently enthusiastic about things and ideas; but he shrank from what he felt to be the indecency of expressed emotional intimacy with other human beings.

Intellectually, the child was almost preternaturally bright and precocious. At the age of ten he was chosen by his schoolmasters to deliver an hour-long funeral oration on Ronsard, in Latin, before a large and brilliant audience. If the large and brilliant audience had been able to understand him, he could have delivered an equally effective oration in Greek, a language he had learnt at almost as early an age as John Stuart Mill and by the same conversational methods as had been used to teach Montaigne his Latin.

Along with this intellectual precocity there went a no less extraordinary forwardness in matters of religious devotion. At the age of four, we are told, the child was brought down to the dinner table one day when his parents were entertaining a distinguished company of guests. Let us try to visualize the scene, to translate it from the telegraphic shorthand in which Father Joseph's first biographer records it into language a little more adequate to the events described.

Next to his proud but rather anxious mother sits the tiny boy, dressed already in a miniature edition of a grown man's clothes and looking almost indecently "cute" in his claret-coloured doublet and starched ruff. From the other end of the table his father tells him to get up and he obeys with a baby solemnity that delights them all. They ask him what he means to do when he is a man, how he likes his baby sister, when he is going to learn to ride. Finally, a magistrate puts him a question with a double meaning. The innocence of the answer raises a laugh which the child is utterly at a loss to understand. Tears come into his eyes; his mother takes him on her knee and kisses him. The guests go back to their eating and the child is set down on a stool and given a sweetmeat, which he eats in silence. His presence is forgotten. Then, suddenly, in a lull of the conversation, he shouts down the table to his father: may he tell them something? Marie tries to check him; but Jean Leclerc is indulgent: little François shall tell them whatever he likes. The child stands up on his stool. Smiling, the guests prepare to heckle and applaud. After the first few words their faces become suddenly serious, and they listen in silence, profoundly touched. The little boy is telling them a story he has just heard from one of the servants of the house, the story of the Passion. He tells of the scourging, the crown of thorns. As he describes the crucifixion, his voice trembles and, all at once, he breaks down into irrepressible sobbing. His mother takes him into her arms and tries to comfort him; but for this unhappiness there seems to be no consolation. In the end she has to carry him from the room.

The child is father of the man. This tiny boy, grief-stricken by the story of his Saviour's death, was destined to become the co-founder and, for many years, the guardian and spiritual director of a new reformed order of nuns, the Calvarians, whose principal devotion was to be directed to the suffering mother at the foot of the cross. He was also destined to become a statesman, absorbed in the most dangerous kind of power politics and to all appearances quite indifferent to the appalling sufferings for which his policy was responsible. The child in tears for Jesus, the grown man meditating himself, and teaching others to meditate, upon the sufferings endured on Calvary—were these the father and the brother of Richelieu's collaborator, of the man who did everything in his power to prolong the Thirty Years' War? This is a question to which, in its proper place, we shall have to try to find an answer. Meanwhile, our immediate concern is with a sixteenth-century boyhood.

At the age of eight, François du Tremblay was sent to a boarding school in Paris. Or, rather, he went there at his own wish; for he actually asked to leave home, on the ground that he was being spoilt by his mother, *qui en voulut faire un délicat.* Once more the child is father of the man. This little Spartan was to come to manhood as the militant Capuchin, eager to undertake all kinds of supererogatory self-mortification, was to grow up as the tonsured and bare-footed politician who, even at the height of his power, even in the extremities of sickness and fatigue, consistently refused to accept for himself any mitigation of his order's Franciscan rule.

At the Collège de Boncourt François learned more Greek and Latin and was no doubt as mercilessly beaten, bullied and ill fed as little boys were in most of the boarding schools of the period. Among his fellow pupils and friends at Boncourt was one of whom we shall hear a good deal in a later chapter of this book, Pierre de Bérulle, future Cardinal, founder of the Oratory, and the most influential member of the French school of mysticism, which flourished during the first half of the seventeenth century. Like François, Pierre was precociously serious-minded. From childhood his piety had been at once ardent and intellectual, spontaneous and learned. At twelve, we are told by a young Protestant lady, who afterwards became a Carmelite, he could discuss theology like a doctor of the Sorbonne. At eighteen he was a controversialist so powerful and acute that Huguenot ministers were afraid of meeting him in public debate.

Pierre was two years older than François, even more intelligent and no less precocious. Moreover, like the younger boy, he was already passionately religious and serious beyond his years. Their friendship was that of two future theologians and mystics. One conjures up a picture of these strange children, squatting apart, in a corner of the school's high-walled playground. The other urchins play ball or exchange those imbecile witticisms which small boys find so exquisitely funny. With a passionate earnestness and in high treble voices, Pierre and François discuss the deepest problems of metaphysics and religion.

When François was ten, there occurred an event which must have provided them with food for many such discussions of the significance of life and the nature of God and man. In 1587 Jean Leclerc du Tremblay died. François loved his father with all the repressed violence of which his passionate, inward-turning nature was capable. His grief on this occasion was profound; and when the first paroxysm was past, there remained with him, latent at ordinary times, but always ready to come to the surface, a haunting sense of the vanity, the transience, the hopeless precariousness of all merely human happiness.

This precocious conviction that ours is a fallen world was confirmed by all that François heard or saw around him. All over France the Leaguers and the Huguenots, assisted by their foreign allies, were busily engaged in trying to do to their unhappy country what the Lutherans and Imperialists, with *their* allies, were to do a generation later to Germany. For a variety of reasons, the Leaguers and the Huguenots did not succeed in destroying France, as Father Joseph's political friends and enemies were later to succeed in destroying Germany. Fifteen years of peace and good management under Henry IV were sufficient to restore the country to prosperity—to fatten it up like a Christmas turkey, against the coming of Richelieu's tax collectors. But while the religious wars lasted, France had to endure all the horrors of massacre and depredation, of plague and famine, of lawlessness and political anarchy. Those who had to live through this bloody chaos came to appreciate the virtues of order and of that institution of monarchy, which alone, at that time, could bring them the order they desired. At the same time the presence of foreigners—Spaniards, Germans, English, who kept the wars on French soil going and exploited France's weakness—served to stimulate French patriotism. It was in these years of civil strife and foreign intervention that François Leclerc became what he was to remain all his life—a firm believer in absolute monarchy and an ardent nationalist. These political convictions were to be elaborately justified in terms of theology, and this justification was to give them added strength; but it must always be remembered that they had their source, not in any abstract theory, but in the brute facts of the boy's experience.

In 1585, life in Paris became so dangerous that Mme Leclerc decided to remove with all her family to Le Tremblay, near Versailles, where she had a fortified house and a band of tenants and farm hands to protect her. Here François continued his education under a private tutor to whom he gave the affectionately respectful nickname of Minos. His studies now included modern languages, especially Spanish and Italian, both of which he subsequently learnt to write and speak almost as well as his own native tongue, the rudiments of Hebrew, philosophy, jurisprudence and mathematics. In the intervals of study he learned to ride and use the arquebus, he wandered in happy solitude through the woods, he indulged his taste for reading. There were not many books at Le Tremblay; but among those few was a copy of Plutarch's *Lives* in translation and a collection of Christian biographies, mostly of hermits. These two books he read and re-read. Plutarch confirmed his innate taste for heroism and the strenuous life; and under the influence of those hermits, his latent sense of the world's vanity grew so strong within him that he felt inspired to write a little treatise on the advantages of the religious life. This was completed shortly before his twelfth birthday and was much admired for its style. Nobody, not even his mother, had sufficient insight to perceive that the really significant thing about this juvenile production was not the absurd, strained elegance of its laboriously imitated form, but its Early Christian substance. Indirectly, in this rather pretentious little piece of abstract argumentation, the child had announced his own intention of some day entering religion. Two and a half years later, when he was fourteen, he made his first, premature attempt to carry out that intention.

This very significant episode was recorded by François himself when, eight years after the event, as a Capuchin novice, he was ordered by his superiors to write an account of his vocation. The document, which bears the curious title, *Discours en forme d'Exclamation,* is still extant. Briefly, this is the story it tells of the events of 1591.

Mme Leclerc was away from home on business, and had left her three children in the care of one of the neighbouring squires. It was a gay household, noisy with a whole troop of young girls. Among these there was one, of about François's own age, at whom the boy found himself looking with an ever increasing persistence. He had known her from childhood (she was probably a distant cousin); but up till that moment neither she nor any other girl had aroused his special interest. This time it was different. In the penitential language of his autobiography, "his concupiscences took fright" and "quivering with a confused well-being, he saw this girl with eyes quite different from those which had been his before." It was one of those overwhelming passions of early adolescence—passions which it is the stupid custom of adults to deride under the name of "calf love," but which are often more violent, more agonizingly intense than anything experienced in later life. When Juliet loved and died, she was no older than François Leclerc at the time of his first and final excruciation of the heart—just fourteen.

"Her whole face," wrote the Capuchin novice in his *Discourse in the form of an Exclamation*, "her whole face shone, her looks darted lightning." In a little while François "had no eyes but for her; his ears were deaf to every utterance but hers; he had given her all his heart, and except in her he could find no rest."

From the first, it was an uneasy passion, troubled with the sense of guilt. Those Plutarchian heroes were there to remind him that love is the enemy of high ambition; those hermits proclaimed the vanity of human wishes; and when he prayed, the old facility of communication between his soul and its God and Saviour was lost. That transfigured face, that young voluptuous body, the smell of her hair, the wild beating of his own heart—these stood in the way of his prayers, filling the whole field of inward vision, eclipsing God. Then one day, something happened. He was playing at cards with the whole troop of them, half a dozen *jeunes filles en fleur*, his own beloved among them, "laughing and joking, open mouthed," when suddenly, without apparent cause, he became aware of what he was doing, and with a fearful lucidity perceived its utter senselessness. He was appalled. Most of us, I suppose, have had a similar experience—have woken up all of a sudden from the sleep of everyday living into momentary awareness of the nature of ourselves and our surroundings.

It is a party in a parlour,
Crammed just as they on earth were crammed,
Some sipping punch, some sipping tea,
And all as silent as could be,
All silent and all damned.

Suddenly to realize that one is sitting, damned, among the other damned—it is a most disquieting experience; so disquieting that most of us react to it by immediately plunging more deeply into our particular damnation in the hope, generally realized, that we may be able, at least for the time, to stifle our revolutionary knowledge. François was one of those to whom such a course is impossible. The devastating consciousness of what he was doing was succeeded almost immediately by a sense of the presence of God—a sense which gave him such extraordinary joy, that there, at the card table, he almost fainted. His companions noticed his sudden pallor and insisted on taking him out into the open air. The bells were ringing for Vespers as they came out into the garden. François at once suggested that they should all go to church. Kneeling there, before the altar, he felt within him the pull of two conflicting loves, profane and sacred. Beside him knelt the girl whose pretty little face his own passion had transfigured till it shone for him, like the face of one who had seen God; before him, above the altar, was the figure of the crucified Saviour. There was a struggle that ended finally in François seeing nothing but "Christ's feet nailed to the cross and seemingly awaiting him, Christ's arms outspread to receive him." To that image of suffering he made a vow consecrating himself definitively to the service of God. Returning to the house, he immediately began his preparations for running away to Paris. He would creep out at night, he would exchange clothes with the first poor boy he met on the road; he would walk the twenty miles to the city and ask to be taken in at that Carthusian monastery, which he had often visited as a child, five or six years before. It was a mad scheme and the servant to whom he confided it that evening, lost no time in telling him as much. François whose native impetuosity was always held in check by excellent judgment, saw that it would be wrong for him to fulfil his vow in this surreptitious way, and decided not to go. Next day, he was given an opportunity to fight God's battle against his inclinations. A great feast was being given in the neighbourhood, and all the young people were invited. There would be dancing, no doubt, and music, and wine, and lights—festive excitements all the more intoxicating for being so rare in the lives of these country-bred children. And, of course, at night, on the way home, languid with excess of gaiety, what opportunities, in the lurching coach, for secret whispers in the dark, for hand-holding and surreptitious contacts! For the lover, it was an occasion not to be missed at any cost; that was why, even at the risk of seeming discourteous and a prig, young François resolved to miss it. He prayed much that day for strength and when the girls were dressed in all their finery and the coach was at the door, he was able to say no to all entreaties, even those of the beloved. In the end they had to drive away without him. It was a victory—but a victory that was succeeded a day or two later by defeat. For before the week was out, he was as much the slave of his passion as he had ever been. The only difference was that he suffered more acutely than in the past from the reproaches of his conscience.

This painful state of things lasted for four months. At

the end of this time two events occurred, two accidents which the Capuchin novice could only regard as providential. Playing with his arquebus, François came very near to killing his own mother. (Mme Leclerc had returned and they were living again at Le Tremblay.) And almost at the same time a band of marauding soldiers passed near the house and unloaded from their packs, among other unwanted articles of plunder, a tattered volume, called *Barlaam and Josaphat.*

In his intense thankfulness for the preservation of his mother's life from the effects of his own negligence, François renewed his vows. This time there was no going back on them. So violently did he break away from the bondage of the preceding months that he could "scarcely bear even to look at" the girl whose caresses he had so ardently desired only a short time before. At the same time he conceived a real horror of women in general and of the love of the sexes. This horror was to remain with him all his life. He could forget it, of course, in the contemplation of God; but when he was out in the world, separated from the divine presence, the old aversion continued to haunt him. In later life, Father Joseph shrank from too close and direct a contact even with his own sister. "I do not care," he used to say, "I do not care to see the sex" (that curious seventeenth-century name for women must have given him a peculiar satisfaction) "except shut up and curtained from sight, like so many mysteries not to be regarded save with a kind of horror." In other words, the only satisfactory woman was a cloistered woman, and the only tolerable way to enjoy female company was through the wicket of a confessional or the bars of a convent parlour. Otherwise, "they should only be visited like wild beasts, whom one is content to see without approaching." The intensity of Father Joseph's aversion was proportionate, no doubt, to the intensity of his early passion and the amount and violence of the force he had to use against himself in order to master it.

And now for that old book, which the soldiers threw aside as they passed Le Tremblay. François picked it up, read it and at once, as he says "fell in love with it." It was as though the voice of God were speaking from its pages, confirming him in his resolution and, for his consolation, expatiating upon the peace and happiness of the spiritual life.

In modern times a whole literature has sprung up around the pious tale which finally determined the future Father Joseph's vocation. *Barlaam and Josaphat* is a major historical curiosity. For this medieval romance about an Indian prince who leaves the life of pleasure, to which his too solicitous father has condemned him, and who embraces the contemplative life under the direction of a hermit, is nothing more nor less than a Christianized biography of Gautama Buddha. Not only in its main lines, but in detail and actually in phrasing *Barlaam and Josaphat* follows the Sanskrit of the *Lalita Vistara.* Nor is this all. The very name of the prince reveals his identity. The story had been originally translated into Greek from an Arabic version, and the Arabic letters for Y and B are easily confused. Josaphat is the corruption of Bodhisat. Barlaam's disciple is the Bodhisattva or future Buddha. It is one of the tragedies of history that Christendom should never have known anything of Buddhism beyond this garbled version of the semi-legendary biography of its founder. In the teachings of primitive, southern Buddhism, Catholicism would have found the most salutary correctives for its strangely arbitrary theology, for its strain of primitive savagery inherited from the less desirable parts of the Old Testament, for its incessant and dangerous preoccupations with torture and death, for its elaborately justified beliefs in the magic efficacy of rites and sacraments. But, alas, so far as the West was concerned, the Enlightened One was destined, until very recent times, to remain no more than the hero of an edifying fairy tale.

In 1594 Henri IV had heard his mass and was in Paris. Order was restored; the city became safe to live in. Mme Leclerc came back to town, and François was sent to continue his studies in what the wars of religion had left of the University—which was so little that, after a few months, the young man decided to remove to another educational establishment, the Academy conducted by Antoine de Pluvinel.

In sixteenth-century France an Academy was a kind of finishing school for young gentlemen. The studies included horsemanship and mathematics, fortification and fencing, military drill, calligraphy and good manners. At Pluvinel's, the most aristocratic and fashionable of all the Academies in France, the regular course of instruction lasted two years; but the already brilliantly accomplished François Leclerc du Tremblay was able to take his degree in gentlemanliness in less than one. By the autumn of 1595 he was ready for the Grand Tour. Accompanied by a trusted old servant and ten or twelve other young noblemen of his own age, he set out for Italy. And what about Barlaam and Josaphat? What about the hermits, and that treatise on the religious life and his vows at the foot of the crucifix? Had they slipped his memory? Had he pushed them impatiently aside along with the other foolishnesses of childhood? Not at all. Nothing had been forgotten, and the old resolutions still stood. He was only waiting for the right moment, the final and unmistakeable call. It might come very soon; it might be delayed perhaps for years. Meanwhile he would obey his mother and do his best to perform all the duties of the estate into which he had been born. For the other young men in his company, this jaunt to Italy was the first exciting opportunity to be free of parental control, and free, what was more, in that promised land of the *Sonnetti Lussuriosi* and Giulio Romano's engravings. For François, on the contrary, it was merely another stage in a process of education that was to equip him, physically and mentally, to accomplish, in some yet undetermined sphere, the will of his God and Saviour. Strong in the vow of chastity he had made after the incident with the arquebus, strong too in his horror and dread of women, he had no fear of the temptations to which his companions, as they rode southward from Paris, were already gleefully promising themselves to succumb. Italy would teach him only what it was right and necessary for him to learn; nothing more.

Once over the border, François did not waste his time. In Florence he studied the language, fencing and, most important, the art of horsemanship, for which, at that period, the Italians were famed above all others. He was an excellent rider and had a passion for horseflesh and all the niceties of equitation—a passion which he was soon compelled to sacrifice to his religious vocation; for a Capuchin might travel only on his own bare feet. From Florence he proceeded to Rome, where he had an opportunity of learning something of the papal foreign office, a model of diplomatic sharp practice unrivalled by anything of its kind in Europe. Turning northward again, François stopped at Loreto for religious reasons; at Bologna, to visit the University; at Ferrara, to pay his respects to the Duke and inspect His Highness's museum of natural history; and at Padua, for a considerable stay to study jurisprudence. The letters which François sent at this time to his mother have been lost. It is a pity; for it would be interesting to know if he made the acquaintance of Galileo, who was then teaching at Padua, or what were the subjects discussed at those informal meetings which were regularly held, out of school hours, at the houses of the professors. From Padua, the young man proceeded to Venice, which was full of exiled Byzantine scholars and was consequently the best place in all Europe for studying Greek. From Venice he crossed the Alps into Germany, of which he saw enough at least to know what the country looked like before the Thirty Years' War. Less than a year after his departure he was back again in Paris.

When the young Baron de Maffliers was presented at court, he made an excellent impression. Gabrielle d'Estrées, the King's young mistress (she was only two years older than François himself) called him "the Cicero of France and of his age." The monarch expressed himself less emphatically, but he too took approving notice of the youth. It was not to be wondered at. François was not only handsome, in a finely aristocratic and aquiline style; he was also very intelligent; behaved himself with discretion beyond his years; had the most exquisite manners; and could converse delightfully about anything—but without ever abandoning that reserve, without ever departing from that caution, with which he tempered his enthusiasm, his teeming imagination, his impulses to immediate actions. Years later, Cardinal Richelieu had two nicknames for his old friend and collaborator—"Ezéchiely" and "Tenebroso-Cavernoso." The names were admirably chosen to describe that curiously complex nature. Ezéchiely was the enthusiast, the visionary, the Franciscan evangelist and mystic; Tenebroso-Cavernoso, the man who never gave himself away, the poker-faced diplomatist, the endlessly resourceful politician. These two strangely dissimilar personalities inhabited the same body, and their incongruous conjunction was an important element in the character of the man whose destiny we have set ourselves to follow.

François spent a full year at court. It was an instructive interlude. In that very co-educational school of the Louvre, he learned all kinds of useful lessons—to listen with an air of respectful interest to royal bores; to suffer high-born fools gladly; to pay delicate compliments to the ladies whose much exposed bosoms filled him with such an intensity of fascinated disgust; to pick the brains of the well informed without appearing to be inquisitive; to discriminate between the important and the unimportant, the genuinely powerful and the merely showy. For the future Secretary of State and diplomat, such knowledge was indispensable.

Early in 1597 François was given an opportunity to continue his education in yet another field; he was sent to get his first taste of war at the siege of Amiens. This fortress, full of munitions and military stores, had been betrayed by a supporter of the League to the Spaniards, who were in turn besieged by a French army under the command of the Constable, Montmorency. Now, Montmorency was the husband of that legitimized daughter of Henri II who, twenty years before, had graciously condescended to be François Leclerc's godmother. He took the boy under his personal care and was much gratified by the way in which he conducted himself throughout the siege. Men began to prophesy that this young Baron de Maffliers would make a first-rate soldier.

Amiens fell in due course, and its fall was an excellent occasion for concluding the war, of which both Henri IV and Philip II were heartily tired. Henri IV, however, had allies, without whose consent he could not make peace. Of these allies, the most important was Elizabeth of England, who had reasons of her own for wishing to prolong hostilities. To secure Elizabeth's assent to peace, Henri IV dispatched to London a seasoned diplomat, Hurault de Maisse, who happened to be a distant relative of the du Tremblays. François made use of the connection to get himself attached to the ambassador's retinue, and in the autumn of this same year, 1597, he landed in England. For a young man in search of an education, London provided golden opportunities. The court was frequented by accomplished and even learned men, with whom one could talk in Latin about Erasmus and the *Iliad* and the new edition of Aulus Gellius. The Elizabethan drama was in full eruption, and the distinguished foreign guests were frequently treated to the, for them, somewhat bewildering spectacle. And all the while, of course, Hurault de Maise was busily negotiating with the Queen and her ministers; François was given the opportunity of studying diplomacy in action and from the inside. Finally, there was the old royal harridan, to whom it was the attaché's special duty to pay court. She, for her part, was delighted to converse with so handsome a young man, so exquisitely brought up and with such an extraordinary mastery of those dead and living languages, which she herself knew so well and was so fond of talking. (When Hurault de Maisse complimented her on this accomplishment, Elizabeth characteristically answered that there was nothing remarkable in teaching a woman to speak; the difficulty was to make her hold her tongue.)

For any other young man, that brief visit in London would have been nothing but a most amusing and perhaps instructive adventure. And, in effect, that was what it was for François Leclerc during the first week or two of his stay. He was excited by the strangeness of all he saw, pleased with his own success, charmed and delighted by the people with whom he came in contact. He enjoyed himself in England, and he liked the English. And precisely because he liked them, his happy exhilaration at being among them suddenly evaporated. These pleasant, friendly people, who spoke Latin with such a deliciously comic accent—they were all heretics, and therefore all irrevocably doomed. The whole nation was doomed. Millions upon millions of men, women and children sunk in a spiritual darkness, through which there was only one road, and that road led directly to everlasting torment. François was appalled at the thought, and his old sense of the vanity of human wishes, the transience and illusoriness of what is commonly called happiness came back upon him with redoubled intensity. Consider these English! How tranquilly they passed their time, as though all were well with them! And yet, within a few short years every one of them would be in hell. As for himself, kind Providence had decreed that he should be born a Catholic. But even that inestimable godsend was no sufficient guarantee of real happiness. He was only potentially saved. To the very last moment of his life, sin might undo the effects of baptism. Hell remained, not indeed the certainty it was for Elizabeth and the aged Burleigh and all the rest of them, but a terrifying possibility, even a probability if he continued to lead his present worldly life. Wealth, honours, military glory, the flattering attentions of a king, the compliments of a royal paramour—what was the worth of such trifles in comparison with eternal salvation and the doing of God's will on earth?

It was with such questions ringing in his ears that the Baron de Maffliers returned to France in the first weeks of 1598. Arriving in Paris, he went at once to see his confessor, Dr. André Du Val, who listened attentively to what he said and gave him to read a little book that had been published during his absence in England. It was entitled *Bref Discours sur l'Abnégation Intérieure*, and its author was none other than Pierre de Bérulle, then a young priest, studying theology at the Sorbonne.

Inward abnegation! The words seemed magically apposite. François read the book and then re-read it, with passion. It was another *Barlaam and Josaphat*—but with the added advantage that its author was alive and .in Paris. At once he sought out his old schoolfellow. Bérulle received him with delight; and from that time forth, François was seen no more at court, and avoided all the acquaintances he had made there. Consciously and deliberately, he was preparing for the moment, which he now divined was very close at hand, the solemn moment when he should be called to break with his past and begin an entirely new existence.

The little world into which he was now introduced by

Bérulle and Du Val was a truly extraordinary society, composed for the most part of people in whom the highest intellectual powers were accompanied by an intense religious fervour and, in some cases, by rare and striking spiritual gifts. Its central figure was a woman, Mme Acarie, and it was around her that the others, men and women, lay and religious, respectfully gravitated. Born in 1566, Barbe Avrillot was married at the age of sixteen to a man who, like her own father, belonged to the *noblesse de robe*. Pierre Acarie was one of those restless, clever fools, who have to be continually "doing something," and whose total lack of judgment makes them always choose to do something futile or disastrous. Most of his large fortune he dissipated in financing persuasive swindlers. Passionately the politician, he espoused the cause of the League with so much ardour that, after the triumph of Henri IV, he was deprived of his post, exiled from Paris and, committing some further imprudence, came near to losing all that remained of his property and even his life. He owed his safety to the untiring efforts of a wife whom he had consistently maltreated. It was not until she was twenty-two that Mme Acarie discovered her religious vocation. Reading a book of devotion, she came upon the phrase: *"Trop est avare à qui Dieu ne suffit"*—too covetous is he to whom God is not enough. The effect of these words was extraordinary; "it was as though God had struck her with a thunderbolt." She became a different person—one who knew by immediate intuition that the kingdom is within, that God can be progressively experienced, that it is the duty of human beings to begin here and now the unimaginable task of becoming "perfect as their Father in heaven is perfect."

At the time of François Leclerc's return from London, Pierre Acarie had been in exile for more than three years and his wife and six children, temporarily reduced to complete penury, were living with the Bérulles. Their house in the rue Paradis and, later, when Pierre Acarie's fortunes had been somewhat restored, the Hôtel Acarie became for the religious life of France what the Hôtel de Rambouillet was to be, a generation later, for French literature and French manners.

Mme Acarie's influence was felt only by her contemporaries; for, unlike St. Teresa, whom she resembled in her ceaseless practical activity no less than in the eminence of her mystical gifts, she left no record of her experiences in writing. She is known to us only in her biography (which was written by Dr. André Du Val) and in the records left by the men and women who knew her. From these it is evident that nobody could be with her, even for a short time, without recognizing that here was a person, different from ordinary human beings, not only in degree, but actually in kind. Mme Acarie was one in whom the process of illumination and sanctification has gone so far that the merely human element is no more than a thin pyscho-physical shell enclosing a core of constantly realized divine immanence.

Some saints have charmed their contemporaries; Mme Acarie's sanctity was of a more awe-inspiring kind. St. François de Sales, who was her friend and acted for a time as her confessor, wrote of the "infinite respect" in which he held her; and it was the same with all who approached this extraordinary woman. Those who knew little of the spiritual life were further impressed by the physical phenomena which often accompanied her mystical states—by those trances and ecstasies, which she tried so hard to control and which, along with all experienced directors, then as now, she regarded not so much as a symptom of divine grace as of her own weakness. (Mme Acarie also received the stigmata, but managed to conceal the marks from those who surrounded her. The fact, which she confided to only three people, of whom Bérulle was one, was known only after her death.) Late in the eighteenth century, Barbe Acarie was formally beatified; unofficially, however, her sanctity had been universally recognized during her life time. Even professors of theology, like Du Val, could not fail to perceive who and what she was. In 1594, by a kind of providential practical joke, Du Val, the fabulously learned schoolman had been introduced to Mme Acarie. For the first time in his life, this expert in the science of deity found himself in the same room with someone whose acquaintance with the subject was not merely discursive and intellectual, but immediate and intuitive. Within the first five minutes, he had recognized that, whereas he himself knew all *about* God, this woman knew God directly. With an entirely admirable humility, the theologian placed himself under the spiritual guidance of the unlearned mystic, and from that time until her death in 1618, Du Val remained Mme Acarie's faithful pupil and most trusted friend.

One of the members of Mme Acarie's circle was a certain Capuchin friar, whose name in religion was Father Benet. This Father Benet had been born in the early 1560's at Canfield in Essex, the son of a prosperous squire called Fitch. As a young man, William Fitch went up to London to study for the law. The reading of some bootlegged volume of Catholic devotion converted him all of a sudden from a life of dissipation to seriousness and the old religion. To study Catholic theology was impossible in England; accordingly the new convert crossed the channel and made his way to Douai, where he enrolled himself at the English college. In 1586, he took the habit of a Capuchin and from the first days of his novitiate in Paris revealed himself as a man of the highest spiritual gifts. His contemporary influence was at least as great as that of Mme Acarie—probably even greater; for, as Brémond puts it, Benet of Canfield was "the master of the masters," the teacher of a whole generation of saintly mystics, who were responsible, by their doctrine and example, for that great renascence of personal religion, which revitalized French Catholicism during the first half of the seventeenth century. Mme Acarie herself was a disciple of Father Benet. The story of their relationship is a curious one. That phrase, *"trop est avare à qui Dieu ne suffit,"* had opened up for Barbe Acarie the kingdom of God existing, latent and unrecognized in her own spirit. The experience of divine grace was too much for her physical organism; ecstasies and trances became embarrassingly frequent. Her mother-in-law showed a pained disapproval; her husband exploded in indignation. Doctors were summoned and she was bled to the verge of collapse; the local parson was asked to give her a good talking-to, which he did, sometimes even in public. It was all of no avail; Mme Acarie continued to experience mystical graces and, in spite of all her efforts, continued to be subject to periodical trances and ecstasies. Finally, in 1593, Father Benet was sent for. Already accepted as an authority on these high spiritual matters, the Capuchin pronounced unhesitatingly that Mme Acarie's experiences were of divine origin; and he proceeded to instruct the young woman in the elements of that mystical theology, of which her conventionally pious upbringing had left her completely ignorant. Thanks to Father Benet, Mme Acarie came to know what was happening to her; how she stood in relation to the mystics who had preceded her; what spiritual discipline she ought to undertake; and how she should prepare herself to receive the divine graces.

Bérulle owed even more to Father Benet than did Mme Acarie. The Capuchin taught him, not merely the technique of meditation and contemplation, but also a complete theory of mysticism—a theory which, as we shall see in the next chapter, differed in certain important respects from the traditional theology of Dionysius and his followers down to the time of St. John of the Cross, and whose propagation by Bérulle and the members of his school was to affect the whole future course of Christian mysticism.

Bérulle and Mme Acarie were Father Benet's most influential pupils; but there were many, many others of lesser note. "God alone knows," writes his contemporary biographer, "the number of religious who, with the aid of his documents, delivered by word of mouth and in writing, have raised themselves to sublime states of perfection."

It was from this master of the masters that François Leclerc received his initiation into the "unitive life." Father Benet and, to an even higher degree, Mme Acarie possessed that profound insight into character, which comes to men and women of advanced spirituality and which is technically known as the discernment of spirits. It is recorded of Mme Acarie that she could distinguish infallibly between those who had been graced with a gift for contemplation and those who had not, and that she considered it very unwise to impose a mystical education upon the latter. The fact that Father Benet undertook to teach him, and that Mme Acarie saw no objection to it, seems on the face of it sufficient proof that François had in him the makings of a genuine mystic. It is the business of his biographer to discover why and in the name of what religious principle this potential John of the Cross preferred to become the right-hand man of Cardinal Richelieu.

Mme Acarie, as I have said, was an active mystic. The house in the rue Paradis was the rallying point of all those, lay or religious, who took an interest in the reform of existing monastic orders or the creation of new congregations. At the same time, it was the headquarters of a very efficient organization for the distribution of charity. Contributions came from the most unexpected sources. For example, each time the King sat down to play for high stakes, he would propitiate the Almighty and sacrifice to the goddess of luck by sending five and twenty crowns to Mme Acarie for her good works. Voluntary helpers distributed the sums collected and undertook the labour of visiting the poor, the sick, the imprisoned. It was labour far from light or agreeable. Paris at the beginning of the seventeenth century was an overgrown medieval city, undrained, unswept, pestilential and brutalized with overcrowding. The hospitals were like charnel houses, and the prisons like hells on earth. It was in this frightful Paris of the poor and the criminal that, as one of Mme Acarie's helpers, the youthful Baron de Maffliers began a new chapter of his education. He had tasted successively of learning, travel, courts, war and diplomacy. Now, under the tutorship of Father Benet and Mme Acarie, he was being given a first-hand experience of divine illumination on the one hand and the darkness of human misery and wickedness on the other.

François Leclerc's unofficial novitiate was interrupted after a few months by a curious episode. Secretly, without telling a soul, he left home and headed post-haste for the south. His destination was the Grande Chartreuse, in the hills above Grenoble. Was it on the advice of Du Val or Father Benet or Mme Acarie that the young man made this decision to become a Carthusian monk? One may be permitted to doubt it. St. Bruno's medieval imitation of primitive Egyptian monasticism had survived almost unchanged through the centuries, "never reformed because never deformed," a venerable institution, but somewhat out of touch with the life of an age which was busily engaged in modernizing the old religious organizations and creating a multitude of new ones. His friends in Mme Acarie's circle would almost certainly have advised him to join some other, newer order than the Carthusian. The young man's choice was probably due in part to the impression left upon his mind by the visits he had made in childhood to the Charterhouse of Paris; in part, we may guess, to the fact that, by taking the Carthusian habit, he would be performing an act of self-abnegation, the most complete of which he was capable. It was not that the Carthusian rule was more rigid and mortificatory than all others. The Capuchins, to take but one example, treated their bodies with no less severity. But the Capuchins were actives as well as contemplatives, whereas the Carthusians lived immured and in almost perpetual silence. To a man of François Leclerc's ardent temperament and busy intellect, this total retirement from the world of men must have seemed the final and absolute sacrifice of self. The child, who had begged to be sent to a boarding school for fear his mother might turn him into a molly-coddle, had grown up into this young man, hungry for a life of confinement, and enforced inactivity—hungry for it precisely because he knew it would be the most difficult of all for him to bear.

He set out, then, fully resolved to make the supreme sacrifice of all his inclinations; but on the road, near Nevers, something happened to make him change his mind. He heard an inward voice telling him to return at once to Paris, and that he should not enter religion without first obtaining his mother's consent. He obeyed. St. Bruno lost a monk, but St. Francis gained a friar and Cardinal Richelieu, a secretary of state for foreign affairs.

As François had foreseen, when he left home without taking leave of even his mother, Mme Leclerc had no intention of helping her eldest son to abandon a world in which he might reasonably expect to make a brilliant military or administrative career. Moreover, she had long been negotiating for an heiress, and now the girl had been as good as promised her. With the dowry, François could restore the family fortune, sadly diminished since M. du Tremblay's death, could buy a good position for his young brother and see to it that his sister got a satisfactory husband. Not to mention, of course, all the things that money would permit him to do for himself. And now the boy was talking about throwing it all up and going into a cloister. The folly of it! And, after all she had done for him, the ingratitude! Stubbornly, during the months that followed his return from Nevers, she fought against her son's vocation; and, no less stubbornly, the young man defended it. In the end, torn by conflicting allegiances, he fell sick. The illness dragged on and grew worse, until at last Mme Leclerc's maternal solicitude got the better of her ambition. Reluctantly and conditionally, she assented to a compromise. She would let him enter religion on condition that he chose an order whose rule would permit her to go on seeing him. At this, the divided allegiances were reconciled; François began at once to recover. After some hesitation, he decided in favour of the Capuchins. Father Benet of Canfield was consulted; and by him, in his capacity as Warden of the Capuchin convent of the rue Saint-Honoré, François was given a written "obedience" and sent to the house of novices at Orleans. Secretly, as on the previous journey, he left Paris; and this time there was no turning back. On February 2nd, 1599, he put on the habit of a Franciscan novice.

That he had done wisely to leave home without saying good-bye to his mother was proved a short time later, when Mme Leclerc appeared at the convent gates accompanied by a high legal dignitary and bearing a royal injunction that commanded the Capuchins to give her back her son. There was one last prolonged discussion. The mother's tone was violent; the son's gentle, but unshakeably resolute. She declared that she had never really given her consent; that he was a runaway and the friars no better than kidnappers; that he was neglecting sacred duties, condemning his brother and sister to penury, breaking her own heart. François replied that God had called him and that to neglect this summons would be a sin. His words were spoken with such a moving sincerity, that

Mme Leclerc was touched, wavered and finally broke down in tears. She gave him her blessing, burnt the royal *lettre de jussion* and left him to the church. From having been the implacable enemy of her son's vocation, Mme Leclerc henceforth became its most ardent friend. In her mind, this interview produced the effects of a conversion. She turned from worldliness to a piety which her son fostered by a long series of spiritual instructions; she devoted herself to good works. Her reward, in this world, was to live long enough to see Father Joseph making a career for himself incomparably more brilliant than any she could have hoped for the Baron de Maffliers.

At this point it will not, I think, be out of place to give a brief description of the order within whose ranks the one-time baron had now irrevocably chosen to lead the rest of his life. The history of Franciscanism is the history of a long-drawn-out struggle between a pious worldly wisdom on the one hand and, on the other, uncompromising primitive Christianity. Francis himself had stood for primitive Christianity; his successor, Brother Elias, for worldly wisdom. During the first generations of Franciscanism a party of Moderates was opposed by a party of "Zealots" or "Spirituals"; but in the course of time the names were changed. In later centuries the cause of worldly wisdom is represented by the "Conventuals," while over against them stand the "Observants," so called because they tried, albeit with considerable reservations, to observe St. Francis' original rule. Custom and finally papal authority had stabilized the position of these two branches of Franciscanism, when, with the Counter-Reformation, a new enthusiasm for reform began to spread through the church. Among the Franciscans we have the reforms represented by the Alcantarines, the Recollets, the Reformati and finally, the Capuchins. This order had its first beginnings in Italy about the year 1520, was regularized by a papal bull of 1538 and had begun to do fairly well, when its third Vicar, Bernardino Ochino, turned Calvinist and, in 1543, fled first to Geneva, then to England, where he became a prebendary of Canterbury and wrote a kind of cosmic allegory, in which Lucifer raises up the Pope as Antichrist, only to be thwarted in his machinations by the providential appearance of Henry VIII. Not unnaturally, the new order had to suffer for its Vicar's escapades and for a time there was even talk of dissolving it altogether. Finally, however, it was spared and its privileges restored. Within a few years it had become, next to the Company of Jesus, the most powerful instrument in the church's entire armory.

The Capuchin rule was a nearer approximation to St. Francis' original than that of any of the other Franciscan orders. Thus, the law enjoining poverty was strictly observed. Neither overtly, nor covertly, by a subterfuge, might the monastic houses own any property. The wants of their inmates were to be supplied exclusively by begging, and the convent was not allowed to accumulate stores for more than a few days. No friar might use or even handle money. (When representing the King on diplomatic missions, Father Joseph, as we shall see, was compelled to accept, albeit reluctantly, a dispensation in regard to this matter.) The Capuchin's habit was of rough grey cloth and so rarely replaced that most of the friars were permanently dirty and in tatters. To the hardships of poverty were added those of a rigid discipline. Fasts were numerous in the Capuchin's life and penances severe. A midnight service cut short the hours of sleep. Over and above the time set for the canonical offices, two hours were reserved for private prayers.

Outside the convent, the life of the friars was one of incessant activity. Their work was to preach, save souls and help the poor. Abroad, among the infidels, and at home, among heretics and "libertines," the Capuchins were the great missionaries and converters of the period. Where the spirit of Catholicism had become lukewarm, they were the great revivalists. Nor were their ministrations exclusively spiritual. They worked hard to palliate the chronic miseries of the poor, and wherever disaster struck, they were always present—as stretcher bearers with the armies; as intercessors for the lives of the conquered; as nurses and grave diggers in times of pestilence; as relief workers among the famine-stricken. It has been pointed out that, between 1500 and 1600 the popular attitude towards the regular clergy underwent a profound change. At the earlier date, monks and friars were regarded either with an angry resentment or else with mere derision. And such attitudes were already traditional. The fury of the first Reformers recalls that of the author of *Piers Plowman*; the humorous contempt displayed in the *Epistolae Obscurorum Virorum* is fundamentally the same attitude adopted by Boccaccio and Chaucer. Reformation produced Counter-Reformation. By the end of the sixteenth century the friar of popular imagination is no longer the lecherous and greedy incubus depicted in the *Decameron* and the *Canterbury Tales*. He is the new model Capuchin, the man who respects his vows, who shares the hardships of the poor and is always ready to be a help in trouble. Disinterestedness and active kindness wield an extraordinary influence over men's minds and are the sources of a curious kind of non-compulsive power. In the first fifty years of their existence the Capuchins had thoroughly earned this power and influence. It is one of the tragedies of history that this moral force should everywhere have been exploited, by the rulers of church and state, for the furtherance of their own generally sinister ends. This harnessing by evil of the power generated by goodness, is one of the principal and most tragic themes of human history.

Austerity of life, the assumption of voluntary poverty, a charity of collaboration, not of patronage—these were the characteristics that had earned for the Capuchins the respect and affection of the masses. It was for precisely the same reasons that the order appealed so strongly to men of a certain type in the very highest classes of society. François Leclerc was by no means the only gentleman-friar. Many noblemen and even some persons of royal blood had joined and were to join the order. What attracted them was precisely the thing that might have been expected to repel them—the extreme severity of the rule, the evangelical poverty, the familiar contact with the poorest and humblest. Of those who are born with silver spoons in their mouths, the greater number are only concerned to keep and, if possible, increase their privileges. But at all times there has been a minority of men and women, on whom the possession of privileges has acted as a challenge to their latent heroism, a spur to renunciation. The underlying motive is sometimes a genuine love of God, but more often a kind of pride. The privileged individual wants to prove that he is somebody on his own account and apart from his bank balance and his social position, that he can win the race against all comers, even when he starts from scratch. A course of noble actions begun in pride may be continued in pride, so that the last state of the hero is not appreciably better than the first. On the other hand, it sometimes happens that noble actions begun in pride transform the doer, who ends his career as someone fundamentally different from, and better than, the person he was when he started. There are fashions in magnanimity, and the opportunities for heroism change from age to age. Thus, in recent years, young people with too many privileges have sought a life of heroic austerity in politics, or sport, or science. They have flung themselves into unpopular political movements, gone mountain climbing or big-game hunting, campaigned against disease, volunteered in other people's wars. For the over-privileged of an earlier age, fighting and exploring strange lands also offered excellent opportunities for heroism and renunciation; but they were opportunities that public opinion thought less highly of than those provided by organized religion. "This is a soldier's life," François wrote to his mother a short time after his entrance into religion, "but with this difference: that soldiers receive death for the service of men, whereas we hope for life in the service of God." To François Leclerc's counterpart in the modern world, the equivalent of becoming a Capuchin would have been to join the Communist Party or enlist for service in the Spanish war. But the equivalent would not be complete; for the life of a Capuchin was a soldier's life with a difference—a soldier's life with the addition of another dimension, that of eternity. It is the existence of this other dimension which imparts to certain biographies of earlier times their peculiar poignancy. Even the baldest recitals of these lives have about them some of the depth and intensity of significance, which distinguish Claudel's extraordinary Catholic fantasy, *Le Soulier de Satin.* Consider for example, the life story of that Père Ange who, in 1600, performed the ceremony of our young novice's final and definitive reception into the Capuchin order. Like the future Father Joseph, Père Ange had been a gentleman—a gentleman of a lineage incomparably more illustrious than that of the Leclercs. Before his entry into religion, this friar was known as Henri de Joyeuse, Comte de Bouchage. One of his brothers was a cardinal and had held successively the three archbishoprics of Toulouse, Narbonne and Rouen. Another, Anne de Joyeuse, had died at Coutras in 1587, leading the troops of the League against Henry of Navarre. At the time of his death he had been admiral of France, duke and peer, Governor of Normandy and, by his marriage to Marguerite de Lorraine-Vaudémont, brother-in-law to Queen Louise, the wife of his master and passionately devoted friend, Henri III. Yet another brother, Antoine Scipion, had been Governor of Languedoc. These family connections, the support of his brother-in-law, the Duc d'Epernon, and finally the friendship of the King seemed to guarantee for young Henri de Joyeuse the most brilliant future. But in 1587, his wife died and, a few days later, he carried out an intention which he had had in mind even at the height of his courtly successes: he became a Capuchin. The letter sent on this occasion by Henri III to the Provincial of the order, is still extant. "*Mon Père,*" he wrote, "I know you love me. I am infinitely obliged to you for it; but in order to make this obligation extreme and to give me a great contentment, let me beg that neither now nor in the future (as I am sure that you will not refuse so just a request) shall Frère Ange, whom I hold as dear as if he were myself or my own child, stir from the convent of Paris; and I implore you with all my heart, give me this joy, which will be extreme, that I may still see him and recommend myself to his prayers." The Provincial doubtless obeyed; but the unhappy King had all too little time in which to recommend himself to his friend's prayers. A year after the letter was written, the Duc de Guise was assassinated at Blois and, before another year had passed, the League took its revenge and the last of the Valois kings was lying dead, with Friar Clement's knife in his bowels. His favourite, meanwhile, was happily begging his bread, preaching, nursing the sick and learning the art of mental prayer from Father Benet of Canfield.

Insofar as the Capuchins meddled in politics, they were, at this time, supporters of the League against the new and not yet Catholic king. It was in his capacity as member of an illustrious family of Leaguers that Père Ange was chosen, in 1592, to carry out a strange political mission in Provence, the Lyonnais and Languedoc. He was to try to persuade the governors of the southern provinces (all of them more or less closely related to him) to form a new political federation, independent of the rest of France and under the suzerainty of the Pope. Several months of negotiation had convinced him that the scheme was unworkable, when the news came that his brother, the Governor of Languedoc, had lost his life in an unsuccessful operation against the royal forces. Antoine Scipion was the last lay Joyeuse. Of the two surviving brothers, one was a cardinal, the other a Capuchin—neither of them available for military service. But the people insisted on having a Joyeuse to lead them. Enormous crowds surrounded the Capuchins' headquarters at Toulouse, shouting "We want Père Ange, we want Père Ange" and (a touch so true to mob psychology as to be positively Shakespearean) threatening to burn down the convent if they didn't get him. Rome was consulted; dispensations procured; and at last the day came when, in solemn ceremony, Cardinal de Joyeuse received his brother, dressed all in black in sign of inward mourning for his change of condition, and, in the presence of a great congregation, buckled to his side the sword he had abandoned five years before. Père Ange had been transformed into the Duc de Joyeuse and Governor of Languedoc. For the next few years he governed his province and did battle against Henri IV. But with Henri's conversion and the pacification of France under a Catholic monarch, the League lost its reason for existence. Like other governors of provinces, the Duc de Joyeuse made his peace with the King. Henri IV, who knew how to choose his servants and collaborators, confirmed him in his titles and estates and created him a Marshal of France. Popular clamour had dragged Père Ange from the convent, and now it looked as though royal favour would keep him out. But the mourning garments he had put on in 1592 were the emblems of a genuine regret; and meanwhile his friends in the convent of the rue Saint-Honoré were not idle. "Where is that unitive and ecstatic life," Father Benet of Canfield wrote to him in an impassioned letter, "where the coarse habit, the thick cord, the patched cloak, where are the fasts, the disciplines, the meals of bread and water, the humilities of kissing the ground and sweeping the house? The mirror of France, is it spotted? Is he fled from the battle, that valiant captain among the Friars Minor? Is he slain, that child of St. Francis and the seraphic rule? Can it be that Frère Ange is dead? I am distressed for thee, my brother Jonathan. . . .

"And as for this, that on the outside of this letter I style you de Joyeuse, and within I call you my brother—be not surprised thereat; for it is only without and externally that you are de Joyeuse, but inwardly you are Frère Ange. And not only ought you to be Frère Ange, but also you cannot ever be anything else, even with the Pope's dispensation."

Father Benet spoke truly; having once tasted of "the unitive and ecstatic life," Henri de Joyeuse could not now be anything but Brother Angel. After seven years as governor, commander, duke and courtier, he returned to the order. That was in 1599, the year of François Leclerc's novitiate. In 1600, as we have seen already, it was the newly revived Père Ange who officiated at the reception of the newly created Father Joseph.

III

The Religious Background

IN ALL that concerned his personal religion, Father Joseph remained to the end of his life the faithful disciple of Benet of Canfield. If we would understand the pupil, we must familiarize ourselves with the teachings of his master. But in order properly to evaluate these teachings, we must first know something about the mystical tradition on which they are based and from which they significantly diverge.

In literary form, the mystical tradition makes its first appearance in the Upanishads, the earliest of which are supposed to date from about the eighth century before Christ. In these Hindu scriptures, we find a certain metaphysical theory of the universe and of man's relation to it. This theory is summarized in the phrase *Tat tvam asi*—thou art that. Ultimate reality is at once transcendent and immanent. God is the creator and sustainer of the world; yet the kingdom of God is also within us, as a mode of consciousness underlying, so to speak, the ordinary individualized consciousness of everyday life, but incommensurable with it; different in kind, and yet realizable by anyone who is prepared to "lose his life in order to save it." This metaphysical theory was an attempt to explain a certain kind of immediate experience, and in India it was always taught in conjunction with certain technical instructions regarding the ethical and psychological means whereby men might come to that experience, or, to use the language of the metaphysical theory, might realize the Brahman or ultimate reality latent within them.

Among the early Buddhists, the metaphysical theory was neither affirmed nor denied, but simply ignored, as being meaningless and unnecessary. Their concern was with the immediate experience, which because of its consequences for life, came to be known as "liberation" or "enlightenment." The Buddha and his disciples of the southern school seem to have applied to the problems of religion that "operational philosophy" which contemporary scientific thinkers have begun to apply in the natural sciences. "The concept," says Professor Bridgman in his *Logic of Modern Physics,* "is synonymous with the corresponding set of operations." "A question has meaning, when it is possible to find operations by which an answer can be given." Assertions which do not lend themselves to operational verification are neither true nor false, but without meaning. Buddha was not a consistent operationalist; for he seems to have taken for granted, to have accepted as something given and self-evident, a variant of the locally current theory of metempsychosis. Where mysticism was concerned, however, his operationalism was complete. He would not make assertions about the nature of ultimate reality because it did not seem to him that the corresponding set of mystical operations would admit of a theological interpretation. Mystical operations, he believed, yielded a sufficient answer to such psychological questions as What is liberation? or, What is enlightenment? They did not, in his opinion, yield a sufficient answer to the question What is Brahman? or, What is God?

Christianity started out with a metaphysical system

derived from several already existing and mutually incompatible systems. Jesus seems to have taken for granted the existence of the personal deity of the Old Testament; but at the same time he seems to have used a purely mystical approach to the kingdom of God which he actually experienced within his soul. These two elements, the traditionally Hebraic and the mystical, with its insistence on inward experience, were also present in the doctrine of St. Paul, together with others which have added further complications to Christian theology. Of mysticism in the early Church we know very little. Such psycho-physical phenomena as rapture, glossolalia, visions and revelations were common among the early Christians, and highly esteemed. These manifestations often occur in individuals whose religion is the very reverse of mystical; on the other hand, it is a fact of observation that they sometimes occur as by-products of a genuine mystical experience. We shall probably be fairly near the truth if we guess that there was, in the early Church, much corybantic revivalism and a little mystical contemplation. By the fourth century, as Cassian bears witness, a well-defined mystical philosophy and discipline had been developed among the solitaries and coenobites of the Egyptian desert. Cassian's dialogues with the Egyptian fathers were known to the medieval contemplatives and influenced their theories, habits of life and methods of devotion. Much more influential, because written by one who was a consummate literary artist as well as a knower of God, were St. Augustine's "Confessions." Before becoming a Christian, Augustine had been a student of Plotinus, and the God with whom he sought union was that neoplatonic "something not susceptible of change," which lies behind and is the source of all personal manifestations of deity. Plotinus was interested in oriental thought and as a young man accompanied the Emperor Gordian's expedition to the East, in order to pick up first-hand information on the subject of Persian and Indian philosophy. His one, ultimate reality which cannot be understood except through a direct mystical experience bears a close resemblance to the Brahman which is also Atman, the That which is at the same time Thou. During the fourth and fifth centuries, neoplatonism and along with it, at several removes, the most valuable elements of Hindu religion, entered Christianity and became incorporated, as one of a number of oddly heterogeneous elements, into its scheme of thought and devotion. St. Augustine, as we have seen, played an important part in this Christianizing of oriental mysticism. Even more important was the part played by the unknown Syrian writer of the fifth century who, in order to ensure the widest possible circulation for his writings, put them forth under the name of Dionysius the Areopagite, St. Paul's first Athenian convert. The pious fraud was admirably successful. Dionysius the Areopagite was read with the reverent attention due to his all but apostolic position. This was unfortunate in some ways, fortunate in others; for his books were of very unequal value. On the debit side of the account must be placed the two disquisitions on the heavenly and ecclesiastical hierarchies respectively. The first helped to justify the idolatrous polytheism, into which popular Christianity has always tended to degenerate; the second had a certain undesirable political significance insofar as it affirmed the divine origin of the Church's temporal organization. Over against these, on the credit side, must be set two very remarkable books,

Concerning the Divine Names and *Concerning Mystical Theology*. Using philosophic material derived from neoplatonism and various oriental sources, and drawing upon his own first-hand experience, their author sets forth the mystical tradition in its most austere, Vedantic form. Translated into Latin by Scotus Erigena, in the ninth century, these books were widely read during the whole of the Middle Ages and exercised an extraordinary influence. Accepting the Areopagite's theology and psychology as given, the medieval mystics proceeded to work out for themselves the operations corresponding to these concepts, operations which—in India, in the Egyptian desert, among the Sufis, wherever contemplation has been practised—have always resulted in the same sort of philosophy. In the literature which these contemplatives left behind them, we can read a description of such operations and of the spiritual discoveries which were made possible by their means.

Benet of Canfield was a learned man and had read, not only the Areopagite, but also all the important medieval and sixteenth-century mystics, for whom the writings of pseudo-Dionysius had been an inspiration and a comforting guarantee of their own orthodoxy. An artist is born with certain talents, specifically his own; but he makes use of those talents within the framework of the current artistic tradition. It is the same with the mystic, whose religious life is constituted by the interaction between inborn spiritual aptitudes and the tradition within which he thinks and works. What was the nature of the tradition, at once philosophical, ethical and psychological, in which Father Benet had been brought up? To answer this question I shall briefly summarize a little book that is one of the finest flowers of medieval mystical literature. Composed by an anonymous English author of the fourteenth century, *The Cloud of Unknowing* is at once profoundly original and completely representative of its class. Its author was a man who combined high spiritual gifts and a remarkable literary and philosophic talent with a deep knowledge and love of tradition. Within the compass of that small book the whole medieval development of Dionysian mysticism is exhibited in its essence, and at the same time, as a modern Catholic writer, Father John Chapman remarks, "it seems to sum up the doctrines of St. John of the Cross two hundred years beforehand."

That Father Benet was acquainted with this book is certain; for, in his admirable commentary on *The Cloud,* Father Augustine Baker, the English Benedictine monk and mystical theologian, who was an almost exact contemporary of Father Joseph, records that his own manuscript copy of the book had "belonged to the private library of Father Benet Fitch, our countryman, the Capuchin, author of the book called *The Will of God,* and upon his death was found among other books in his library." Richly did it deserve its place there!

The book's title implies its central doctrine. "The cloud of unknowing" is the same as what the Areopagite calls the "super-luminous darkness"—the impenetrable mystery of God's otherness. Ultimate reality is incommensurable with our own illusoriness and imperfection; therefore it cannot be understood by means of intellectual operations; for intellectual operations depend upon language, and our vocabulary and syntax were evolved for the purpose of dealing precisely with that imperfection and illusoriness, with which God is incommensurable.

Ultimate reality cannot be understood except intuitively, through an act of the will and the affections. *"Plus diligitur quam intelligitur"* was a commonplace of scholastic philosophy. "Love can go further than understanding; for love enters where science remains out of doors. We love God in his essence, but in his essence we do not see Him."

The author of *The Cloud* concerns himself very little with metaphysical speculations. To him, as to the Buddha, thinking about problems to which, in the nature of things, vocalized thought can give no answer seems a waste of time and an obstacle in the way of spiritual advance. Nor is he interested to quote other men's opinions. "Once men thought it a meekness to say nought of their own heads, unless they confirmed it by scripture and doctors' words; now it is turned into curiosity and display of knowledge." Because of these views about learning and speculation, he leaves unexplained the details of the philosophical system which underlies his practical mysticism. But from all he says it is evident that he takes for granted the hypothesis then current among mystical theologians as to the relation existing between God and man. According to this hypothesis, there exists within the soul something variously called the "synderesis," the "spark," the "ground of the soul," "the apex of the higher will." Of this divine element in their being men are, for the most part, unaware, because all their attention is fixed on the objects of craving and aversion. But, if they choose to "die to self," they can become aware of the divine element within them and, in it, experience God. For those who so desire and are prepared to fulfil the necessary conditions, the transcendent can in some way become immanent within the spark, at the apex of the higher will.

This theory bears a close family resemblance to that which, from time immemorial, has been fundamental to Indian thought. But whereas the oriental mystics have never shrunk from establishing a complete identity between the "spark" and God Himself, the Christians have generally adopted a more cautious attitude. "Thou are That," affirm the Indians; the Atman is of the same substance with Brahman. A Sufi mystic could say, "I went from God to God until they cried from me in me, 'Oh, thou I.' " For Christian thinkers, creature and creator were incommensurable, and the possibility of union with God did not imply a substantial identity of the "spark" with that with which it was united. Some statements of the German and later Flemish mystics have, it is true, a positively Indian ring about them; but it was precisely for this reason that such writers as Eckhart were suspect to the ecclesiastical authorities. In this respect the author of *The Cloud* is strictly orthodox. Man's soul can be "oned with God"; but it is not for that reason of the same substance as God. "Only by his mercy without thy desert art thou made a god in grace, oned with him in spirit, without separation, both here and in the bliss of heaven without any end. So that although thou be all one with him in grace, yet thou art full far beneath him in nature." This "oneing" of the godhead with the spark in the soul can never be complete in the present life. The full beatific vision is reserved for eternity—indeed, in some sense, *is* eternity. For the soul, "is immortal inasmuch as it is capable of the beatific vision." *Ut beatificabilis, est immortalis.* In the flesh, men are not strong enough to bear the plenary experience of God without physical injury or death. In the words of Cardinal Bérulle, "God is infinitely desirable and infinitely insupportable. And when it pleases him to apply himself to his creature, without proportioning himself to his creature, he cannot be supported by the created being, which feels itself engulfed, ruined by this infinite power." Similarly, the Indians affirm that more than a certain amount of the highest *samadhi* is fatal to the body of him who experiences it.

So much for the metaphysical system underlying *The Cloud.* Our author accepts the current hypotheses without discussion. What interests him is something else—the facts of empirical experience which originally called for interpretation in terms of such hypotheses, and the means whereby such facts might be reproduced in the souls of those who desire to experience God. Only by implication and incidentally is the book a philosophical treatise; explicitly it is a handbook of mystical practice, a guide to a certain way of life—the way of spiritual perfection.

The author of *The Cloud* prefaces his volume by an urgent and emphatic recommendation to "whatsoever thou be that this book shall have in possession" that "thou neither read it, write it or speak it, nor yet suffer it to be read, written or spoken, by any other or to any other, unless it be by such a one, or to such a one as hath (in thy supposing) in a true will and by a whole intent purposed him to be a perfect follower of Christ." The reason for this recommendation is simple. *The Cloud* is a book for those who are already well advanced on the road of mystical education. It is not a primer. True, "the work of this book," as the author calls the art of achieving mystical union with God, is necessary, not merely for a few, but for all. "For want of this working a man falleth ever deeper and deeper into sin, and further and further from God."

For this reason the command to be "perfect even as your Father in Heaven is perfect" is incumbent upon every man and woman. "There is no Christian, whatever anyone may say, who is not bound by the duties of his profession at the baptismal font, to undertake the study and practice of mystical theology." So, continuing a venerable and orthodox tradition, wrote the Carmelite, Father Leon of St. John, an eminent contemporary of our own Father Joseph. But, like all other studies and practices, those of mystical theology must begin at the beginning. And the beginning is a long-drawn process of moral amendment, discursive meditation and training of the will. Hence the paucity of mystics; for the world is mainly peopled by Micawbers, optimistically convinced that something or somebody will turn up and get them out of the difficulties from which, as a matter of cold fact, they can be saved only by their own efforts. Many, in this case all, are called; but few are chosen, for the good reason that few choose themselves.

The author of *The Cloud* assumes that his readers have already taken the first steps and are persistent in their resolve to be "perfect followers of Christ." To these he imparts the work appropriate to the second, or higher stage of contemplative life. This work consists in the cultivation of the art of loving God for himself alone and as he is in himself—not for what the worshipper can get out of him and not as he is after passing through the refractive medium of a human personality. "Lift up thine heart to God with a blind stirring of love; and mean himself and none of his goods." These "stirrings of love" must be blind, because, if God is to be experienced as he is in himself, he must be loved with a pure act of the will, unmitigated by discursive reasoning. There must be no vain and distracting attempt to comprehend what is in its nature incomprehensible. The work of the contemplative is to train himself in abstraction from all creatures, above all his own feelings, wishes, memories and thoughts. He must "tread them under the cloud of forgetting," and, having done so, must beat "with a naked intent," a "blind stirring of love" upon the "dark cloud of unknowing" within which God as he is in himself is forever wrapped from human sight. If he beats persistently enough upon the cloud, if the "dart of his longing love" is sharp enough, if the "cloud of forgetting" between this love and his own personality is sufficiently thick, it may be granted to the contemplative to see God, if not yet face to face, at least less darkly than at first. This is as far as the active work of contemplation can hope to go. But it sometimes happens, as our author and his fellow mystics insist, that this active contemplation gives place to a passive contemplation, in which God is the agent and his worshipper but an instrument which he uses for his divine purposes. In these cases God "sends out a beam of ghostly light, piercing this cloud of unknowing that is between thee and him." It is an act of special grace, in no way dependent upon the efforts of the contemplative; therefore, the mystics are all agreed, nothing can profitably be said of passive contemplation except that it does sometimes occur. (It may be remarked that this distinction between active and passive contemplation seems to correspond to the distinction made by Indian writers between the lower and higher levels of *samadhi*. Couched in whatever language and formulated at whatever period, mystical theories are based upon the empirical facts of mystical experience. It is therefore not to be wondered at if such theories reveal fundamental similarities of structure.)

Selfhood is a heavy, hardly translucent medium, which cuts off most of the light of reality and distorts what little it permits to pass. The Old Adam cannot see God as he is in himself. The aspiring contemplative must therefore rid himself of selfhood. The author of *The Cloud* assumes that the person for whom he writes has already obtained sufficient mastery over his passions and has learned, in his meditations, to exclude the discursive, analytical intellect from a sphere in which its workings serve only to inhibit the direct experience of reality. But the passions and the discursive intellect are not the only components of the self; there is also a great psychological province to which the name most commonly given by mystical writers is "distractions," a province little touched upon by ordinary moralists and, for that reason, worth describing in some detail. Contemplatives have compared distractions to dust, to swarms of flies, to the movements of a monkey stung by a scorpion. Always their metaphors call up the image of a purposeless agitation. And this, precisely, is the interesting and significant thing about distractions. The passions are essentially purposeful, and the thoughts, the emotions, the phantasies connected with the passions always have some reference to the real or imaginary ends proposed, or to the means whereby such ends may be achieved. With distractions the case is quite different. It is of their essence to be irrelevant and pointless. To find out just how pointless and irrelevant they can be, one has merely to sit down and try to recollect oneself. Preoccupations connected with the passions will most probably come to the surface of consciousness, but along with them will rise a bobbing scum of miscellaneous memories, notions and imaginings—childhood recollections of one's grandmother's Skye terrier, the French name for henbane, a white-knightish scheme for catching incendiary bombs in mid air—in a word, every kind of nonsense and silliness. The psycho-analytical contention, that all the divagations of the subconscious carry a deep passional significance, cannot be made to fit the facts. One has only to observe oneself and others to discover that we are no more exclusively the servants of our passions and our biological urges than we are exclusively rational; we are also creatures possessed of a very complicated psycho-physiological machine which grinds away incessantly and, in the course of its grinding, throws up into consciousness selections from that indefinite number of mental permutations and combinations struck out in the course of its random functioning. These permutations and combinations of mental elements have nothing to do with our passions or our more rational mental processes; they are just imbecilities—mere waste products of psycho-physiological activity. True, such imbecilities may be made use of by the passions of their own ends, as when the Old Adam in us throws up a barrage of intrinsically pointless distractions in an attempt to nullify the creative efforts of the higher will. But even when not so used by the passions, even in themselves, distractions constitute a formidable obstacle to any kind of spiritual advance. The imbecile in us is as radically God's enemy as the passionate and purposeful maniac, with his insane cravings and aversions. Moreover, the imbecile remains at large and busy, when the lunatic has been tamed or actually destroyed. In other words, a man may have succeeded in overcoming his passions, in replacing them by a fixed one-pointed desire for enlightenment, and yet still be hindered in his advance by the uprush into consciousness of pointless distractions. This is the reason why all advanced spirituals have attached so much importance to these imbecilities and have ranked them as grave imperfections, even as sins. It is, I think to distractions, or at least to one of the main classes of distractions, that Christ refers in that strangely enigmatic and alarming saying, "that every idle word that men shall speak they shall give account thereof in the day of judgment. For by thy words shalt thou be justified and by thy words shalt thou be condemned." Verbalized imbecilities, spoken irrelevances, all utterances, indeed, that do not subserve the end of enlightenment, must be condemned as being barriers between the soul and ultimate reality. They may seem harmless enough; but this harmlessness is only in relation to mundane ends; in relation to the eternal and spiritual, they are extremely harmful. In this context, I would like to quote a paragraph from the biography of that seventeenth-century French saint, Charles de Condren. A pious lady, named Mlle de la Roche, was in great distress, because she found it impossible to make a satisfactory confession. "Her trouble was that her sins seemed to her greater than she was able to say. Her faults were not considerable, nevertheless she was quite unable, she said, ever to express them. If the confessor told her that he was content with her accusation, she would answer that she was not satisfied with it and that, since she was not telling the truth, he could not give her absolution. If he pressed her to tell the whole truth, she felt utterly incapable of doing so." Nobody knew what to say to this unfortunate woman, who came in time to be regarded as not quite right in the head. Finally, she addressed herself to Condren, whose comments on her case are of the greatest interest. " 'It is true,' he said, 'that you have not adequately expressed your sins; but the fact is that, in this life, it is impossible to represent them in all their hideousness; we shall never know them as they really are until we see them in the pure light of God. God gives you an impression of the deformity of sin, by which he makes you feel it to be incomparably greater than it appears to your understanding or can be expressed by your words. Hence your anguish and distress . . . You must therefore conceive of your sins, as faith presents them to your mind—in other words, as they are in themselves; but you must content yourself with describing them in such words as your mouth can form.' " All that Condren says about poor Mlle de la Roche's no doubt very venial sins applies with equal force to distractions. Judged by everyday human standards, they seem matters of no account. And yet, as they are in themselves, as they are in relation to that "pure light of God," which they are able to eclipse and darken, as the sun is darkened by a dust storm or a cloud of locusts, these trifling imperfections have as much power for evil in the soul as anger, or an ugly greed, or some obsessive apprehension.

The psycho-physical machine, which produces distractions as a by-product of its functioning, works on materials derived from the external world. This, so far as civilized man is concerned, is mainly a human world, made in his own image—a projection and material embodiment of his reason, his passions and his imbecilities. To distractions within correspond the external distractions of civilized life—news, gossip, various kinds of sensuous, emotional and intellectual amusements, novelties and gadgets of every sort, casual social contacts, unnecessary business, all the diversified irrelevances whose pointless succession constitutes the vast majority of human lives. Because a large part of our personality is naturally imbecile, because we like this imbecility and have a habit of it, we have built ourselves a largely imbecile world to live in. Deep calls to deep; inner distractions evoke outer distractions and in their turn the outer evoke the inner. Between congenitally distracted individuals and their distracting, imbecile environment there is set up a kind of self-perpetuating resonance.

Fate which foresaw
How frivolous a baby man would be—
By what distractions he would be possessed,
How he would pour himself in every strife,
And well nigh change his own identity—
That it might keep from his capricious play
His genuine self, and force him to obey
Even in his own despite his being's law,
Bade through the deep recesses of our breast
The unregarded river of our life
Pursue with indiscernible flow its way;
And that we should not see
The buried stream, and seem to be
Eddying at large in blind uncertainty,
Though driving on with it eternally.

But often, in the world's most crowded streets,
But often in the din of strife,
There rises an unspeakable desire
After the knowledge of our buried life;
A thirst to spend our fire and restless force

In tracking out our true, original course;
A longing to enquire
Into the mystery of this heart which beats
So wild, so deep in us—to know
Whence our lives come and where they go.
And many a man in his own breast then delves,
But deep enough, alas! none ever mines.

Every sensitive human being has at one time or another realized the pointlessness and squalor of the common life of incessant and reiterated distractions, has longed for one-pointedness of being and purity of heart. But how pitifully few have ever chosen to act upon this realization, have tried to satisfy their longing! None has written more eloquently of the misery of the distracted life than Matthew Arnold. And yet, though he was fairly well versed in Christian literature, though, as a young man, he had been profoundly impressed by an early translation of the *Bhagavad-Gita,* he sought no practical remedy for that misery and denied, even as a matter of theory, the very possibility of such a remedy existing. The best he can offer is merely the symbol, the distorted human reflection of a remedy.

Only—but this is rare—
When a beloved hand is laid in ours . . . ,
A bolt is shot back in our breast; . . .
A man becomes aware of his life's flow
And hears its winding murmur . . . ,
And then he thinks he knows
The hills where his life rose
And the sea where it goes.

Note the sad lucidity of the phrase, "he thinks he knows."

More romantic and optimistic, Browning would have asserted emphatically that the man *did* know the secret of life every time his "world-deafened ear is by the tones of a loved voice caressed." Matthew Arnold was too realistically minded to fall into such a confusion, and too honest to pretend that he believed the flattering doctrine which equates those two incommensurables, the human and the divine. Those who enjoy the natural ecstasies of passion and affection do not know; they merely think they know. And for the unlucky ones who do not happen to have a beloved hand to clasp there is nothing but to

> demand
> Of all the thousand nothings of the hour
> Their stupefying power;
> Ah yes, and they benumb us at our call!

But they benumb us only for a little while, and then the old misery returns more unbearable than ever. In the theological language of John Tauler (or whoever it was that wrote "The Following of Christ"), "each sin begetteth a special spiritual suffering. A suffering of this kind is like unto that of hell, for the more you suffer, the worse you become; this happeneth to sinners; the more they suffer through their sins, the more wicked they become, and they fall continually more into them, in order to get free of suffering."

Like so many poets and moralists before him, Arnold had stated a problem to which there is no practical solution, except through some system of spiritual exercises. In the overwhelming majority of individuals, distraction is the natural condition; one-pointedness must be acquired. One-pointedness can, of course, be turned to evil purposes no less than good. But the risk of actualizing a potential evil must always be run by those who seek the good. In this case, the good cannot be achieved without one-pointedness. That Arnold should have failed to draw the unavoidable conclusion from the premises of his own thoughts and feelings seems puzzling only when we consider him apart from his environment. The mental climate in which he lived was utterly unpropitious to the flowering of genuine mysticism. The nineteenth century could tolerate only false, ersatz mysticisms—the nature-mysticism of Wordsworth; the sublimated sexual mysticism of Whitman; the nationality-mysticisms of all the patriotic poets and philosophers of every race and culture, from Fichte at the beginning of the period to Kipling and Barrès at the end. Once more, Arnold's "sad lucidity" did not permit him to embrace any of these manifestly unsatisfactory substitutes for the genuine article. He chose instead the mild and respectable road of literary modernism. It was a blind alley, of course; but better a blind alley than the headlong descent, by way of the mysticisms of nationality and humanity, to war, revolution and universal tyranny.

The acquisition of one-pointedness and the cultivation of genuine mysticism were tasks no easier in the fourteenth century, or the seventeenth, than under Queen Victoria; they merely seemed more reasonable, more worthy of consideration by men of culture and intelligence. No concern for his intellectual respectability deterred the author of *The Cloud* from telling his pupils the best ways of approaching God and repressing or circumventing the distractions, which interpose themselves between the soul and ultimate reality. He wrote; and those who read his book—even those who read it without the smallest intention of following his instructions—regarded him as an eminently sensible person, treating of a highly important subject.

In *The Cloud* a number of different methods for dealing with distractions are described. There is the method which consists in fixing the unstable mind by means of what the Indians call a *mantra*—a word or short phrase constantly repeated, so that it fills, so to speak, the whole conscious and subconscious foreground of the personality, leaving the something that exists in the background (the higher will of scholastic psychology) free to beat with its blind stirrings of love against the cloud of unknowing. Another method may be described as the method of repression and inattention; distractions are "trodden down under the cloud of forgetting"—not with a vehement effort of the will (for such efforts tend to defeat their own object and to strengthen, rather than weaken the forces of distraction), but by a gentle turning away towards the object of contemplation. The distraction is ignored; one "looks over its shoulder" at what lies beyond and, deprived of the attention which gave it life, the distraction perishes of inanition. Sometimes, however, it happens that distractions make their assault in such force that they cannot be defeated or avoided by any of the foregoing methods. In this case, says our author, it is best to yield to them, to allow them to swarm over the mind like a conquering horde. Meanwhile, the mind should make itself conscious of its humiliating defeat, should dwell upon its own abjectness in being unable to resist the enemy. From this realization of impotence may spring a livelier sense of the greatness and goodness of God and, with it, new stirrings of love, new power to beat with naked intent upon the cloud of unknowing.

It should be noted here that, in the higher stages of contemplation, all thoughts and feelings, even the holiest, must be counted as distractions, if they hold back the higher will from its blind beating against the cloud. Like Eckhart, like St. John of the Cross and indeed like all the great mystics of the Dionysian tradition, our author is emphatic on this point. "Weep thou never so much for sorrow of thy sins, or of the passion of Christ, or have thou never so much thought of the joys of heaven, what may it do to thee? Surely, much good, much help, much profit, and much grace will it get thee. But in comparison of this blind stirring of love, it is but little that it doth, or may do, without this. This by itself is the *best part* of Mary, without these other. They without it profit but little or nought. It destroyeth not only the ground and the root of sin, but also it getteth virtues. For if it be truly conceived, all virtues shall be subtly and perfectly conceived, felt and comprehended in it, without any mingling of thine intent . . . For virtue is nought else but an ordered and measured affection plainly directed unto God for himself."

Discursive meditations on the passion are profitable at an earlier stage of the contemplative life; for those who are far advanced along the road of perfection, they are distractions interposed between the soul and the dark cloud of godhead. The same is true of meditations on one's own sins. Our author takes it for granted that his pupils have confessed and been absolved of their old sins and are doing their best to live virtuously as "perfect followers of Christ." For those who have reached this state, a constant dwelling upon past offences and present shortcomings, is not merely of no special profit, it actually tends to increase their egotism—and egotism is nothing but the root of evil, the settled propensity to sin. Like the idea of God, the idea of sin must not be analysed by the contemplative. "Hold them all whole these words; and mean by sin a lump, thou knowest not what, none other thing but thyself." Sin is the manifestation of self. Men commit evil and suffer misery, because they are separate egos, caught in time.

> I am gall, I am heartburn. God's most deep decree
> Bitter would have me taste; my taste was me.
> Bones built in me, flesh filled, blood brimmed the curse;
> Selfyeast of spirit a dull dough sours. I see
> The lost are like this, and their scourge to be
> As I am mine, their sweating selves; but worse.

This anguish at being a separate, God-excluding self is the final act of repentance for the ultimate sin. "Thou shalt find, when thou has forgotten all other creatures and all their works—yea! and also all thine own works—that there shall remain yet after, betwixt thee and thy God, a naked knowing and a feeling of thine own being." This knowing and feeling of our own being is the trespass which cannot be forgiven unless and until we work to have the unitive experience of God. Conversely the knowing and feeling of self "must always be destroyed, ere the time be that thou mayest feel verily the perfection of this work." How may this sense of separate individuality be destroyed? Only by "a full special grace full freely given by God, and also a full according ableness on thy part to receive this grace . . . And this ableness is nought else but a strong and a deep ghostly sorrow. . . . All men have matter of sorrow; but most specially he feeleth matter of sorrow that knoweth and feeleth that he *is*. All other sorrows in comparison with this be but as it were game to earnest. For he may make sorrow earnestly that knoweth and feeleth not only *what* he is, but *that* he is. And whoso never felt this sorrow, let him make sorrow; for he never yet felt perfect sorrow."

When he has sorrowed for the sin of his separate individuality, the contemplative must take the unanalysed sense of his own being and annihilate it in a sense of the being of God. He must work until the blind stirring of love, the beating against the cloud of unknowing, the naked intent to be made one with God as he is in himself, have actually taken the place of his sense of self, so that when he knows and feels his own being, he knows and feels as much at least of the being of God as he has been able to experience through the veils of the divine darkness.

Such, in briefest summary, is the teaching of *The Cloud of Unknowing*, a teaching which, as I have said before, is the same in every essential as that of all the great masters of the Dionysian tradition. In the years that immediately followed his conversion, Benet of Canfield made himself familiar with this tradition, and when he himself came to teach the art of mental prayer to others, he remained in all points but one its faithful continuator.

Father Benet did most of his teaching by word of mouth or by means of manuscript instructions specially prepared for each of his pupils. Early in the 1590's, however, he composed a full-length treatise on mystical practice and mystical theology. Manuscripts of this were communicated to selected individuals and religious communities, and many copies of the book were made, generally without the friar's authorization. Finally, in the first years of the new century, a pirated version of the work, very inaccurate and with additions by some other hand, found its way into print. In defense of his doctrine, Father Benet was compelled to publish the book as he had written it. Under the title, *The Rule of Perfection, reduced to the sole point of The Will of God,* it appeared first in French, then in the author's Latin translation, published at Cologne in 1610. Several editions were called for, and it was translated, in part, into English (1609) and in its entirety into Italian (1667). In spite of its considerable contemporary success, *The Rule of Perfection* was, within a hundred years, completely forgotten and is now very hard to come by, in any edition or language.

All mystics are agreed that knowledge of ultimate reality comes only to those who have killed out the Old Adam and conformed the personal will to the will of God; conversely, that killing out of the Old Adam and the conforming of the personal will to God's will can only be consummated by those who are in process of acquiring the knowledge of ultimate reality. Some mystics have laid the greatest stress upon one aspect of this double, reciprocating process; some upon the other. Father Benet was one of those to whom it seemed best and most natural to emphasize the voluntary aspect of enlightenment. As the title of his book implies, he was primarily concerned with a technique for the daily and continuous losing of one's personal life in order to gain divine life, for eliminating the personal will in order to make room for the will of God. His aim was to show how everyday, active life could be made to subserve contemplation, and how the spirit of contemplation could be made to animate and transform active life. In all its editions his book was preceded by an engraved frontispiece, certainly conceived and perhaps (for it is of a touching incompetence and amateurishness) actually executed by Father Benet himself. The lower part of this engraving shows the Saviour at prayer on the Mount of Olives, with the disciples asleep in the background and, in the sky, an angel presenting a chalice. Below are inscribed the words, *Non mea voluntas sed tua fiat.*[1] The upper part of the engraving is filled by an elaborate circular diagram, curiously like one of those symbolic *mandalas,* into which the Buddhists contrive to cram such a wealth of doctrinal significance. Facing the frontispiece is a page of print, in which Father Benet has explained the significance of his diagram. "This figure in the form of a sun represents the will of God. The faces placed here in the sun represent souls living in the divine will. . . . These faces are arranged in three concentric circles, showing the three degrees of this divine will. The first degree signifies the souls of the active life; the second, those of the life of contemplation; the third, those of the life of supereminence. Outside the first circle are many tools, such as pincers and hammers, denoting the active life. Inside the third circle is Jehovah. But round the second circle we have placed nothing at all, in order to signify that in this kind of contemplative life, without any other speculations or practices, one must follow the leading of the will of God. The tools are on the ground and in shadow, inasmuch as outward works are of themselves full of darkness. These tools, however, are touched by a ray of the sun, to show that works may be enlightened and illuminated by the will of God.

[1] Not my will be done, but Thine.

"The light of the divine will shines but little on the faces of the first circle; much more on those of the second; while those of the third are resplendent. The first show up most clearly; the second, less; the third, hardly at all. This signifies that the souls of the first degree are much in themselves; those of the second degree are less in themselves and more in God; while those of the third degree are almost nothing in themselves and all in God and absorbed in his essential will. All these faces have their eyes fixed on the will of God." The text of *The Rule of Perfection* is in the nature of an extended commentary on this symbolical frontispiece.

Father Benet begins by classifying the will of God under three heads; Exterior, Interior and Essential. The exterior will of God is "a certain light, norm or rule that guides us in active life"; the interior, "a brightness that directs us and supports the soul in contemplation"; and the essential, "a splendour that governs and perfects the spirit in the supereminent life." The first exercise that the aspirant must learn is the "practice of the intention of the will of God." There are six grades of this intention, which must be actual, unique, willing, indubitable, clear and prompt.

When one intends actually, one notes within oneself the actual remembrance of the will of God; and one excludes thereby the sins of forgetfulness and mental dissipation. "This forgetting," writes Father Benet, "is a common error that brings immense harm, depriving us of an incredible amount of light and grace." To intend uniquely, is to conceive of God's will as the sole and simple end of all one does or suffers. By this act one excludes all other selfish or merely irrelevant ends.

God's will must not be done in a grimly stoical spirit,

but with full inclination and a sense of peace and joy. In other words, the intention must be willing. To intend willingly excludes strain, worry and gloom, and makes the soul capable of receiving the Holy Spirit, of whom it is written, *"Factus est in pace locus ejus."*[2]

Intending indubitably, one excludes all vacillation; for one believes firmly that the work undertaken for the will of God is really God's will.

Clarity of intention refers to the quality of the faith involved. One clearly conceives the eternal and divine significance of one's actions in the world of creatures.

Finally there is the act of prompt intention, which excludes dilatoriness and sloth.

The practice of these six grades of intention is prescribed by Father Benet at every stage of the spiritual life, from the most rudimentary to the most advanced. The exercise is a very difficult one, but it is obvious that anyone who has learned to carry it out faithfully has gone far in the direction of transforming his entire life into a continuous act of prayer and contemplation.

A question that naturally arises, as we read this section of the book, is the following: How do we know which acts are in accord with God's will and which are not? Father Benet tries to answer—not, it must be admitted, with entire success. He divides acts into three classes, those commanded, directly or indirectly, by divine authority; those prohibited; and the indifferent. In regard to the first two, God's will is clear, because there are laws and commandments which embody an objective norm of conduct. In regard to the third, what counts is the intention. For in matters indifferent, "the work accords with the

[2] In peace is his place established.

intention, not the intention with the work." If, while doing an indifferent thing, we dedicate our action to God, the doing of it will actually be the will of God. To go for a walk or to eat one's dinner, consciously, for God's sake is better, so far as one's own soul is concerned, than the performance of intrinsically meritorious acts for one's own advantage. All this is good as far as it goes; but unfortunately it does not go far enough. Father Benet says nothing whatever about a whole class of acts which, so far as their earthly consequences are concerned, are more important than any others: I mean, those acts which the individual performs, not for his own sake, but on behalf and for the advantage of some social organization, such as a nation, a church, a political party, a religious order, a business concern, a family. There are no moral problems more difficult than those connected with this class of actions. All the more reason, then, that in a treatise on the practice of God's will they should be thoroughly examined. Father Benet chose to ignore them. In this, he followed the example of all too many Christian moralists, belonging to both the great ethical traditions—the mystical, "theocentric" tradition and that other "anthropocentric" tradition derived from Stoicism. If Father Joseph deviated from the way of perfection into power politics, the fault must be attributed in part, at least, to his upbringing. Benet of Canfield never discussed the relationship between political action on the one hand and, on the other, the unitive life, the doing of the will of God. In a later chapter, it will be necessary to examine this relationship in some detail.

The second part of *The Rule of Perfection* deals with the interior will of God—that "brightness which directs and supports the soul in contemplation." According to Father Benet the interior will of God is realized in stages, of which he counts five, namely, manifestations, admirations, humiliations, exultations and elevations. (The list, as one reels off the polysyllables, seems a trifle ridiculous. But then so do all classifications. Compared with the manifest continuity of nature, what could be more absurd than the elaborate hierarchy of names devised by men of science? And yet, without such a hierarchy of names, there could be no analysis of the world about us and no intellectual understanding. It is the same with the higher psychology. Its experiences are continuous and direct; but they cannot be described or theorized about, and the conditions of their realization cannot be taught, except in terms of a hierarchy of analytical names. So long as we remember that "words are signs of things" and avoid the all too common and absolutely fatal mistake of "making things the signs of words," classifications can be of the utmost value to us. With this parenthetic warning, let us return to Father Benet's polysyllables.)

Manifestations, which are those experiences of the divine presence that ordinarily accompany the first stages of the contemplative life, follow normally from the exercise of pure intentions in regard to the exterior will. The mechanism is simple: purity of intention in action produces a dying away of passions and affections directed towards mundane objects; the dying away of passions and affections produces tranquillity of mind, which in turn produces the inward silence in which the soul can begin to experience the immanent divinity.

Admirations arise when the contemplative gains a direct experience of God's infinite greatness, together with a correlated experience of his own intrinsic nothingness.

Humiliations are a further fruit of the sense of personal nothingness, and are valuable as providing an antidote to that complacency, into which beginners so easily fall after their first experiences of divine graces.

God's goodness in uniting himself with the soul in spite of its abjectness produces exultations. This spiritual joy makes sweet the progressive denial of self which is the necessary condition of progressive advance in the way of union. In Father Benet's own words, it "makes us despise carnal consolations, makes easy things that seem impossible, opens the way to heaven."

Finally, the contemplative reaches the stage of elevations. These are the "blind stirrings of love" which result in union. *Quis adhaeret Deo, unus spiritus est.*

Of the third part of his book Father Benet says specifically that it is not for beginners. Its subject is the essential will of God, and the practices it inculcates are the equivalents of pure intention and contemplation on a higher stage of that ascending spiral, which is the way of perfection.

The essential will of God is that the soul should become united with God's essence. In this union, the soul is passive, God alone active. All the soul can do is to expose itself, utterly naked of its will, to the will of God, and to use "a subtle industry" in order to strip away the last shreds of its selfhood.

Father Benet begins by describing two approaches to the supreme task of doing the essential will of God. The first is through a consideration of the imperfections in one's acts of contemplation. Imperfections exist at every

ACTION, CONTEMPLATION, UNION

Engraved frontispiece to the Latin edition of *The Rule of Perfection* by Benet of Canfield

stage of the spiritual life. In the early stages, they are gross and palpable. But as the mind becomes increasingly illuminated, these disappear and are replaced by faults of a more subtle nature. No spiritual, however far advanced, can ever afford to relax his watchfulness; for in an illuminated mind, the tiniest imperfection can effectively hinder union with God.

The contemplation of advanced spirituals has three common defects. First, it may be too fervent, in which case the soul is not peaceful enough to receive God. Second, the soul may retain a subtle image of what is in itself imageless, the essence of God. Thirdly, the soul may conceive of God as being somewhere else than "in its own ground," "at the apex of the higher will." All these defects can be remedied by suitable acts of "denudation." Emotionality and images can be stripped away; and when they have been stripped away, it will be found that the soul has become fit for the consciousness of God as pure immanence.

The second approach to the doing of God's essential will is through Annihilation, which is the final, consummating stage of the long-drawn process of getting rid of self-will.

Annihilation is classified by Father Benet as passive and active. Passive annihilation occurs, when God actually makes himself present to us in contemplation. Active annihilation is the being dead to the world while working in the world, the dwelling inwardly in eternity while outwardly operating in time. Both types of annihilation are necessary; but active annihilation is the higher and more perfect condition.

Concerning passive annihilation, Father Benet has little

to add to what was said of contemplation in the preceding section of his book. Distractions are touched upon, and the contemplative is advised to avoid and circumvent, never to fight against the intruding irrelevances. "For the more a man operates, the more he is and exists." But the more the man exists, the less God exists within him.

It is for an analogous reason that the advanced contemplative should avoid in his meditations all particular aspects of the divine life, and content himself with a "simple regard" directed to God in his totality.

Active annihilation is obtained through a process of "recording," a kind of continuous, effortless awareness of God, and through a pure faith, which conceives of God as really present even in those circumstances, in which there is no sensible inward evidence of that presence and no reason for inferring it.

In this third section of "The Rule," the right relationship between action and contemplation, between man in time and God in eternity, is discussed at length and with great subtlety. Here, I can only summarize what Father Benet says about that shrinking from outward works, into which so many spirituals fall, out of a fear of being distracted from their contemplation of God. This shrinking, he insists, defeats its own object and is in fact the final and greatest obstacle to perfection. For "the more the soul fears and retreats from outward works, the more the images of these things stamp themselves upon her. Furthermore, she tends to attribute to them the place and standing of God. God must be recognized as being everywhere and, for the contemplative, his presence should do away with outward things. Instead of that, the soul that is afraid of outward things gives so much place to them that their presence does away with God." The spiritual who knows only passive contemplation tends to introvert his mind away from things, to retreat from them into an inward act of contemplation. But this does not abolish the problem of outward works; it merely postpones it to another occasion. Moreover, introversion implies extraversion, the attitude of the average sensual man who regards outward things as fully real and worthy of being treated as ends in themselves. "I say, then, that introversion must be rejected, because extraversion must never be admitted; but one must live continuously in the abyss of the divine essence and in the absolute nothingness of things; and if at times a man finds himself separated from them (the essence and the nothingness), he must return to them, not by introversion, but by annihilation." The learning to live in constant active annihilation is probably the most difficult and exacting of all human tasks; but to those who fulfill it comes the reward that came to Brother Lawrence and St. Teresa, to Mme Acarie, to Father Benet himself and, indeed to all the great mystics; the experience of living simultaneously in time and eternity, among men and in God; the peace and bliss, here in this earthly life, of the beatific vision. The state to which Father Benet gave the name of active annihilation has been described, not only by Christian mystics, but also by the contemplatives of other faiths—by Hindus, by Buddhists, by Taoists, by the Sufis. All are agreed in regarding it as the highest, the most perfect condition to which the human consciousness —purified, one-pointed, radically transformed—can attain.

Up to this point *The Rule of Perfection* contains nothing which might not be found in the writings of any of the great contemplatives of the Dionysian tradition. But from now on Father Benet leaves the path of pure, undogmatic mysticism followed by his predecessors, to take another, more specifically Catholic road.

Father Benet departs from traditional mysticism by insisting that even the most advanced contemplatives should persist in "the practice of the passion"—in other words, that they should meditate upon the sufferings of Christ, even when they have reached the stage at which it is possible for them to unite their souls with the Godhead in an act of "simple regard." The Dionysian mystics, whose religion was primarily experimental and who were consequently ready to adapt Catholic dogma to direct and immediate experience, had always maintained the contrary. In the higher stages of orison, they had insisted, all ideas and images, even ideas and images connected with the life of Christ, must be put aside, as distractions standing in the way of perfect union.

In his commentary on *The Cloud of Unknowing* Father Augustine Baker specifically comments on Father Benet's departure from the traditional teaching. "I ask you to observe," he says, "that he (the author of *The Cloud*) leaves no room for the exercise of the passion, so long as one is enabled in this exercise of love. This love is directed to the pure divinity, without the use of any image, either of our Saviour's humanity, or of any other creature. So that, according to our author's teaching throughout this book, if one be enabled for the said exercise of the love of the divinity, and that during his whole life, he must not leave it to go and exercise himself in the passion, much less in any inferior matter. And in this point our author agreeth fully both with the author of *Secrets Sentiers* and with what I myself have affirmed in my treatise on the exercise of the passion, wherein we differ from the opinion of Father Benet Fitch in the third book of his *Will of God* and from some others also, who would have some exercise of the passion in all states."

Father Benet himself was no less clearly aware than Father Baker of the novelty of his doctrine in this respect. There is no attempt in *The Rule of Perfection* to conceal or gloss over the break with tradition. On the contrary, it is admitted, and a whole chapter is devoted to an elaborate attempt to justify it. Unhappily Father Benet's essay in justification is one of those, to us, completely fantastic rigmaroles, so dear and apparently so convincing to the medieval and early-modern theologian. Dozens of quotations from the Old and New Testaments are strung together in support of the contention whose truth it is desired to demonstrate. A few of these quotations have some slight bearing on the point at issue; but most are perfectly irrelevant and must therefore be subjected to a process of arbitrary interpretation. This makes it possible for any statement to have any meaning whatsoever. Thus, Father Benet is able to find the confirmation of his teaching even in the anecdote of Rahab. That line of scarlet thread, which the whore of Jericho attached to her window, as a sign to the invading Israelites, prophetically signified that "God wishes us to place the red and bloody passion of Christ in the window of our inward house, which is our understanding, to the end that we may always meditate upon it and contemplate it." That this sort of thing should ever have carried conviction to anybody seems now completely incomprehensible. The fact that it actually did so is a salutary reminder that the frames of reference within which men do their reasoning and feeling do not remain the same, and that at any given moment of history certain thoughts are strictly unthinkable, certain sentiments, impossible to experience. Father Benet's real reasons for teaching that the practice of the passion should be continued at every stage of the contemplative life were doubtless the following: first, he himself was strongly attracted to acts of personal devotion; second, he was a Franciscan, and Franciscan devotion had always been especially concerned with the passion; and, thirdly, he felt (as many theologians before and after his day have felt) that the empirical mysticism of the Dionysians was, in its higher stages at least, too undogmatic to be truly Catholic. From our particular perch in time we look back and wonder why on earth Father Benet couldn't baldly have said so, without bringing in Rahab and all the other nonsense. Meanwhile the odd fact remains that, owing to the nature of the frames of reference within which he thought and felt, justification in terms of a Bronze Age harlot seemed to Father Benet intrinsically more convincing than justification in terms of psychology and religious history.

The thesis which Rahab serves to justify is that contemplation of the passion is more pleasing to God than contemplation of the divinity. "One should not leave the passion to contemplate the divinity, but one should continue both simultaneously." That "simple regard," with which the Dionysians had contemplated the Godhead, should be turned instead on Christ—but not on Christ in his humanity alone; rather as God and man in one person. "The whole difficulty of this simple regard comes from the contradiction which seems to prevent the human reason from being able to contemplate in one simple regard God and man, body and spirit." The difficulty, says

Father Benet, can only be overcome through a sustained act of faith which, while the mind dwells on the image of Christ on the cross, absorbs and annihilates that image in God's essence. From a psychological point of view, this whole passage is peculiarly interesting. It reveals Father Benet as a true mystic, very far advanced on the road to union, and yet constrained, by the logic of the theology he has accepted as true, to turn back from ultimate reality towards a particular manifestation of reality, from the direct intuition of God to imaginings and discursive reasonings connected with a person.

Such, then, were the doctrines which the youthful Baron de Maffliers received from his first master in religion, and which, as Father Joseph, he was later to reproduce, in a simpler and more systematic form, for the benefit of his converts and the novices entrusted to his charge. The friar's own method of orison has been described at length in the first chapter, and it is unnecessary to add any further details here. Suffice it to say that his *Introduction à la vie spirituelle par une facile méthode d'oraison* is an excellent specimen of its kind, well balanced, practical, distinguished by sound sense no less than by eloquence. In spite, however, of all these merits, it was little read. Like *The Rule of Perfection*, Father Joseph's "Introduction" was soon forgotten, and exercised no appreciable influence on the course of religious life during the seventeenth century. To develop Father Benet's doctrine, to introduce it to a wider public, was to be the work not of Father Joseph, but of his friend and fellow disciple, Pierre de Bérulle. The history of this accomplishment and of its unforeseen consequences is only indirectly relevant to our main theme, but it is intrinsically so interesting and instructive that I make no excuse for briefly summarizing it here.

"An able thinker of our time," writes Bérulle, "has maintained that the sun is at the center of the world, not the earth; that the former stands still, while the latter moves in relation to it. This novel opinion, not widely accepted in the science of the stars, is useful and should be followed in the science of salvation." This Copernican revolution in theology was Bérulle's reaction to the intense personalism of the then fashionable Jesuit devotion, based upon the "Spiritual Exercises" of St. Ignatius Loyola. At the beginning of his "Exercises," Ignatius had, it is true, reaffirmed the fundamental Christian doctrine that man's end and purpose in this world is the glory of God. But having made this affirmation he proceeded to write a book, in which the predominant role is played by the human individual. The exercises are a gymnastic of the personal will; so much so that, instead of being an end in itself, the worship of God is made, in some sort, an instrument to be used by the gymnast in establishing self-control. For this ptolemaic system of religious thought and feeling Bérulle substituted a thorough-going theocentrism. God is to be worshipped without regard even to one's spiritual profit. He is to be worshipped for his own sake, in an act of adoration and awe. He is to be worshipped as he is in himself, the sovereign and infinite being. To worship this sovereign and infinite being adequately, a man would have himself to be infinite and possess the highest reality. In practice, God has only once been worshipped as he should be worshipped and that was by Christ, who being God as well as man, was alone capable of giving the infinite adoration due to an infinite and eternal reality.

All this is strictly in accord with the Dionysian tradition. All good contemplatives are religious Copernicans, and, in genuine mysticism, the theocentric hypothesis is axiomatic. Bérulle's contribution to religious thought and practice consists in this; that he developed and systematized traditional theocentrism, while at the same time he developed and systematized into an elaborate "Jesus-centrism" the aberrant mystical doctrine which he had learned from Father Benet.

In discussing the reasons for Father Benet's departure from the Dionysian tradition, I suggested that one of these might be found in the friar's sense of the essential un-Catholicness of pure mysticism. That this was true of Bérulle is certain. Writing of the school, of which Bérulle was the founder, Brémond says that "its spirituality continually refers to and derives authority from the dogmas of the Church." Bérulle possessed undoubtedly a great aptitude for the mystical life; but before being a mystic, he was a Catholic. For him, theology, the gospel story and ecclesiastical tradition were fundamental data, antecedent to personal experience, which was something to be bent and moulded into conformity with them. The contemplatives of the Dionysian tradition, on the other hand, had adapted dogma to their own experience, with the result that, in so far as they were advanced mystics, they had ceased to be specifically Catholic. To a non-Christian, this seems the supremely important, the eminently encouraging fact about mysticism—that it provides the basis for a religion free from unacceptable dogmas, which themselves are contingent upon ill established and arbitrarily interpreted historical facts. To certain pious Christians, on the other hand, mysticism is suspect precisely because of its undogmatic and unhistorical character. (Karl Barth, for example, regards it as nothing but "esoteric atheism.")

Bérulle knew and respected the mystics of the Dionysian tradition, but he preferred not to follow them. Instead, he devoted all the energies of a powerful intellect to the creation of a new, mystico-Catholic philosophy of life. In this philosophy, the raw materials of Catholic dogmas and popular Catholic devotion were worked up into a finished product of high spirituality by means of techniques borrowed from the Dionysian contemplatives. The result was in the highest degree remarkable; but it was not mysticism. It was not mysticism because though the approach was the same as that of the Dionysian contemplatives, the object approached was not the imageless Godhead of their direct experience and of their theology. The revolution which Bérulle accomplished at the instigation of Benet Fitch and under the influence of Catholic thought and practice was more than Copernican. Not content with affirming that the sun was the center of the world, he insisted that there were several suns. To theocentrism he added Jesus-centrism and even Virgin-centrism—the contemplation of Christ and his mother in and for themselves. These two new suns assumed such importance for Bérulle that, they came, in his system, very largely to eclipse the great original sun of the Godhead. "Each man," he wrote, "is but a part of which Jesus is the whole. It is not enough for a man to be subordinated; he must be disappropriated and annihilated, and appropriated to Jesus, subsisting in Jesus, grafted in Jesus, living and operating in Jesus." Substitute "God" for "Jesus," and the passage might have been written by the author of *The Cloud of Unknowing*. The same significant similarities and differences can be found in the devotional practices of Bérulle and his followers on the one hand and of the Dionysian contemplatives, represented by the author of *The Cloud* on the other. For Bérulle, as for the earlier mystics, the end and purpose of orison is the annihilation of self through self-abandonment to the divine will. The act of self-abandonment begins with adoration or admiration—" a sublime, rare and ravishing occupation," in Bérulle's words—and goes on to "adherence," which is a process of cleaving to that which one had adored, of immersing onself in it, of transubstantiating the soul into what it contemplates. But here again, where the earlier mystics had insisted that adoration should beat upon the imageless cloud which envelopes the Godhead, Bérulle advocated "adherence" and finally "servitude" to Christ and even to the Virgin. Urban VIII, who raised him to the cardinalate, gave him, along with the Hat, the title of "apostle of the Incarnate Word." The nature and scope of Bérulle's more than Copernican revolution was not only recognized by his contemporaries; it was also officially approved.

"Virtue," the author of *The Cloud* had written, translating directly from Richard of St. Victor, "is nought else but an ordered and measured affection, plainly directed unto God for himself." St. Augustine had expressed the same idea in a phrase: Love, and do what you will. A man who has learnt to love God intensely and unremittingly can safely do what he wishes, because he will never wish to do evil.

Bérulle and his followers often contrasted their method with that of the pagan and non-mystical moralists. The moralist, they pointed out, seeks to become virtuous by strengthening his self-conscious will. His method consists in making a succession of resolutions to demonstrate some particular virtue. The carrying out of these resolutions is virtue in action, and may be expected, in the long run, to establish a habit. The defect of such a method, as the psychologists of every time and country have pointed out, is that it engages only the superficial levels of the mind and leaves the sub-conscious more or less unaffected. But it is from the sub-conscious that our impulses to action, our cravings and aversions, mainly spring. It follows, therefore, that the moralist's method of training is fundamentally unsatisfactory. "We should accomplish our acts of virtue," says Bérulle, "more through relation and homage to Jesus Christ than out of desire for the same virtue in itself." And we should do this, not only because all true religion is theocentric, but also because theocentrism produces better ethical results than anthropocentrism and moralism. For, as one of Bérulle's contemporaries and followers remarks, "when one wishes to dye a piece of white stuff scarlet, one can set about it in two ways; either by applying the color to the stuff, a process which takes much time, labour and trouble; or by dipping it into the dye, which is done without any trouble. It is the same with the virtues; virtue is a dye in the heart of Jesus Christ, and when, by love, by adoration and by the other duties of religion, a soul plunges into it, it easily takes this dye." This plunging into the dye is accomplished by means of "adherence," by a process of active and yet resigned and self-immolating exposure of the soul to the divine object of its adoration, which in Bérulle's devotional practice is generally Christ and sometimes the Virgin, seldom, as with the true mystic, that imageless Godhead which direct experience reveals as the ultimate reality.

The effects of Bérulle's more than Copernican revolution were profound, far-reaching and mainly disastrous. From the end of the seventeenth century to the end of the nineteenth, mysticism practically disappeared out of the Catholic Church. As of all historical events, the causes of this disappearance are many and complex. There can be no doubt, however, that among these causes the Bérullian revolution must take an important place. By substituting Christ and the Virgin for the undifferentiated Godhead of the earlier mystics, Bérulle positively guaranteed that none who followed his devotional practices should ever accede to the highest states of union or enlightenment. Contemplation of persons and their qualities entails a great deal of analytic thinking and an incessant use of the imagination. But analytic thinking and imagination are precisely the things which prevent the soul from attaining enlightenment. On this point all the great mystical writers, Christian and oriental, are unanimous and emphatic. Consequently the would-be mystic who follows Bérulle and chooses as the object of his love and contemplation, not the Godhead, but a person and personal qualities, thereby erects insurmountable barriers between himself and the higher states of union.

In this context it is interesting to compare Bérulle and Bérullism with Ignatius Loyola and the Jesuit school of devotion. Loyola seems to have been a born mystic who rejected the gift of passive contemplation in favour of active meditation based on analytic thought and imagination. Anthropocentric and moralistic, his Spiritual Exercises lie outside the field of mystical literature and make little appeal to persons of mystical temperament. Brought up on these exercises, the Jesuit theologians were mostly ignorant of the highest mystical states and, being ignorant of them, denied their very possibility and regarded with suspicion or even actively persecuted those who insisted that such states existed. The influence of Bérulle and his followers was of a subtler kind; for they revolutionized mysticism from within. Unlike Loyola, Bérulle did not reject his own mystical gifts. He preached the theocentrism traditional among mystics up to the time of St. John of the Cross, and he practised their traditional "adherence." Hence the appeal of his writings to the mystically minded; hence the depth and inwardness of his influence; hence, too, the fatal consequences of his subordination of direct mystical experience to personalistic theology. Bérulle no doubt sincerely believed that the soul could adhere to the Incarnate Word or to the Virgin in exactly the same way as it could adhere to God, and with the same consequences. But, psychologically, this is impossible. There cannot be adherence to persons or personal qualities without analysis and imagination; and where analysis and imagination are active, the mind is unable to receive into itself the being of God. Bérulle taught potential mystics to follow a path which could not, in the nature of things, lead to the ultimate goal of mysticism. It was a path that would lead them to virtue; for (as Coué sufficiently demonstrated in our own day) imagination is more effective in this respect than will; a soul can be made virtuous by being dyed in its own mental image of another's goodness. It was also a path that would lead them to intense, affective devotion to divine persons, and to untiring activity on their behalf. But it was not a path that would lead to union with ultimate reality. Like the Jesuits, the followers of Bérulle were condemned, by the very nature of their devotions, to a spiritual ignorance all the more fatal for imagining itself to be knowledge. It was the prevalence of this ignorance among sincere and virtuous men that led to the reaction against mysticism in the second half of the seventeenth century. The aberrations of the Quietists were used to justify the violence of this reaction. But, as a matter of fact, neither Molinos nor Mme Guyon wrote anything that a little common sense cannot easily neutralize. The real objection to the Quietists was that they were continuators of that Dionysian tradition of mysticism whose last great representative had been St. John of the Cross. They were out of place in a world where Jesuitism and Bérullism were just coming to their devotional consummation in the cult of the Sacred Heart. (Jean Eudes, beatified as the Father, Doctor and Apostle of that cult, was a Bérullian, and the revelations of Margaret Mary Alacoque were sponsored by the Jesuits.) By the end of the seventeenth century, mysticism has lost its old significance in Christianity and is more than half dead.

"Well, what of it?" it may be asked. "Why shouldn't it die? What use is it when it's alive?"

The answer to these questions is that where there is no vision, the people perish; and that, if those who are the salt of the earth lose their savour, there is nothing to keep that earth disinfected, nothing to prevent it from falling into complete decay. The mystics are channels through which a little knowledge of reality filters down into our human universe of ignorance and illusion. A totally unmystical world would be a world totally blind and insane.

From the beginnings of the eighteenth century onwards, the sources of mystical knowledge have been steadily diminishing in number, all over the planet. We are dangerously far advanced into the darkness. By a tragic irony (due, of course, to the ignorance that accompanied their good intentions) the ecstatic Father Benet, the brilliant and saintly Pierre de Bérulle take their place among the men who have contributed to the darkening of the human spirit.

IV

The Evangelist

IN THE foregoing chapter I have painted in some detail the religious setting, historical, contemporary and personal of Father Joseph's life. It was against this fixed backdrop of an intense Catholic devotion, partly mystical, partly imaginative and emotional, that the episodes of his political career were acted out; and it was in relation to it that they had to be explained and justified in his own mind.

During the first years of his life as a Capuchin, Father Joseph's activities were exclusively religious. His career began, as we have seen, with a year's novitiate at Orleans. After his profession in Paris he was sent to the Capuchin seminary at Rouen. Here the course of studies ordinarily lasted four years; but the new pupil was already so far advanced that he was altogether excused the preliminary year of philosophy and one of the three subsequent years of theology. His reputation at the seminary was that of a young religious graced with notable spiritual gifts, fervent in prayer, indefatigable in good works, burning with the holy ambition to become a saint. He practised supererogatory austerities in the matter of food and labour; he kept such a careful watch over pride that he was never heard to speak of his past life, his present wishes or his future projects; he was eager in all circumstances to do more than his duty. That Spartan taste of his for the uncomfortable and the strenuous continually manifested itself, sometimes in the oddest ways. For example, it was his custom, during certain of the prescribed periods of prayer, to worship standing, barefooted on the flagstones. When sleepiness overtook him (which it sometimes did, as he was in the habit of shortening his nights with contemplation) he would combat it by standing on one leg. The practice was not generally approved of in the seminary; but when warned of the dangers of excess, the need of discretion even in matters of piety, Father Joseph would answer that the kingdom of heaven is taken by violence, and continue his prayers to the accompaniment of excruciating muscular strain.

All this was a sign of most commendable zeal; but what chiefly interested his superiors was the fact that their new pupil seemed to have a definite gift of orison. Father Benet had taught him the theory and practice of his own kind of modified Dionysian mysticism; and the young Capuchin had brought to his devotions that obsessive, hallucinatory preoccupation with the sufferings of Calvary, which had haunted his mind from earliest childhood. The result was a type of mental prayer which his superiors described as an orison of "seraphic and crucified love." Intensive practice of this form of contemplation (to which the young seminarist gave many more hours than the two, which the Capuchin rule prescribed for mental prayer) led not infrequently to ecstasy and the seeing of visions. If we add to all these the fact that he had eloquence and a talent for religious controversy and religious exhortation, we shall not be surprised at the extraordinarily favourable judgement passed upon him by Ange de Joyeuse. "Father Joseph," he declared in 1601, when the young man was still at the Rouen seminary, "is the perfect Capuchin and the most consummate religious of his province, indeed of the whole order."

Benet of Canfield was at this time lying in an English prison, from which he was not delivered until 1602. But though absent, his influence over his young pupil's mind was still strong. How strong we may judge from the books which Father Joseph read most. The list begins with St. John's Gospel and the Epistles of St. Paul, goes on to St. Augustine's *Confessions* and *Soliloquies,* Dionysius the Areopagite's *Mystical Theology* and *Divine Names,* the mystical writings of Hugh and Richard of St. Victor and St. Bernard, and ends with Ruysbroeck and two lesser contemplatives of the fifteenth and sixteenth centuries respectively, Henry de Herp and the Benedictine Abbot, Blosius. It is a little library of the purest mystical tradition.

Father Joseph's superiors expressed their high opinion of him by acts no less than words. In 1603, a few months after he had left the seminary, the young man was appointed reader in philosophy at the convent of the rue Saint-Honoré. His career as a theologian and man of learning was cut short, after only a year, by an aggravation of that progressive defect of vision which advanced throughout his life until, at the end, he was nearly blind. Henceforward the scholar's world of books was closed to him; but the world of men lay still wide open.

In 1604 he was ordained, received his license to preach and was sent to take charge of the novices at the Capuchin house of Meudon. Here he set to work, with an energy always tempered by tact and skill, teaching the new-made friars those arts of mental prayer which he himself had learned from Benet of Canfield only a few years before.

To help his pupils, he reduced the essence of the spiritual life, with its three stages of purgation, illumination and union, to a series of thirty-six rhymed quatrains; and for each novice he wrote out a set of spiritual instructions specially designed for his individual needs.

To his work within the convent he added another labour—the re-evangelization of the neighbouring countryside. Meudon and, along with it, all the other villages in the neighbourhood of Paris had suffered extremely during the wars of religion. Not content with despoiling the people's farms and shops, the marauding soldiers had pillaged and often wrecked the churches. In some communities all organized religious activity had come to an end; and of the parish priests who remained many had succumbed to the influence of their anarchic surroundings and were leading lives of a far from edifying character. With the approval of his superiors, Father Joseph set himself to recover this spiritually devastated area for the church. His missionary efforts were crowned with immediate and startling success. Whenever he preached, thousands would come from miles around to listen to his impassioned eloquence. Churches and convent chapels were too small for such congregations and soon he was speaking in the open air. Many of his listeners went through the crisis of conversion, and everywhere the habits of traditional piety were re-established. So great indeed, was the throng of those desiring to be confessed and take communion that additional friars had to be sent for from Paris to cope with them. Well schooled in humility, Father Joseph displayed no personal satisfaction at his triumph, which he regarded as a particularly good opportunity for practising the "active annihilation" of self in the divine will. Preaching, he tried to remain continuously aware that he in himself was nothing and God, everything; that this eloquence, which made the people groan aloud in fear of hell, weep for their offences, raise supplicating hands towards the mercy seat, was not *his* eloquence, but the word of God finding utterance through him, the utterly unworthy instrument of God's will. From the active annihilation of preaching, he would retire at night to his cell and there, in the dark silence, would give himself up to passive annihilation in an act of mental prayer. A few hours of sleep, and he was at work again, strong in powers and energies not his own, at peace and happy in the conviction that his true vocation had been revealed to him. The service to which he was called was that of an evangelist and missionary.

This was now obvious, not only to himself and his companions, but also to his superiors. So obvious, indeed, that, in the autumn of 1605, he was relieved of his teaching at Meudon and appointed Warden of the Capuchin house at Bourges. Here, he would have relatively little to do within the convent walls and would therefore be able to devote the best part of his energies to the work of evangelization outside.

At Bourges, he was no less successful with an educated, urban audience than he had been among the peasants of Meudon and the neighbouring countryside. At the request of the city fathers he delivered a series of addresses which were so well attended that he had to move from the conventual church to a much larger building. The subject of these addresses, which generally lasted two hours, was the art of mental prayer. In the succeeding years we shall find him returning again and again to this topic. By word of mouth and in written summaries, which he left with his auditors to be copied and circulated in manuscript, he urged upon all Christians, the desirability, nay, the absolute necessity of the mystical approach to God. In one such summary written at about this time he says emphatically that "a man who neglects this duty of orison is blind indeed, not knowing his friends from his enemies. One can never sufficiently regret the loss entailed by this slothful neglect, a loss of the inestimable graces brought to the soul by conversation with God." Even during the years when he was acting as Richelieu's coadjutor, he still remained, with one side of his being, the faithful pupil of his first master, Benet of Canfield.

Father Joseph was not allowed to remain for long at Bourges. His talent for preaching was too valuable to be lavished on a single congregation, and in the early spring of 1606 he was called to preach the Lenten sermons in the cathedral of Le Mans. Nothing remarkable happened here, except that a hysterical woman heard him preach, and conceiving a violent passion, tried to seduce him. For a man who regarded uncloistered females as wild beasts and horrific mysteries, the temptation was not too serious; and after having converted his fair assailant, Father Joseph proceeded to Angers, and from Angers to Saumur. To be chosen to preach at Saumur was a very special honour; for Saumur was one of the walled cities assigned by the Edict of Nantes to the Huguenots. Under the administration of its very capable and active governor, Du Plessis-Mornay, it had become a centre of Calvinist illumination. An academy had been founded not long before, where young men were taught by eminent professors, recruited not only from among the French Huguenots, but from every part of Protestant Europe as well. Saumur also had a seminary for the training of future ministers, and a well-equipped press, where Protestant controversialists—Du Plessis-Mornay himself among them—could print their books and pamphlets.

In this thriving Calvinist city (later to be ruined and half depopulated by the Revocation of the Edict of Nantes) a Catholic minority enjoyed liberty of worship and had its church assigned to it. Here Father Joseph preached and gave addresses on the art of orison; and here, as was his custom, he wrote out the substance of these addresses to serve as a handbook for his listeners, when he should be gone. In the intervals of preaching and instructing, he consulted with the more influential members of his flock about the possibility of founding a Capuchin convent in their city. Hitherto Du Plessis-Mornay had refused to admit the friars into his Calvinist preserves. Father Joseph did not yet know how this formidable opposition was to be broken or circumvented; but he was determined that, somehow or other, Saumur should get its Capuchins. At the meeting of the Chapter of his province, which was held that same summer in Paris, he broached the subject in a speech. His colleagues and superiors approved his design and, at the end of August, he left Paris with the new post of warden of the convent of Rennes and a commission to take appropriate steps for establishing the friars at Saumur.

For the young Capuchin, this commission was to have profound and far-reaching consequences. The pious plot to get the better of Du Plessis-Mornay was the first link in a long chain of unforeseeable circumstances that drew him at last to the very pinnacle of political power. It all began with his visit to the abbey of Fontevrault. Fontevrault was the parent house of a twelfth-century order of monks and nuns, all of whom were under the rule of its Abbess. The order was immensely rich, had scores of subsidiary houses all over the country and recruited its nuns from the most aristocratic families. The Abbess was one of the great dignitaries of the Gallican church. As befitted the holder of so important a position, "Mme de Fontevrault" was almost never below the rank of a duchess and frequently above it; for the profitable charge was often given to princesses of the blood. The incumbent in 1606 was an elderly aunt of Henri IV, called Eléonore de Bourbon. Her exalted rank and the fact that Fontevrault was distant only a few miles from Saumur made of Mme de Bourbon the obviously fitting person to deal with Du Plessis-Mornay. To her then, Father Joseph was sent. She listened favourably to his request and wrote at once to the governor of Saumur. Du Plessis-Mornay disliked the friars; but he could not afford to offend a close relation of the King's. He gave his consent to the founding of a Capuchin house at Saumur; but followed up this action by privately doing everything in his power to prevent his consent from doing the Capuchins any good. All the obstructive machinery of the law was set in motion, and for three long years the royal edict which granted the Capuchins a right to found a convent at Saumur, failed to obtain the necessary registration from the local Parlement. But the friars were persistent and at last, in 1609, the foundation stone of the new convent was solemnly laid. Father Joseph had triumphed. But he was not to enjoy his triumph. What he had hoped and expected from his enterprise at Saumur was the privilege to serve as a missionary among the heretics. What it actually led to was a very different kind of career.

Mme de Bourbon was very favourably impressed by the young friar who had been sent to see her. His zeal and piety were exemplary, his judgment was no less remarkable than his ardour; and, what was more, under the ragged habit and the unkempt beard, he was an aristocrat, consummately well educated and of the most polished address. Once a gentleman, always a gentleman; nothing could disguise the fact that Father Joseph had been the Baron de Maffliers. Great nobles, ministers of the crown, princes and princesses of the blood—with this particular friar such people felt at home. He was "one of us," a member of their caste. Besides, in the words of a contemporary, "his conversation was ravishing, and he treated the nobility with infinite dexterity." Mme de Bourbon was as much ravished as all the rest of them. When the business on which he had been sent was finished, she consulted the young man about her own troubles. These were not inconsiderable. Without being scandalous, life in Fontevrault and its dependent houses was exceedingly worldly. These convents were like very exclusive country clubs for women. Of the three monastic vows, that of chastity was observed in them fairly scrupulously; that of obedience, only grudgingly, and that of poverty, not at all. The nuns enjoyed their own private incomes and lived surrounded by their own possessions and domestics. Mme de Bourbon was pious in a vague sort of way, and would have liked to do something about her order. But what? But how?

Father Joseph discussed the matter with the Abbess and her coadjutrix and niece, Mme Antoinette d'Orléans.

Much more intensely and deeply religious than her aunt, this princess had long dreamed of creating within the order of Fontevrault, or outside it, a congregation of pure contemplatives. This young mystic with his energy and his gift for business, was exactly the counsellor and helper she had always hoped to find.

Father Joseph worked out two plans, one of mild reformation for Mme de Bourbon and the more worldly ladies of Fontevrault, the other, radical, for Mme d'Orléans and such nuns and novices as might wish to share with her a strictly cloistered life of contemplation. With these genuine enthusiasts for a mystical and ascetic religion like his own, Father Joseph was able to co-operate enthusiastically and with the greatest satisfaction. Not so with Mme de Bourbon and the worldly party. The young man desired only one thing, to go on being an evangelist and an apostle of mysticism; and now, by an unfortunate concatenation of circumstances, here he was, inextricably involved in a labour which he found peculiarly distasteful—the reformation of nuns who didn't want to be reformed, even in moderation, and who were rich and powerful enough to hamper their reformer at every turn. But the talents he displayed in the performance of this ungrateful task were so conspicuous, that he was never allowed to throw it up and return to his missionary labours. Warden successively of the convents of Rennes, Chinon and Tours, he was constantly recalled to Fontevrault. There, among those great ladies in religious fancy dress, he strove heroically to annihilate the last traces of his own personal feelings towards the task that had been assigned to him. It was God's will that this task should be accomplished and he was merely the instrument of God's will. Daily and hourly he renewed his resolution to do that will—actually, uniquely, *willingly*. . . .

Meanwhile, the fact remained that the job of reforming Fontevrault was peculiarly difficult and delicate. Two heads being better than one in such affairs, Father Joseph turned for assistance and advice to the bishop of the neighbouring see of Luçon, a young man still in his twenties, but enjoying already a high reputation for ability and reforming zeal. The name of this precocious ecclesiastic was Armand Jean du Plessis de Richelieu. The two men met, discussed the immediate business at hand, exchanged views on matters of more general interest, and parted as admiring friends. Another link in the chain of Father Joseph's destiny had been forged.

The work of reformation dragged on for years. In 1610 Father Joseph was transferred from the province of Paris to that of Tours, in order that he might be more continuously at Fontevrault, and from this time until 1613 he lived for months at a stretch in one or other of the convents of the order, assisting Mme d'Orléans in the creation of her little community of contemplatives, and trying to persuade the members of the Fontevrault country club to behave a little more like the nuns they were supposed to be. The problems with which he had to deal were suddenly complicated by the death of old Mme de Bourbon. The appointment of her successor belonged to the crown, and the crown at this moment was represented by the regent, Marie de Medicis, who chose the Duchess de Lavedan. Before and after this appointment the Queen Mother sought the advice of Father Joseph and, like everyone else who met him at this time, conceived a very high opinion of his virtues and abilities—an opinion which she retained until that day in 1630, when her flight to Brussels finally removed her from the French scene. Once again, circumstances were conspiring to draw the missionary away from his preaching into the world of high politics.

It would be unprofitable to describe in detail the work which Father Joseph accomplished at Fontevrault and the neighbouring abbey in which Mme d'Orléans had installed those nuns who genuinely desired a life of austerity and orison. Suffice it to say that thanks to him the behaviour of the worldly ladies became more decorous and that finally in 1617, the community founded by Mme d'Orléans was promoted, by a papal bull, to the rank of a new and independent order, the Congregation of Our Lady of Calvary. This last labour was carried to a successful conclusion in the teeth of the most determined resistance on the part of the new Abbess of Fontevrault, who was jealous of her authority and hated a reform, however intrinsically excellent, which threatened to deprive her of any of her subjects.

Of the two founders of the Calvarian order, Mme d'Orléans died in 1618, only a few months after it had been declared independent of Fontevrault. Dying, she bequeathed to Father Joseph the task of steering the new congregation along the road which together they had mapped out. It was the road which, from the time of his first entrance into religion, the Capuchin had chosen for himself—the road of mortification, mystical orison and the intensive, hallucinatory practice of the passion of Christ. For almost as long as he could remember Calvary had filled his imagination; and it was to Calvary that the new congregation was dedicated. To imagine themselves in the position of Mary at the foot of the cross, to feel themselves into her thoughts and the emotions she had felt during her son's long agony—this was to be the principal devotion of the nuns; for the rest, they were to practise the art of mental prayer as systematized by Father Joseph out of the writings of Benet of Canfield. To their guidance, their spiritual and even their intellectual education, Father Joseph gave henceforth unstintingly of his time, his talents and his energies. Even at the height of his political power and under the heaviest pressure of business, he never neglected the Calvarians. Whenever he was in Paris or in one of the other towns in which a Calvary had been established, he found time to give at least one day in every week to the instruction and encouragement of the nuns. He composed for their use a small library of treatises on prayer, on morals, on philosophy, on theology, besides a great number of letters on the day-to-day problems of the spiritual life. Much of this material still survives, but has never been printed. According to the computations of the only modern scholar who has had access to them, Father Joseph's treatises and spiritual letters to the Calvarians would fill, if published, thirty octavo volumes of five hundred pages apiece. Most of this great mass of material was composed at a time when the Capuchin was acting as Secretary of State for Foreign Affairs and Apostolic Commissary for Missions—two whole-time jobs, to which he added this third, of spiritual director to an entire congregation of religious. Vicariously, in these cloistered contemplatives, he was able to give himself to that life of orison, which Father Benet had taught him to love, but which Richelieu and the affairs of state made it impossible for him to lead in person. The glory of France, the humiliation of the House of Austria—these meant a great deal to a patriot who was convinced that a triumph for his country was also a triumph for God. But the spiritual well-being of his nuns and their progress in the art of mental prayer were of no less moment in Father Joseph's eyes. To the very end, the power politician tried his best to remain a mystic.

While engaged on his delicate and distasteful business at Fontevrault, Father Joseph was appointed to be coadjutor to the Provincial of Touraine; and a little later, when he had won his freedom from the worldly ladies and had only Mme d'Orléans and her contemplatives to think of, he became Provincial. The Capuchin province of Touraine included not merely the district around Tours, but the whole of Poitou and much of Brittany and Normandy as well. As overseer of this great domain, Father Joseph regarded it as his duty to become acquainted personally with every friar within its borders. The frequent journeys of the preceding years gave place to an almost continuous wandering, by forced marches, back and forth across the face of the country. During this period of his life he must have walked literally thousands of miles. And what miles! In our minds the name, "France," calls up visions of a beautifully tidy country of well-tilled fields and well-trimmed woodlands, covered with a network of admirable roads and dotted with substantial villages and towns. At the beginning of the seventeenth century this France was far removed in the yet unrealized future. The country was dark with great forests, hardly less wild than those which Caesar had traversed during the Gallic wars. Wolves abounded; and in some parts of the country bears were still met with, and beavers. Of the open land, outside the forests, much was still undrained. Great areas which are now under the plough were then malarious swamps, waterlogged during all but the driest months of the year. Such roads as there were partook of the nature of the ground they traversed and, in wet weather, were impassable for wheeled traffic and difficult even for horsemen and foot passengers. The owners of the land lived in castles and fortified manors, many of which are still standing, but those who actually cultivated it were housed in mud and wattle huts so flimsy in their squalor that most of them have disappeared without leaving a trace of their existence. The ordinary poverty of the peasants under feudal lords had been made acute by the devastations of the civil wars; but now, with the return of peace under Henri IV it was reverting to the merely chronic condition then regarded as prosperity. Of the men who had done the fighting in those civil wars, many were now unemployed and had taken to pimping and thieving in the towns and highway robbery in the country. The decaying bodies of some of these malefactors dangled conspicuously from wayside gibbets. But more were still at large, and travellers went armed and, if possible in considerable bands. Father Joseph was fortunate in possessing nothing except the Capuchin's reputation for active charity and an austere life. He might be set upon by wolves, might contract malaria or typhus, might be drowned while trying to cross a flooded river; but it was very unlikely that he would be killed by bandits. The treasures which the Provincial of Touraine was laying up, as he visited the monasteries under his charge, were not of the kind that would buy anything a highwayman was likely to desire.

To Father Joseph these interminable cross-country marches were less fatigues to be dreaded than welcome opportunities for meditations, which it was legitimate to prolong from the moment of his departure at dawn to the end of the day's journey at sunset.

Among the friars of his province Father Joseph had a reputation for firmness in action tempered by an extraordinary gentleness and humility of manner. Abuses were promptly corrected, discipline enforced, the necessary reprimands and punishments unfailingly administered, but always with mildness, always with an insight into character almost amounting to that attribute of the saints which is technically called "the discernment of spirits."

In such intervals as were left between his journeys, Father Joseph continued to preach and write. It was at this time that he composed, for the novices of his province, that *Introduction to the Spiritual Life* of which we have already spoken and in which he set forth most fully his theory and practice of the mystical life. We have seen that he had written similar treatises in the past; but this was by far the most complete and elaborate—for the good reason that this alone was intended for publication.

During this period of his life, Father Joseph had time to practise his peculiar method of mystical and imaginative orison with more than ordinary persistence. He experienced in consequence a renewal of the phenomena that had accompanied his early devotions at the Rouen seminary. He saw visions, received revelations, passed into ecstasy. There were times when he could hardly speak of the sufferings of Christ without falling into a rapture. On at least one occasion this happened to him in the pulpit. Mentioning the crucifixion, he was so much moved that his senses left him, he fell down in a faint and remained for some time afterwards in a state almost of catalepsy.

Such physical symptoms are generally regarded by experienced mystics as signs, possibly of divine grace, but certainly of human weakness, and probably also of inadequate training in, and injudicious practice of, the art of orison. At the same time, of course, they testify to the intensity of the experience which produced them. About Ezéchiely there was nothing lukewarm or half-hearted.

Of his psychic experiences, Father Joseph spoke little; but there is no doubt that he attached great importance to them. In later years, he made use of visions and revelations—sometimes his own, more often those of the Calvarian nuns under his charge—as significant factual data, to be taken into account in framing policies and conducting military campaigns. He might have spared himself the trouble. These apocalypses neither made him infallible, nor detracted from his native sagacity as a politician. It is worth remarking that Father Joseph's all too human and anthropocentric attitude towards such by-products of the religious life was not universally shared by his contemporaries. Here is the judgment which was passed upon them by Jean-Jacques Olier, founder of the seminary of Saint-Sulpice and a worthy pupil of Bérulle's greatest disciple, Charles de Condren. "Revelations," he writes, "are the aberrations of faith; they are a distraction that spoils simplicity in relation to God, and that embarrasses the soul, making it swerve from its directness towards God, and occupying the mind with other things than God. Special illuminations, auditions, prophecies and the rest are marks of weakness in a soul that cannot suffer the assaults of temptation, or bear anxiety about the future and God's judgment upon it. Prophecies are also marks of creaturely curiosity in a being towards whom God is indulgent and to whom, as a father to his importunate child, he gives a few trifling sweetmeats to satisfy his appetite." How far this is from Father Joseph's or, for that matter, from Pascal's hungry craving and superstitious reverence for signs and miracles! Olier had achieved a degree of intellectual austerity, of annihilation, as Father Benet would have put it, to which these others were far from having attained.

V

The Approach to Politics

Now that Fontevrault had been reformed, it looked as though Father Joseph might be able to get back to the work he loved best, the work of which he could not but feel that it was his true vocation. There were so many things to do—heretics to be won back to the Church, lukewarm and complacent Catholics to be awakened from their fatal apathy, and everywhere a minority of the devout to be taught the true art of mental prayer. So many things to do; but, at the head of a whole province of friars, how much he might hope, with God's help, to accomplish! He rejoiced at the thought of all that it might be granted to him to do and suffer in this missionary service.

But again destiny intervened and, because it corresponded to one of the sides of his double nature, because it was intrinsically like the Tenebroso-Cavernoso in him, proved too strong for the Franciscan evangelist. In the persons of Richelieu and the Queen-Mother, high politics had already distantly beckoned to him. Now, suddenly, in the last weeks of 1615, they were all around him. Without warning, he found himself in the midst of a civil war and in the position to negotiate a settlement.

The murder of Henri IV had left the government of France in the hands of his widow who ruled as regent during the minority of Louis XIII. The portraits of Marie de Médicis reveal a large, fleshy, gorgeously bedizened barmaid; and the records of her administration prove her to have been even stupider, if that were possible, than she looked. With this unintelligence there went an almost abnormal coldness of temperament. Her only strong passions were for power, which she was incapable of exercising, and for expensive bric-a-brac, especially jewels, for which she indebted herself and the national treasury to the tune of millions. To love, maternal no less than sexual, she seems to have been almost insensible. She was an unaffectionate wife, a continent widow and a neglectful and even heartless mother. (The Dauphin was brought up at Saint-Germain, where Marie seldom troubled to visit him. Indirectly, however, she played a decisive part in his education; for she gave and constantly reiterated the most formal orders that the child should be birched every morning before breakfast for the offences of the previous day. The practice was continued even after Louis had become King of France.) The only person for whom Marie seems genuinely to have cared was the little deformed maid, who had been the companion of her unhappy childhood, Leonora Dori, called the Galigai. This woman was treated by her mistress with a positively imbecile indulgence. Her husband, the Florentine adventurer, Concini, was made prime minister and a marshal of France, while the Galigai herself dictated the policy of the country, appointed ministers, judges, bishops, ambassadors, governors of provinces (always for a financial consideration) and, by taking bribes and stealing from the government, amassed in a few years a fortune running into millions of crowns.

Corrupt rule by foreign gangsters can hardly be popular, and Marie de Médicis' government was duly hated by nobles and people alike. It was hated, what is more, without being feared; for to corruption it added inefficiency and weakness. The civil wars of the later sixteenth century had restored to the great French magnates much of the power, the quasi-autonomy that had been theirs in the Middle Ages, before the rise of the absolute monarchy. Strong in the loyalty and approval of the Third Estate, Henri IV had reduced the nobles to obedience. By its ineptitude and corruption, the regency fairly invited them to reassert their independence of the crown. When they rebelled, it was ordinarily Marie de Médicis' policy to buy them off with enormous gifts of money, land and preferment. The nobles accepted, swore fealty and, a few months later, began again. It was the Third Estate that suffered from the disorder and that paid the bills. But in spite of this, in spite of the universal detestation inspired by the Queen Mother's Italian favourites, the people remained unswervingly loyal to the crown—partly from a reasoned belief that the crown would protect them from the intolerable tyrannies of the local magnates, lay and ecclesiastical, partly out of traditional sentiment. How strong that sentiment was the people proved again and again during these troubled years.

In seventeenth-century France, the divine right of kings was a fact of crowd psychology. Thus, it was not only because they were oppressors that the clergy and nobility were disliked; it was also because they were insufficiently respectful to the King.

O noblesse, ô clergé, les aînés de la France,
Puisque l'honneur du roi si mal vous maintenez,
Puisque le tiers état en ce point vous devance,
Il faut que vos cadets deviennent vos aînés.[1]

[1] O nobility and clergy, you elder sons of France, since you so ill maintain the King's honour, since the Third Estate surpasses you in this point, your juniors must now become your elders.

So wrote a popular rhymer of this period, and in 1614, at the meeting of the States General (the last before 1789), the Third Estate offered a resolution to the effect that "there is no power, spiritual or temporal, which has any right over the kingdom." It was a declaration of revolutionary royalism, directed against the nobles and the Roman hierarchy.

In 1615 the magnates were at it again. The Prince of Condé, the Dukes of Bouillon, Longueville, Mayenne, Nevers—all of them governors of provinces and possessors of private armies—rose in revolt against the central government. The real motive of their rebellion was the same as ever—to increase the power and wealth of the nobility at the expense of the crown. The avowed motive, ironically enough, was to support the Third Estate in its assertion of the divine right of the King to rule without interference. Not, of course, that Condé, the leader of the rebellion, took any interest in the lower classes, or desired the royal power to be strengthened. If he backed up the resolution of the Third Estate, it was because such an action might win him the support of the people in general and of the Protestants in particular. These last approved of the resolution for the same reason as Marie de Medicis disapproved of it—because it was anti-papal. Condé hoped to use the force of religious prejudice to back up his own and his friends' demand for cash and power.

The rebellion started in the late autumn of 1615. The rebels collected an army, the government collected an army. It looked this time as though there might be real fighting. Then suddenly, out of the blue, Father Joseph made his appearance. The winter was one of the worst in living memory and an epidemic of what seems to have been influenza was killing its thousands in every town and village; but the Provincial of Touraine was carrying out his tours of inspection as usual. At Loudun, he found himself all of a sudden at the very heart of the rebellion.

To serve as peacemaker was one of the duties of a Capuchin. Without waiting for instructions from his superiors, Father Joseph resolved immediately to present himself to Condé. It was not difficult for him to obtain an audience with the prince. As Provincial, he was a person of some authority; besides, his younger brother, Charles du Tremblay, was one of Condé's gentlemen in waiting. He was received; he talked with the prince, he sat down to long discussions with the assembled council of magnates. Speaking with the authority of a man of God and with the passionate eloquence of the born preacher, he adjured them to spare their country the horrors of civil war, to return to their obedience to the King. The magnates raised objections, put forward their claims and aired their grievances. At once, the preacher gave way to the diplomatist, Ezéchiely to Tenebroso-Cavernoso. With fascinating skill and those perfect manners which he had learnt at M. de Pluvinel's Academy, he reasoned with them, he cajoled; occasionally, too, he permitted himself an outburst of blunt frankness, such as a gentleman may be excused for giving vent to, when speaking to his equals. Then, all of a sudden, the tone would change again, and he was once more the visionary friar, licensed by his habit to denounce wrong doing even in the highest place, to give warning even to princes of its fatal consequences in this world and the next. Such, throughout his career, was to be Father Joseph's method of negotiation. Combining in his own person the oddly assorted characters of Metternich and Savanarola, he could play the diplomatic game with twice the ordinary number of trump cards. It must not be imagined that he acted on these occasions with deliberate insincerity, that he consciously rang the changes on his dual rôle. No, he actually *was* both Ezéchiely and Tenebroso-Cavernoso; and he was really convinced that the policies pursued so skilfully by the latter were no less in accordance with God's will than the preaching and teaching which were the life-work of the former.

After spending a week with the insurgents, Father Joseph obtained their leave to present their case to the Queen Mother and her advisers, who were quartered, with their forces, at Tours. He did so and, on the advice of the papal nuncio, was appointed by Marie de Médicis as her unofficial agent to negotiate terms of settlement.

At Tours, he renewed his acquaintance with the Bishop of Luçon. Richelieu had entered public life in the preceding year as a representative of the clergy at the States General; had ingratiated himself to the Queen Mother by a speech full of the most outrageous flattery; had paid court to Concini and the Galigai; and had been rewarded for his pains with the post of almoner to the child queen, Anne of Austria. He was now prowling in the neighbourhood of the court, hungrily on the look out for an opportunity to snatch the smallest morsel of that political power which he felt was due to his extraordinary abilities. Whenever he was forewarned of the friar's journeyings, Richelieu would drive out in his coach to meet him. For a mere duke or prince of the blood, Father Joseph would not break the rule which forbade him to ride a horse or sit in a carriage. But Richelieu as a bishop had a right to his obedience. His command was a momentary dispensation from pedestrian travel. When the lackeys jumped down and opened the carriage door for him, he could climb in with a good conscience and in the knowledge that his behaviour was, ecclesiastically speaking, perfectly regular.

Seated side by side in the swaying coach, the two men talked at length and confidentially—about the current rebellion, about the weakness of the government, about the state of the country at large, about the menacing designs of Spain, about the troubles brewing in the Germanies, about the plight of Rome, caught between its avowed enemies, the Protestants and its yet more dangerous and sinister friends, the Hapsburgs. On most points the friar and the bishop found themselves in full agreement. Both were convinced that the crying need of France was for a strong central government; that the power of the nobles and the Huguenots must be broken and the King made sole master of his realm. Both wished to see the Gallican church reformed and revivified. Both were convinced that France was one of the chosen instruments of Providence and that the country should be made powerful, to the end that it might play, in the affairs of Christendom, that leading rôle to which God had unquestionably called it. But whereas Richelieu was convinced that the proper policy for this more powerful France must be specifically anti-Spanish and anti-Austrian; Father Joseph, on the contrary, thought of collaboration between the great Catholic powers against the heretics. First among equals, the Bourbons were to work with the two branches of the Hapsburgs for the reconstitution of united Christendom. And, with this, his tone would change; Tenebroso-Cavernoso would give place to Ezéchiely. Richelieu would listen, and then as the prophetic thunders died away, would quietly remark that while, of course, every good Catholic desired to see Christendom more united, the fact remained that for a hundred years now Spain and Austria had been trying to dominate all Europe. France was encircled by their territories. Spanish armies were on every frontier; Spanish ships came and went from Biscay to the Netherlands. Sooner or later, it would be necessary to teach these Hapsburgs a lesson.

"But the integrity of the Church," the friar protested, "the seamless garment. . . ."

"Woven," the Bishop drily interrupted, "in Madrid and embroidered at Vienna."

And so the discussions went on. In spite of their disagreements on the matter of foreign policy, Father Joseph's admiration for the young bishop daily increased. Among all the corrupt, self-seeking, hopelessly incompetent creatures who gravitated, either as friends or foes, around the young King and his vain stupid mother, Richelieu seemed to him the only person capable of giving to France the things of which that distracted country stood so sorely in need—internal peace, a strong government, the reform of abuses. The more he thought and prayed over the sorry state of the kingdom, the more clear it became to him that here, in the Bishop of Luçon, was the man whom God had chosen to be his instrument. He resolved henceforward to do everything in his power to help his friend to accomplish his manifest destiny. On all his visits to Tours he found opportunities of recommending Richelieu's abilities to the Queen Mother. Later, when the Capuchin had departed for Italy, Marie de Médicis followed his advice and appointed M. de Luçon to continue and complete the work of appeasement which had been begun at Loudon.

In the negotiations which led up to the peace of Loudun Father Joseph displayed to the full his extraordinary political talents. His chief opponent in the diplomatic game was the Protestant Duke of Bouillon, a man of such force and ability that he was able to hold out for years against Richelieu in a condition of almost complete political independence. At the end of these negotiations Bouillon paid the friar a tribute, of which any politician might be proud. "This man," he said, "penetrates my most secret thoughts; he knows things that I have communicated only to a few people of tried discretion; and he goes to Tours and returns, on foot, in the rain, the snow and the ice, in the most frightful weather, without anybody being able to observe him. I swear, the devil must be in this friar's body."

The treaty was finally concluded as the result of a decisive intervention by Ezéchiely. Condé fell sick of the prevailing influenza and seemed for a day or two at the very door of death. Father Joseph chose this moment to represent to him, in the most solemn manner, the dangers to which he would be exposing his soul if he died leaving his country a prey to civil war. The prince was so terrified that, though he recovered and lived to make a nuisance of himself for many years to come, he promptly made his peace with the Queen Mother, as Father Joseph had insisted that he should.

The treaty of Loudun settled nothing; for the magnates were to rebel many times more before they were finally curbed by Richelieu. It was decisive only for Father

Joseph. The negotiations with Condé and Bouillon had revealed him to those in authority as a consummate politician. Henceforward he would never be allowed to give himself exclusively to the life of a missionary and mystic. Even if Richelieu had never come to power, Father Joseph would still have played a part, albeit a subsidiary part, in the political life of his time. At Loudun his destiny had drawn him into a position from which he could hardly retreat, even if he had wanted to. And though a part of him *did* want to retreat, though he was often, in the coming years, to protest that political life was like a hell on earth, there was always a Tenebroso-Cavernoso who enjoyed the game he played so brilliantly well, there was always the ardent patriot who *knew* that God's purposes and those of the French government were at bottom identical.

Among the great nobles assembled at Loudun there was one, the Duke of Nevers, with whom Father Joseph had many long and private conversations. The historical significance of this personage was in no wise due to his native abilities. Like Dryden's Zimri, he was a man, who,

> Stiff in opinion, always in the wrong,
> Was everything by starts and nothing long.

Nor did the resemblance end there. He was as vain as Buckingham, as extravagant and ostentatious, as thoroughly unreliable. Perhaps the most remarkable thing about him was the fact, attested on oath by one of his body servants, "that he always slept with his eyes open, and that from those open eyes came rays so frightful that he (the servant) was often frightened and could never get used to them." The secret of the duke's peculiar contemporary importance was due to his genealogical tree.

By upbringing and title, he was French; by birth, Italian, Greek and German. His mother was a princess of the house of Cleves; his paternal grandmother, an imperial Palaeologus; and his father, a Gonzaga. (In a letter to the Queen Mother Nevers once wrote, with more truthfulness than tact, that "it was well known that the Gonzagas had been princes long before the Medici had even been gentlemen.") Being a Gonzaga, he was in the running, should the direct line fail, for one of the most important of the Italian States. Years later, the question of his succession to Mantua led to war between France and Spain, and the settlement of the quarrel was to call for Father Joseph's most astute diplomacy. At present, however, it was not as a Gonzaga, but as a Palaeologus, that the duke aroused his interest. The sultans had ruled in Constantinople for more than a hundred and fifty years; but among the conquered and downtrodden Greeks the memory of political freedom and their last emperors was still very much alive. The Duke of Nevers was a descendant of those emperors and it was therefore to him that the people of the Morea had recently sent a delegation, begging him to put himself at the head of a projected uprising of Christians against their Turkish overlords. The Duke was to bring his name and a store of munitions; the Greeks promised to do the rest. Nevers, who had a thirst for glory as well as a keen sense of his own hereditary eminence, was greatly tempted. But though foolish and impulsive, he had at least sense to know that the Ottoman empire could not be overthrown by an undisciplined force of Greek mountaineers, even under the command of a Palaeologus. If the uprising was to be successful, it must be supported by a military and naval expedition fitted out by the great powers of Western Europe. But would the great powers consent to use their resources in this way? That was the question. And that was the subject of those long intimate conversations between the duke and Father Joseph.

In an age when there were no Westerns or detective stories, the most exciting reading matter an imaginative boy could get hold of was probably to be found in the chronicles of the crusades. To a child of François du Tremblay's time, the infidels occupied the place reserved in the minds of a more recent generation of schoolboys for the Redskins. Most men, as they grew up, forgot about the infidels, just as they now forget about the Indians. Not so François du Tremblay. Entering the cloister, he found himself in a world where the infidels were a constant subject of conversation and even of prayer. St. Francis had been deeply concerned with missions, martyrdom, and the recovery of the Holy Places. This concern had become a tradition among his followers. All Franciscans, including of course the Capuchins, took a kind of professional interest in crusading. To this professional interest, Father Joseph added his own private enthusiasm. Ever since childhood, Calvary had been the home of his imagination. The Holy Places were as dear to him as his native land. To deliver them was a matter of spiritual patriotism. From the premise of Christ's sufferings, the logic of emotion and imagination led to the conclusion that crusading against the Turks was among the Christian's highest duties. Father Joseph's meditations upon this theme had often crystallized into visions and auditions; God had commanded him to work for the crusade, had seemed obscurely to promise success. And now, suddenly, providentially, here was the last of the Palaeologi; and the Greeks had begged him to come and lead them against the infidels. It was a new vocation, a call to tasks even higher and more glorious than those of preaching to the indifferent and the misguided. Ezéchiely's enthusiasm blazed up. And simultaneously Tenebroso-Cavernoso surveyed the political scene and found the juncture peculiarly favourable for a crusade. The existing equilibrium in Europe was desperately unstable. The Hapsburgs, as Richelieu was never tired of pointing out, were planning, in the name of the Counter-Reformation, to impose their direct rule or their influence upon the whole of Europe. Alarmed by the Spanish-Austrian menace, the Protestant powers were uneasily preparing for a war, which was expected to break out on the expiration of the twelve-year truce between Spain and Holland, in 1621, but which actually began in 1618, with the revolt of Bohemia against the Emperor. Under the Queen Mother's regency, the traditional anti-Spanish policy of France had been reversed; but it was sufficiently obvious that fear of Hapsburg domination must sooner or later cause a return to the strategy of François I and Henri IV. Meanwhile, all the states of Germany had been building up their armies; the huge military machine of Spain had reached a perfection unknown since the time of the Romans; Dutch naval power was growing; the Swedes had started to apply scientific methods to warfare. All Europe fairly swarmed with soldiers, ready at a word to march. Scoffers might regard a crusade as absurd and chimerical; but at this particular moment of history, a shrewd politician could find a great deal to be said for the idea. If a crusade could be organized in time, the war which everyone regarded as inevitable might be averted and the great powers reconciled in their effort against a common enemy. Ezéchiely's dream of a reunited Christendom would be realized. Events were to prove the plan unworkable. But, if we grant for the moment the desirability of slaughtering huge numbers of Moslems, we are forced to agree with Father Joseph that, in this second decade of the seventeenth century, there was no more far-sighted policy than that of a great international expedition against the Turks. The immediate, practical problem was that of persuading the great powers to accept so far-sighted a policy. Richelieu, when consulted, shook his head and enumerated the obstacles which would have to be surmounted. But the others would not allow their enthusiasm to be damped; and in the end the bishop agreed to do what he could to forward the scheme, on condition that the Duke of Nevers should join forces with Father Joseph in pressing his own claims to political power.

No crusade could possibly be launched without the express approval and encouragement of the Holy See. As soon, therefore, as the necessary permissions could be obtained and the necessary arrangements made, Father Joseph set out, on foot as usual, for Rome. The crusade was not his only business, nor was Nevers the only important personage whom he represented. From Condé he carried explanations, apologies and a plea to be forgiven for his recent co-operation with the Huguenots; from Marie de Médicis a message of greeting; from Mme d'Orléans, a reminder that her Calvarians were still waiting for the bull that would make of them an independent

MARIE DE MÉDICIS

Artist unknown

congregation; and from his own order, a request for the right to organize missions among the heretics of Poitou.

Camillo Borghese, who ruled in Rome as Paul V, was a man of an intensely legalistic turn of mind, a stickler for the letter as against the spirit, a martinet. But though he started by feeling rather suspicious of the friar's hints of visions and revelations, that "ravishing conversation," "that infinite dexterity in dealing with the nobility" soon had their usual effect. The Pope was impressed and finally convinced. He promised to support the scheme for a crusade with all the machinery of the Church. But before official representations could be made, it would be necessary, he insisted, that the friar should sound out the various governments concerned. When Father Joseph left Rome in the spring of 1617, he took with him the definite promise of bulls for the Calvarians and the missions of Poitou, and a pontifical letter addressed to the court of Spain and empowering him to negotiate for the crusade. His stay in Rome had been long—about eight months in all—but he had achieved everything he set out to accomplish there. More than that, he had made the acquaintance of some of the highest dignitaries of the Roman Curia, and had left them all profoundly impressed by his zeal, his integrity and his outstanding talents. The weeks at Loudun had made of him a man to be reckoned with in France; the months at Rome, a figure of some consequence within the Church. From this time forward we find him exchanging letters with nuncios, legates, cardinals, even the papal secretary of state.

Another man would have been exultant; but Father Joseph was perpetually on his guard against such lapses into pride and vanity. He had long since schooled himself out of the external manifestations of personal satisfaction or displeasure; and to a considerable extent, no doubt, he had suppressed even their inward manifestations. The only emotional indulgence he permitted himself, as he hastened northward, through Umbria and Tuscany, was versifying. Under the stimulus of repressed elation, his mind fairly seethed with poetic imagery. In the intervals between his meditations he composed and committed to memory an astonishing number of verses in French and Latin. In the dead language he began and, at the astonishing rate of two hundred lines a day, half finished a full-length epic about Turks and crusaders. In French he expressed his feelings in a series of religious lyrics, one of which—a long rhapsody on the spring-time as the symbol of eternal life—contains these really charming stanzas on the nightingale.

En mille tours il façonne
De sa voix les longs replis:
Ainsi tout le ciel résonne
De mille choeurs accomplis.

Aisément l'on ne peut dire
De ce long chant nuit et jour,
S'il meurt, s'il pâme, ou soupire
De tourment, d'aise ou d'amour.

Quand par les champs je m'égaye,
En quelque air dévotieux,
Ce chantre jaloux s'essaye
D'élever sa voix au cieux.

Mais en plus pleine musique
La violente douceur

De l'harmonie angelique
Repond aux voix de mon coeur.

Ces oisillons qui rassemblent
En un leurs accents divers
Aux motet des Saints ressemblent
Unis en tout l'univers.[2]

Versifying, praying, singing hymns in competition with the innumerable nightingales of the Italian spring, Father Joseph entered Turin. Here once again he became the diplomat. The prophetic eloquence, the ravishing conversation, the infinite dexterity with the nobility—all were brought out; but without much success. Charles Emanuel of Savoy had a war with Spain on his hands and was in no position to think about crusades against the Turks. After a few weeks, Father Joseph took the road again, crossed the Alps by forced marches and reached Paris in early June. During the twelve months of his absence, many strange things had happened in that exalted political world, into which his destiny was slowly but surely drawing him. In the autumn of 1616, Richelieu had been made a member of the Council of State and appointed minister for war and foreign affairs. That supreme power at which, from earliest manhood, he had steadily aimed, and which he had pursued by ways so devious and often so degrad-

[2] In a thousand turns he fashions the long windings of his voice, so that the sky resounds with consummate singing. Of this song that continues night and day it is hard to say whether it dies, or swoons, whether it sighs with torment, bliss or love. And when, walking in the fields, I lift up my heart in some hymn of praise, this envious singer also tries to raise his voice to heaven. But in mid-music, the violent sweetness of the angelic harmony makes answer to the voices of my heart. These little birds, that join their various accents in a single theme, are like the choir of the saints united throughout the world.

ing, seemed now within his grasp. Then, suddenly, the Queen Mother's system of education bore fruit, and the fruit was terrible. The boy who had been whipped every morning was now legally as well as in name the King of France. His mother, however, still continued to treat him as a child and to keep all the power in her own and the Concinis' hands. By force of habit and from sloth and diffidence, Louis XIII had hitherto silently acquiesced in this state of things. Then, without warning, he took his revenge for all his mother's long neglect, all those thousands of cold-blooded and methodical birchings. He gave orders to the captain of the guard that Concini should be arrested, adding that, if he resisted he might be killed. It was a death warrant. Concini was shot as he entered the Louvre, and a few hours later his naked and mutilated body was hanging by the heels from the gibbet on the Pont Neuf, while the mob danced around, howling with bestial glee. Even on the following afternoon the crowd was still so dense that Richelieu's carriage was held up for many minutes at the approach to the bridge, and the future cardinal was given ample opportunity to observe what happens to unpopular ministers when they lose the King's favour. For him, the moral of the revolting spectacle was clear: "If ever you get political power," that poor gelded and gutted carcass proclaimed, "take very good care to stick to it." For the eighteen years of his dominion, Richelieu never ceased to act upon this precept. Meanwhile, of course, the game was up, at any rate for the time being. Too unimportant to suffer Concini's fate, the Bishop of Luçon followed the Queen Mother into exile. For the next four years the country was ruled by Luynes, a middle-aged country gentleman, for whom the young Louis had conceived the most intense affection and admiration, on account of his skill in falconry.

Father Joseph remained loyal to his exiled friend, and patiently awaited the opportunity to bring him back to power. For the time being, however, there was no hope for the Bishop of Luçon. Luynes hated and feared him for his ability, and to Louis he was repugnant as a creature of his mother's ignoble favourite. Father Joseph bided his time and continued to work on his great project of the crusade. From the reports which came in from Nevers, who was visiting the various courts of Germany, and from his numerous ecclesiastical correspondents, he learned that his plan was winning a fair measure of approval among all except the Spaniards. He decided that it was time to make use of his pontifical letter to Philip III. The Procurator of the Capuchin order had given him "obediences," entitling him to travel as much as he liked, and in the spring of 1618, a few days after Richelieu had been separated from the Queen Mother and sent into a remoter exile at Avignon, he set out with two companions for the south. At Poitiers the journey was unexpectedly interrupted. A few days before his arrival, his old friend and collaborator, Antoinette d'Orléans, had died, leaving the newly established Congregation of Calvary without a head. While Father Joseph was at Poitiers, settling the troubled affairs of his Calvarians, an odd piece of news was brought to him. The Emperor's representatives in Bohemia had been thrown out of a third story window of the palace at Prague. The long anticipated war had begun—the war that was destined, though nobody dreamed that such a thing was possible, to last for thirty years.

As soon as the new abbess was elected, and her rule securely established, Father Joseph hastened on to Madrid, at such a rate and through summer weather so torrid, that both of his companions died before the journey was completed. Of tougher constitution and supported by a more indomitable spirit and a more constant practice of the divine presence, Father Joseph reached his destination in safety and at once plunged into negotiations with the Duke of Lerma and his royal master. The reception accorded to the Pope's representative was courteous and cordial in the extreme; the idea of the crusade was pronounced to be eminently catholic and meritorious. But when it came to the question of the means by which this pious approval in principle might be translated into active diplomatic, military and naval co-operation with France, Father Joseph found that he was dealing, not with obedient sons of the Church, but with Spanish nationalists. Simultaneously, of course, the Spaniards made a corresponding discovery about Father Joseph. Having a beam in one's own eye may actually sharpen one's vision for similar beams in the eyes of others. To Lerma and his master it was abundantly obvious that, though the friar sincerely believed that a crusade would be highly pleasing to God, he was also convinced that France should lead the crusade and derive the chief benefits from it. Father Joseph rationalized this last belief by an appeal to history. France had played the chief part in earlier crusades—had played it because it was evidently the will of Providence that she should do so. If France were to play any part below the highest in the present crusade, it would be a rupture of historical tradition and a flouting of God's will. Therefore, France must play the leading part. It seemed an irrefragable argument, to a Frenchman. To the Spaniards, unfortunately, it was less convincing. All they felt certain of was that a crusade such as Father Joseph projected would strengthen France at the expense of Spain. Experience had taught them that the old crusading motto, "*Gesta Dei per Francos*"[3] could all too easily be transformed in practice into "*Gesta Francorum, gesta Dei*";[4] and they shrewdly suspected that some such transformation had actually taken place inside the tonsured skull of Father Joseph. After four months of strenuous and perfectly ineffective negotiations, the friar was forced to return home, with nothing but the vaguest promises, the most noncommittal of good wishes.

Spanish coolness and the rigours of winter on the Sierras had no power to chill Father Joseph's enthusiasm. On the way home he composed a long lyrical rhapsody on the liberation of the Greeks from Turkish bondage. Two stanzas of this poem are peculiarly illuminating. "*Si, pour te soulager,*" he writes, apostrophizing Greece,

> *Si pour te soulager, l'univers je tournoie,*
> *C'est trop peu pour mes voeux;*
> *Dans une mer de sang il faut que je me noie*
> *Pour éteindre mes feux.*[5]

In other words, Father Joseph's zeal for a crusade was too burningly hot to be extinguished by anything short of a

[3] God's deeds by means of the French.

[4] The deeds of the French are the deeds of God.

[5] If, in order to succour thee, I overturn the whole world, it is all too little for my wishes; to quench the fires of my ardour, I must drown me in a sea of blood.

sea of other people's blood. Few political idealists have spoken so frankly about the consequences of their idealism. The reason, it may be, is that few political idealists have spent half a lifetime brooding upon the torture and death of a man-god, by comparison with whose sufferings those of ordinary human beings are so infinitesimal as to be practically negligible. And when the sea of blood had been spilled, what then? Most political idealists have no doubt at all; liquidate the people who don't agree with you, and you will have Utopia. Again Father Joseph is strangely free from illusions and strangely frank about that freedom.

J'ignore où mon dessein, qui surpasse ma vue,
Si vite me conduit;
Mais comme un astre ardent qui brille dans la nue,
Il me guide en la nuit.[6]

The results of any plan of action are always unknown and unknowable; the plan must be pursued for its own sake, as an end in itself. This is the bald truth about politics; but how few politicians have ever had the perspicacity to see it or the courage, if they have seen it, to tell the disquieting truth!

The crusade against the Turks remained to the end of his life one of Father Joseph's principal concerns. True, by 1625 he was forced to admit that any scheme for an international expedition would have to be abandoned, probably for many years to come. The reasons for this abandonment were the troubled state of Europe and the persistent opposition of the two branches of the House of

[6] I know not whither my design, whose end I cannot see, is leading me so swiftly; but like a bright star blazing in the sky, it guides me through the night.

Hapsburg. This opposition to the crusade transformed Father Joseph's early Spanish policy into an intense and fixed dislike of "the hereditary enemy." At the beginning of the Thirty Years' War he was whole-heartedly on the side of the Emperor against the Elector Palatine and the Protestants. Of the imperial victory of the White Mountain, in 1620 he wrote enthusiastically: "Satan has lost one of his horns and Jesus, expelled from these regions, will be re-established in Bohemia." A few years later he was doing everything in his power to make Satan's horn grow again. Why? Because a Hapsburg triumph would be dangerous to France and an obstacle to the launching, under French auspices, of a great crusade against the infidel. The most ardent of Catholics, he came to believe that Catholic Austria and Catholic Spain were a menace to the best interests of Catholicism. This view was far from unorthodox; for it was shared by no less a person than the Pope. As an Italian prince, the Pope had very good reasons to fear the House of Hapsburg. A too sweeping victory in Germany would make the Emperor and the King of Spain the undisputed masters of the Peninsula.

On his return from Madrid, Father Joseph continued to work with unabated zeal for the crusade. Behind the scenes, he helped the Duke of Nevers to organize the new order of chivalry, which was to form the nucleus of the projected international army. This Christian Militia, as it was called, was to enroll its knights and commanders in all parts of Catholic Europe. Each recruit was to take a crusader's oath and to contribute to the common war chest a sum proportionate to his rank and fortune. The Christian Militia did as well as such an organization could be expected to do in the circumstances. Many nobles and gentlemen joined the order; a considerable amount of money was promised; and questions of leadership and prestige provoked a great deal of heart burning and resulted in interminable disputes. The Militia received its first serious set-back when Philip IV of Spain refused to allow its establishment in any of his possessions. Then, with the absorption of Europe's best energies in the war, the order rapidly lost its reason for existence. In 1625, when Father Joseph obtained its official recognition by Pope Urban VIII, the Christian Militia was for all practical purposes dead and buried.

Nevers' war effort was not confined to organizing an order of chivalry. He raised troops in his domains and had a number of fine ships built to transport them to Greece. As commander of his little navy, he engaged a well-known Norman pirate, who had specialized in the Mediterranean and possessed an unrivalled knowledge of Levantine waters. Father Joseph did what he could to help the potential Emperor of Byzantium in these preparations, none of which, however, bore any fruit. The troops evaporated, the ships were seized by a Protestant squadron from La Rochelle, the pirate returned to his own line of business, and finally the Duke of Nevers himself got bored with crusades and began to think about other things.

> Blest madman, who could every hour employ
> With something new to wish, or to enjoy!

Only Father Joseph remained, a voice crying in the wilderness; and soon that voice would be changing its tune, would cry no longer for the destruction of the Turk, but for the humiliation of the Hapsburgs. But before abandoning (how reluctantly!) his policy of a-crusade-in-our-time, Father Joseph made one last and most extraordinary contribution to the cause. In 1617, on his way back from Rome, he had begun the composition of his Turciad. Thirty-five miles, three hours of meditation and two hundred hexameters—such was the daily programme of that strenuous journey. In the years that followed, and on the roads of France and Spain, he completed and polished the work. By 1625 the epic, in four thousand six hundred and thirty-seven lines, was complete. That year he took with him to Rome the two printed copies which constituted, so far as can be discovered, the first and only edition of the work. One copy was for Urban VIII, the other for Cardinal Barberini, his nephew and papal secretary of state. Himself a distinguished classical scholar and the author of many elegantly turned verses, many truly Ciceronian briefs and bulls, Urban VIII was delighted with the poem, which he called "the Christian Aeneid." The Abbé Dedouvres, who some forty-odd years ago discovered the only surviving copy of the Turciad, is unable, as a conscientious Latinist, fully to endorse this pontifical judgement. Father Joseph, he has to admit, was apt to make regrettable confusions of moods after declarative verbs and in indirect interrogations. At the same time the copulative conjunction is all too frequently separated from the negation. As for his prosody, it shows too many elisions of monosyllables, while there is persistence of the short syllable in no less than forty-four sigmatisms. Nor is the Turciad entirely above reproach in matters of scansion. Thus, *concidit* is treated as a dactyl, when in fact it is an antibacchius. Worse still, *inscitiam,* which is manifestly an epitrite III, is made to do duty as a choriambus. Grave offences! But let those who are without sin in the matter of false quantities throw the first stone.

Of more interest than the linguistic form of Father Joseph's epic is its extraordinary substance. The Turciad is one of those things in virtue of which plain history is always so much odder than the most romantic of historical novels. A novelist might possibly invent a character who was simultaneously a power politician and a practising mystic. But to fabricate someone who, besides being a power politician and a practising mystic, should also have composed the four thousand six hundred and thirty-seven hexameters of the Turciad is a feat beyond the powers of any literary artist, however greatly gifted. Every human being is an individual slice of history, unique and unrepeatable; but the majority of such slices belong to one or other of a number of familiar and recognizable classes. This is not the case with exceptional individuals. These represent the wildest improbabilities, such as only life can make actual; for life alone possesses the resources and the patience to go on playing the lotteries of heredity and environment until the necessary number of one-in-a-million chances turn up simultaneously, and an exceptional individual appears and runs his course. That is why truth is so much stranger, richer and more interesting than fiction.

The Turciad opens with the description of a public meeting of angels called by the Second Person of the Trinity. Addressing the meeting, Christ expresses his distress at Mohammedan supremacy in the Near and Middle East, and urges the heavenly powers to do something about it. Even the Virgin, it is indicated, would be glad to participate in a crusade, if such a thing were proper to her station. From this opening the speaker proceeds to an account of the life of Mohammed, considerably more picturesque than historical. Near Mecca, he tells his auditors, is a cave from which a chimney goes down directly into hell. One day the young Mohammed found his way into this cave and was there kindly received and instructed in the arts of mischief by Lucifer.

This instruction was easy to give; for round the chimney there ran a series of galleries which had been fitted up by the devils as a kind of Museum of Evil. In them had been placed such interesting objects as the tooth of the serpent which tempted Eve; Cain's club; the first iron weapons, invented by Tubal-cain; the emblems of Venus and of Bacchus; all the rich apparatus of sorcery and magic; material illustrative of all the heresies from that of Arius to that of Calvin; and finally the armament, already prepared for future contingencies, to be used in the campaigns of Antichrist. Duly enlightened by his visit to this chamber of horrors, Mohammed was sent home to write the Koran and plan the conquest of the Holy Places. Having obtained the support of the heavenly hierarchies for a crusade, Christ next sets out to work upon the princes of Europe, especially Louis XIII and Philip IV of Spain. By means of a dream he explains to them why a holy war is so urgently necessary.

At this point, for no particular reason, the author of the epic appears on the scene and asks permission to pass on to the general public the substance of what has been imparted to the princes. Leave is given, and he at once embarks upon a theological lecture. After briefly explaining the Holy Trinity, the creation, the fall, free will, angelology, the beatific vision and the New Jerusalem, he concludes, at the end of some seven hundred and fifty lines, with an exhortation to the potential crusaders to ally themselves immediately with the forces of heaven.

The next five hundred and seventy lines are devoted to the account of another public meeting in heaven. This time the audience consists, not of angels, but of saints, who are seated, tier upon tier, in a kind of amphitheatre, in whose arena stand two golden thrones. From the earth comes a squadron of cherubim transporting the European princes, who enjoy the spectacle from a kind of hovering platform composed of the angel's wings. Among the nine choirs of saints, those most useful to crusaders are pointed out to the new arrivals. The list closes with St. Francis, whom Father Joseph relates, by means of an elegant pun, to France.

Sibi nam cognata cohaerent,
Francia, Franciscus, fatalia nomina Turcis.[7]

Suddenly the Second Person of the Trinity appears again, accompanied by the Virgin. All rise and make obeisance, while the two take their places on the thrones prepared for them. In the ensuing silence, Christ calls for the Duke of Nevers. The Archangel Michael picks up the last of the Palaeologi from where he is sitting on the platform of angels' wings, swoops into the arena and deposits him, more dead than alive with terror, at the foot of the thrones. After the Virgin has comforted him with a few reassuring words, Christ proceeds to harangue the duke at some

[7] For cognate things stick together, France and Francis, names fatal to the Turks.

length, reminding him of his imperial origins and the duties they impose on him, reminding him also of his faults and that a crusader must be a man of exemplary conduct. Much moved, Nevers vows to devote the rest of his life to a crusade against the Turks. Whereupon the Virgin invests him with the insignia of the Christian Militia. The proceedings are brought to a close by a long procession of all the heroes who have fought for the Lord against His enemies. Moses and Joshua head the parade, which winds on chronologically through Godefroy of Bouillon to Don John of Austria and the heroes of Lepanto. Needless to say, this is a golden opportunity for Father Joseph to bring out one of those sonorous lists of names, so dear to all writers of epics. With what gusto the pontifical critic must have rolled around his tongue such lines as *"Hunneades sollers et Scanderbegius acer!"*[8]

News of this meeting is brought to Satan and fills him with considerable apprehension. Wistfully, he yearns for the coming of Antichrist; but, as Antichrist shows no signs of appearing, he does what he can on his own account by starting the war in Bohemia. It was a successful manœuvre—just how successful Father Joseph was to discover during the remaining years of his life. In 1625, when the Turciad was completed, he would only admit a local and temporary set-back. The troubles which the fiend had stirred up would soon be settled; united Europe would utterly destroy the Turks and, by this war to end war, inaugurate a golden age of universal peace—under the leadership of France. And the poem ends with yet another dream, a dream in which the author is addressed by the personification of his country, by that France which, be-

[8] Skilful Hunyadi and Scanderbeg the Terrible.

cause he believed her to be the instrument of divine providence, he was able, with a good conscience and without suspecting that he was committing idolatry, to worship as though she were God.

Thus baldly analysed, the Turciad seems almost uniquely preposterous. But apply the same process to Paradise Lost, discount the style, strip away the ornaments, reduce the poem to its naked subject matter, and you have something only a little less absurd. Public meetings of angels, theological discussions between the First and Second Persons of the Trinity, angelic battles, complete with three-dimension strategy, infernal artillery and the divine equivalent of the tank. Was it all merely a matter of literary convention, of a self-conscious imitation of the poetical machinery of another age? Were these strangely materialistic accounts of life in heaven regarded by their authors as being as completely fabulous as that pathetic tale of young Prince Syphilis, which Fracastoro had composed a hundred years before? It would be comforting to believe it; but I am afraid that we are not justified in so believing. In some ineffably Pickwickian way the Apotheosis of Charles V, Paradise Lost and the Turciad were probably conceived by Titian, and Father Joseph and Milton as being something more than merely fantastic. In the case of Titian and Milton this was comprehensible enough; both, in their different ways, were men of exoteric religion. Not so Father Joseph. That he had had some direct, unmediated experience of ultimate reality is unquestionable. In his *Introduction to the Spiritual Life* he had described the soul's union with God. A few years later, and evidently with no sense of incongruity, he was writing the Turciad and writing it in the conviction that, by so doing, he was serving, and in some way telling the truth about, the God whom he had dimly apprehended in the act of contemplation. The fact is, of course, that human beings find no difficulty at all in entertaining, successively or even at the same moment, convictions which are totally incompatible one with another. Indeed, such self-contradiction is the normal and natural condition of man. It suits our book to have different notions at different moments; therefore we have such notions, even though there is no means of reconciling them. Complete consistency comes only with complete one-pointedness, complete absorption in ultimate reality.

In the intervals of working for the crusade, Father Joseph devoted his enormous energies to the organization of missions among the Protestants of Poitou. Nor was it the Protestants only who stood in need of evangelization; for though Catholicism survived in the West, it had been reduced by war, indifference and worldliness to a most abject and unedifying condition. Almost all the abbeys and most of the parishes had passed into the control of the local gentry, who spent the church revenues on themselves and were represented by half-starved and generally illiterate vicars, acting as their bailiffs. "Benefices and even curacies are given to girls as marriage portions, are counted as private property, as well by Catholics as Huguenots, and are sold for cash under contracts drawn up by the notary." This Augean stable of simony and heresy was calculated to rejoice the heart of Ezéchiely. Here indeed was a labour proportionate to his zeal! Starting at first with only seven picked helpers, Father Joseph flung himself into the task of reformation and conversion. His success was spectacular. Hungry for just such a revival of religion, the Catholics responded with enthusiasm. Hardly less eager were the Huguenots who flocked in thousands to see the unfamiliar rites, to hear the liturgical chanting and the sermons. Impressed as much by the austerity of the missionaries' lives as by the eloquence of their preaching, many returned, and considerable numbers were finally converted. Father Joseph was in his element again, doing the work he loved best. But he was now too completely committed to the life of high politics to be able even to imagine that he could become again what he had been—the popular evangelist, the itinerant teacher of the art of mental prayer. His missionary campaigns in the West were periodically interrupted by visits to Paris—visits, in the course of which he was in contact with people of the highest importance, great noblemen, great ecclesiastics, the papal nuncio, Luynes himself and even the King. Louis XIII respected the Capuchin's political judgment and was impressed by his burning eloquence, his mysterious accounts of visions and revelations vouchsafed either to himself or to his Calvarians. Five years before Richelieu became prime minister, Father Joseph was on sufficiently intimate terms with the monarch to be made the confidant of what had happened when, protesting, and with the most intense reluctance, the eighteen-year-old boy had been pushed by Luynes into his consort's bed. No less than Louis himself, his brother Gaston of Orleans, fell under the same prophetic spell and, in spite of Father Joseph's position as coadjutor of the detested cardinal, remained attached to him to the end.

It was during one of Father Joseph's visits to Paris, in February 1619, that a courier brought disquieting news from Blois. The Queen Mother had escaped from the castle, by night, and fled to Angoulême, where she had placed herself under the protection of the Duke of Epernon. A new and more dangerous rebellion seemed to threaten. What was to be done? In his perplexity, Luynes sent for Father Joseph and Bérulle. They advised the immediate dispatch to the Queen Mother of some disinterested person whom she could trust. For example, Father Joseph suggested, her almoner, Bouthillier. Now Bouthillier was dean of Luçon and one of Richelieu's most faithful supporters. The dean was the thin end of a wedge, whose other extremity was the bishop. Bouthillier was sent, and the result was that Marie demanded, as a first condition of peace, that her trusted counsellor should be permitted to come back to her from his exile. Luynes' reluctance to recall a potentially dangerous rival was outweighed by his fear of an immediate civil war. Knowing that Richelieu could be trusted to advise moderation, he accepted the Queen Mother's terms. At the beginning of March, Father Joseph's brother, Charles du Tremblay, was sent posting south, to Avignon, bearing a letter from the King to the bishop of Luçon. Breaking the seal, Richelieu read the command to proceed immediately to Angoulême, to rejoin the Queen Mother. He obeyed with an alacrity which, owing to the wintry weather and the appalling state of the roads, exposed him to considerable dangers. At Angoulême he was joined by Father Joseph and, together, they patched up a precarious agreement between the Queen Mother's party and the King. The peace was not of long duration. A year later, in 1620, the nobles were using Marie's grievances as an excuse for yet another uprising. In the engagement at Pont-de-Cé, the royal forces won a decisive victory. As a kind of consolation prize and to reinforce their loyalty, Marie de Médicis gave orders that her infantry should be permitted to sack the town of Angers, before retiring further south. Father Joseph, who was in the neighbourhood, heard of this and immediately demanded an audience of the Queen. This time the friar's "infinite dexterity with the nobility" gave place to prophetic eloquence. Standing before the Queen, he told her unequivocally that, if she suffered Angers to be sacked, the blood of its people would be upon her head, and that God would damn her everlastingly.

The doctrine of hell fire was not entirely mischievous in its effects. On occasions like the present, for example, it could do excellent service. A stupid, obstinate, heartless creature, like Marie de Médicis, would have been deaf to any appeal to the higher feelings she did not possess, or possessed only in a condition so latent that it would have taken the greatest saint a very long time to bring them into actuality. But the Queen cared intensely for herself, and she believed without doubt or question in the physical reality of hell. Thunderously harping on that portentous theme, Ezéchiely was able to put the fear of God into her. She recalled the order she had given; Angers was saved. Thanks to a certain kind of intellectual "progress," the rulers of the modern world no longer believe that they will be tortured everlastingly, if they are wicked. The eschatological sanction, which was one of the principal weapons in the hands of the prophets of past times, has disappeared. This would not matter, if moral had kept pace with intellectual "progress." But it has not. Twentieth-century rulers behave just as vilely and ruthlessly as did rulers in the seventeenth or any other century. But unlike their predecessors, they do not lie awake at nights wondering whether they are damned. If Marie de Médicis had enjoyed the advantages of a modern education, Father Joseph would have thundered in vain, and Angers would have been sacked.

After the battle of Pont-de-Cé, fighting gave place to negotiations, which finally bore fruit in the Peace of Angers. As a reward for the part he had played in averting further civil strife, in moderating the nobles' demands and in reconciling the King and his mother, Richelieu demanded a cardinal's hat. Luynes made a show of agreeing, sent in a request to Rome that the Bishop of Luçon should be promoted at the earliest opportunity, and accompanied his official letter with a private hint that he was in no hurry to see his rival made a prince of the church. Richelieu did not actually receive his hat till 1622, some months after Luynes' death. Meanwhile the bishop had become too important to be trifled with. As the price of his friendship, or at any rate of his benevolent neutrality, Richelieu demanded and obtained the hand of Luynes' nephew, de Combalet, for his niece, Mlle de Pont-Courlay. It was an excellent match; for, in his brief tenure of office, Luynes had amassed vast fortunes, not only for himself, but for all the members of his needy and undistinguished family. The go-between who actually arranged the marriage was Father Joseph. We cannot doubt that he believed himself to be doing what his master had called the Exterior Will of God.

The abrupt conclusion of the war left the King with a considerable army, fully equipped, but with nothing to do. Luynes was all for disbanding it at once. Not so Father Joseph. Here, he perceived, was an opportunity, which it would be a sin to miss—an opportunity to begin that great work of national unification, of which he and Richelieu had talked so often on the road between Loudun and Tours. The presence of the army was providential; the King must use it to strengthen the royal authority and advance the true faith. Specifically, he should lead it into Béarn, at the western end of the Pyrenees. This native province of Henri IV still enjoyed a kind of autonomy; what was worse, it was so virulently Protestant that for upwards of fifty years, Catholicism had been all but outlawed within its borders. Let the King march at once, resume his father's patrimony and re-establish the true faith.

Louis XIII listened and was inclined to take the friar's advice, which was echoed by Richelieu and the whole Catholic party. But Luynes, who was the most unmilitary of men, objected. The fate of the domestic crusade hung in the balance. Finally, Father Joseph was called to express his views before a meeting of the council, presided over by the King in person. According to Cardinal de Retz, he spoke "like the prophets of the Old Testament" in favour of an immediate march towards the south. The majority was won over and, at the head of an army, whose numbers were swelled by Catholic soldiers from the rebel camp, the King set out on the crusade.

Béarn yielded without a blow, and was formally incorporated into the kingdom of France. Jeanne d'Albret's decrees were rescinded, confiscated church lands were restored to their original owners, and Catholicism was reintroduced into the province. Father Joseph, who accompanied the army, was kept very busy founding convents, re-consecrating churches, organizing the missionaries, who were to win the heretics back to the true faith. Like

Richelieu, Father Joseph did not believe in dragooning the Huguenots into conformity. "Forced religion," he declared, "is no longer religion." Military action against the Huguenots was to be taken not because they were Protestants, but because of their claim to constitute a quasi-independent state within the state of France. Once reduced to obedience, they were to be allowed to worship as they pleased. To convert them would then become the business of Catholic missionaries, such as the Capuchins. Such were Father Joseph's principles in regard to the heretics; and, for the most part, his practice conformed to those principles. There were plenty of Catholics who would have liked to see the Protestants more harshly treated. Thanks to Richelieu, the shrewd, conservative statesman, thanks too, to Father Joseph, the ardent evangelist and missionary, a more tolerant policy prevailed. The result was that, after their political defeat, the Huguenots remained a loyal minority of useful and contented citizens. Louis XIV's persecution of them, in the latter part of the century, was without political or economic excuse; it was an act of what is called "high idealism," in other words of pure and gratuitous bigotry.

From Béarn the royal forces marched on the great Huguenot fortress of Montauban. They were under the command of Luynes, who had been made Constable of France. The contrast between the general's resounding title and his hopeless incapacity as a soldier was a source to all of contemptuous merriment. Weeks passed, and the siege of Montauban had to be ingloriously raised; then after other humiliating failures, the Constable forestalled his imminent fall from the King's good graces by catching typhoid and, in the last days of 1621, miserably dying.

The King was now without either a favourite or a competent adviser, and for the next two and a half years the government was carried on by a succession of feeble and generally unsatisfactory ministries. Coming and going between Touraine and Paris, Father Joseph worked unobtrusively for the advancement of his friend, the new-made Cardinal. The task was not easy. For though Richelieu was by far the ablest man in French public life, the King was reluctant to make use of him. There were many reasons for this reluctance. To begin with, the Cardinal's mere physical presence was extremely repugnant to Louis. Sickly and neurotic himself, the King liked to be surrounded with healthy bodies and healthy minds. He shrank with a kind of disgust from the contact of this invalid priest, whose ordinary restraint of manner concealed nervous abnormalities at least as considerable, in their own way, as his own. Furthermore, Louis was painfully conscious of his own shortcomings; he knew he was slow-witted and ignorant, pathologically moody and vacillating. The Cardinal's prodigious abilities and the almost superhuman quality of his undeviating will were felt by the younger man as a kind of standing reproach and at the same time as a menace to his personal independence. His harsh and loveless upbringing had left him with a fear of being bullied, a mistrust of dominating personalities. Besides disgusting and shaming, the Cardinal actually frightened him. But over and against these private reasons for rejecting Richelieu were ranged all the public and political reasons for accepting him. True, his reputation in certain respects was bad. He had flattered the infamous Concinis and had openly acknowledged himself their creature. Then, while in exile, at Blois, he had kept up a secret correspondence with Luynes, informing him of all the Queen Mother's plans. The information had been useful; but in the giving of it the informer had not increased his reputation for trustworthiness. Meanwhile, the fact remained that he was an incomparable politician and, to all appearances, the only man capable of solving his country's most urgent problems. Louis XIII took his duties as a king very seriously; the fact that he overcame his personal distaste for Richelieu and that he contrived to repress it through all the eighteen years of their association bears witness to the strength of his public spirit. The first and most decisive manifestation of that public spirit came when, yielding to a new irresistible pressure of advice and persuasion, the King admitted Richelieu to the council of state. That was in April 1624. Four months later, came the second. In August of the same year, La Vieuville, the head of the ministry was arrested, and the Cardinal installed in his place. One of Richelieu's first acts as prime minister was to send a letter to the Provincial of Touraine. "Next to God," he declared, "Father Joseph had been the principal instrument of his present fortune," and he begged the Capuchin to come at once to Paris, where there was important work for him to do. The necessary "obediences" were obtained from the general of the order, and within a very short time Father Joseph had taken the place he was to occupy until his death in 1638—the place of unofficial chief of staff for foreign affairs.

VI

The Two Collaborators

FINALLY and unequivocally, Father Joseph had now surrendered to his destiny. His career as an evangelist and a teacher of spiritual exercises was not indeed over—for he continued with almost superhuman energy to instruct his nuns and direct an ever-growing organization of foreign and domestic missionaries—but had become secondary to his career as a politician. From now on he was primarily the collaborator of Richelieu and, in all but name, his country's minister for foreign affairs. In the Capuchin's life, as in the Cardinal's, that summer of 1624 marked a decisive turning point. Having reached this date in our narrative, we may, I think, appropriately devote a few paragraphs to a comparison of the two men, who were henceforward to work together in such intimate collaboration.

In the course of his fruitless visit to Madrid, in 1618, Father Joseph had received from his hosts only one concrete proposition, and that was strictly dishonourable. Important personages in close touch with the government waited upon the friar in his cell at the Capuchin convent, assured him of the high esteem in which he was held by the King, the admiration felt by the Duke of Lerma for his virtues and talents, the desire of both for a better understanding with France and their readiness, if he would support the pro-Spanish policy which had been pursued by Marie de Médicis and had now, with her exile, fallen into discredit, to place at the friar's disposal practically any sum he cared to mention—oh, not for his own use, of course! How could the Reverend Father imagine such a thing? No, no, for some good work in which the Reverend Father was interested—some mission, for example, some new order of religious, dedicated to the contemplation of God's transcendent majesty and beauty. . . .

It was the classic temptation, reserved for souls of quality. The common run of merely animal men and women can be left to Belial—

> Belial, the dissolutest Spirit that fell,
> The sensualest and, after Asmodai,
> The fleshliest Incubus, who thus advised:
> "Set women in his eye and in his walk."

But when fishing for the elect, it is a waste of time to bait the hook with such too, too solid, such obviously unidealistic worms.

> Among the sons of man,
> How many have with a smile made small account
> Of beauty and her lures, easily scorned
> All her assaults, on worthier things intent.

Therefore, Satan concludes,

> Therefore with manlier objects we must try
> His constancy—with such as have more show
> Of worth, of honor, glory and popular praise
> (Rocks, whereon greatest men have oftest wrecked).

Through the Spanish government, Satan set to work on Father Joseph, but with no success. The friar was a good Frenchman, who mistrusted foreigners *et dona ferentes.*

He was also (and this is much more significant) a good Capuchin, who mistrusted money as such.

How Richelieu would have received a similar offer is uncertain. He was as good a Frenchman as Father Joseph; but in that age many good Frenchmen did not scruple to accept substantial gifts and pensions from foreign governments. The current conventions of honour and morality did not unequivocally condemn such practices, which were common among the aristocracies of every country in Europe. This being so, Richelieu would quite probably have seen no reason for refusing such a gift, all the more so as he would not have felt bound by it to keep his side of the bargain. He could have taken the bribe with a good social and political conscience. As for his personal conscience, that would not have been troubled even for a moment. He felt no scruples about money and could indulge his covetousness without a qualm. Such scruples as he had were mainly sexual. He had a high opinion of continence—no doubt because he had a low opinion of women. "These animals," he said of them, "are very strange. One sometimes thinks they must be incapable of doing much harm, because they are incapable of doing any good; but I protest on my conscience that there is nothing so well able to ruin a state as they are." Belial, it is evident, was no more dangerous to the Cardinal than to the friar. But when it came to Mammon, the demon of wealth, and Lucifer, the arch-fiend of pride and power, the case was very different. Richelieu was eaten up by a consuming lust for power. Nor was the reality of power enough; he also desired the appearance of it. There is a story that his uncle, La Porte, was present at a meeting between Richelieu and the Duke of Savoy, when the former took precedence over the latter and, as they walked along, passed first through every doorway. "To think," exclaimed the old gentleman in a kind of rapturous *Nunc Dimittis*, "to think that I should have seen the grandson of lawyer La Porte walking in front of the grandson of Charles V!" Behind that cold, impassive mask of his, the Cardinal rejoiced as whole-heartedly as his bourgeois uncle. These triumphs were profoundly important to him.

No less important were the triumphs he could buy with money—the palaces, the attendants, the plate, the libraries, the great banquets, the gorgeous masques for which bishops acted as choreographers, and the audience consisted of queens and princes, great nobles and ambassadors. The passion for wealth was born and bred in him, and grew with every satisfaction it received. His speech before the States General in 1614 contains a passage which his subsequent behaviour was to render exquisitely comic. Expatiating on the desirability of employing priests in the affairs of state, he declared that the clergy "are freer than other men from the private interests which so often harm the public. Observing celibacy, they have nothing to survive them but their souls, and these do not accumulate earthly treasures." By 1630, the speaker was in receipt of an income of fifteen hundred thousand livres from the accumulation of ecclesiastical benefices alone. His salaries, perquisites and miscellaneous pickings amounted to four or five millions more. Of the grand total, he spent upon himself four million livres (the annual subsidy given by France to her Swedish allies was less than a million), and he put aside at the end of each year enough to make it possible for him to leave to his nephews and nieces an estate valued in the scores of millions. When one considers that the purchasing power of a livre in the early seventeenth century amounted to seven or eight gold francs, one is forced to admit that, for a man whose profession discouraged him from "acumulating earthly treasures," the Cardinal did not do too badly.

Money and power were not the only "manlier objects" for which Richelieu yearned. He also had an itch for literary fame. He employed a committee of five poets to work up his ideas into dramatic form, and when one of them, Corneille, wrote *Le Cid,* the Cardinal was consumed by envy and, through paid critics, tried to prove that the tragedy was entirely undeserving of the praise it had received.

Richelieu's, it is evident from his biography, was a case which can have presented no difficulties to the Tempter. The Satan of *Paradise Regained* is only a shade more intelligent than poor Belial; but to land a pike so frantically greedy as was the Cardinal requires little more than the bare minimum of cunning. Any old "manlier object" was bait enough for Richelieu. To Father Joseph, on the contrary, these glittering tin minnows were of no interest. Bait of a much subtler kind was required for him—something more intrinsically precious than power, cash or fame, some imitation of the real Good much more plausible and specious than a "manlier object." Of such temptations the Satan of *Paradise Regained* makes no mention—for the sufficient reason, of course, that his inventor was not aware of their existence.

By nature and by puritan upbringing, Milton was a proud, stoical moralist. Strenuously cultivating self-reliance and a "self-esteem founded on just and right," he lived his whole life in happy ignorance of the fact that religion consists in the exact opposite of self-reliance and self-esteem—in total self-surrender to a God who is not merely a very virtuous puritan gentleman, considerably magnified, but a being of a wholly different order, incommensurable with man even at his highest and most righteous; incommensurable, and yet suffering himself to be experienced by those who are prepared to accept the conditions upon which that experience may be had: the sacrifice of all the elements of their personality, the respectable no less than the discreditable. Milton's Christ never mentions the final and compelling reason why he must reject the wealth that will enable him to "do good," the power by means of which he may establish "the kingdom of heaven." That reason is that a son of God is what he is in virtue of his continual and perfect practice of God's presence; and that the continual and perfect practice of God's presence is impossible for a soul preoccupied with wealth or power. As it stands, *Paradise Regained* is a curiously uninteresting and obtuse affair. Its versified arguments are wordy battles between a Satan who is only John Milton in his uninhibited day-dreams ("he was of the devil's party without knowing it") and a Saviour who is the same John Milton at his ideally best, in a kind of glorified *de luxe* edition.

A really intelligent Satan would have read the lives of the saints and the writings of the mystics, and, having read, would have known how to deal with such sincere and devoted seekers of perfection as Father Joseph. And, of course, the real Satan, as opposed to the Miltonic invention, *did* know exactly how to deal with him; for the real Satan is the element in every individual being which hinders that being from dying to its selfhood and becoming united with the reality from which it has been separated. This being so, the intelligence, the sensibility, the spirituality of Satan is always exactly proportionate to the intelligence, sensibility and spirituality of the individual in whom he is at work. Milton's Satan has the intelligence, sensibility and spirituality of a great poet who is at the same time a proud, passionate stoic; Richelieu's, of a great statesman, with a similar stoic morality much less effectively in control of passions darker and more destructive. The Satan who tempted Father Joseph into power politics was a different and much more interesting fiend. It was his business to tempt a man who had not only taken vows of poverty and humility, but who had also schooled himself, by a long course of theocentric spiritual discipline, into a condition in which he genuinely did not desire money and was more or less completely indifferent to power. As for fame, contemporary or posthumous, Father Joseph cared nothing for it. As a politician, he worked without show or noise, keeping himself deliberately in the background; as a writer, he courted anonymity in print and was content for the most part to leave his productions unpublished. In a word, the ordinary "manlier objects" with which men of exceptional ability are tempted, made no appeal to him whatever. If this man was to be caught, the fiend would have to become a good deal cleverer and more subtle than the Satan of *Paradise Regained*.

Father Joseph was diverted from the road of mystical perfection by a set of closely related temptations—the temptation to do what seemed to be his duty, to accomplish what was apparently the external will of God; the temptation to be mistaken about God's will and to choose

CARDINAL RICHELIEU

a lower at the expense of a higher duty; and the temptation to believe that a disagreeable task must be good just because it was disagreeable. Let us consider these temptations in detail.

Father Joseph, as we have seen, was intensely a patriot and a royalist. Born and brought up during the civil wars, he had conceived a veritable passion for national unity, for order and for what was then the sole guarantee of these two goods, the monarchy. This passion had been rationalized into a religious principle by means of the old crusading faith in the divine mission of France and the newly popularized doctrine of the divine right of kings. *Gesta Dei per Francos* summed up the first belief; the second was to find its most pregnantly abbreviated expression in Bossuet's dictum: "The King, Jesus Christ, the Church—God under these three names." Hanotaux, the historian of Cardinal Richelieu, writes of the Capuchin that "he gave himself to two high causes, which absorbed his life, God and France, always ready to work and fight for either cause, but never separating one from the other, always responding to the call of an inner conviction, namely that France is the instrument of Providence and French greatness a providential thing." Granted the validity of these doctrines—doctrines which he held with a burning intensity of conviction—it was obviously Father Joseph's duty to undertake political work for king and country, when called upon to do so. It was his duty because, *ex hypothesi,* such political work was as truly the will of God as the work of preaching, teaching and contemplation.

We come now to the second temptation—the temptation to fall into error regarding God's will. One of the immediate reasons for this error has already been stated:

Father Joseph believed that the cause of God and the cause of France were inseparable. We must now inquire why he chose to harbour this belief. There seem to be two reasons. The first is that the circumstances of his upbringing had created habits of thought and feeling which, in spite of his long-drawn effort to kill out the Old Adam in him, he had found it impossible to eliminate. To the second we are given a clue by a penetrating phrase of Victor Cousin's. In one of his studies of seventeenth-century manners, that philosopher-historian remarked of Father Joseph that "he was a man without ambition for himself, but full of a boundless ambition for France, which he regarded as the great instrument of Providence." In spite of his reading of the theocentric moralists, in spite of all the thought he had given to the right relationship between man and God, Father Joseph had failed to see that vicarious ambition is as much of an obstacle to union as personal ambition—that a craving for the glorification of France is merely Satan's "manlier object" at one remove. And whereas personal ambition is regarded by all the moralists as undesirable, only the most advanced theocentrics have detected the perniciousness of vicarious ambition on behalf of a sect, nation or person. For the immense majority of mankind, such ambition appears to be entirely creditable. That is what makes it so peculiarly dangerous for men of good will, even for aspirants to sanctity, such as our Capuchin. Father Joseph had freed himself from personal ambition; but as the devoted servant of a providential France and a divinely appointed Louis XIII, he was able to go on indulging the passions connected with ambition, and to go on indulging them, what was more, without any sense of guilt. To put it cynically, he could enjoy subconsciously the pleasures of malice, domination and glory, while retaining the conviction that he was doing the will of God. To retain this conviction was the more easy for him, inasmuch as he attempted, in Father Benet's phrase, actively to annihilate his political actions, even as he performed them. To what extent such actions are "annihilatable" is another question, which will have to be discussed later. For the present, it is enough to state that such active annihilation was in this case, consistently attempted.

What finally tempted Father Joseph to commit himself definitely to a political career was the fact that a political career was extremely arduous and, to a part at least of his nature, disagreeable. Tenebroso-Cavernoso might enjoy the scheming and the diplomacy, and Ezéchiely might vicariously exult in his royal master's triumphs. But the contemplative who had spent so many hours of each day in communion with God could not but suffer from having henceforward to devote the greater number of those hours to affairs of state. That he should deal with such affairs was, however, his duty and the will of God, who evidently desired to try to the limit his powers of active annihilation. Moreover, a political career was very laborious, particularly when combined, as Father Joseph combined it from the first, with the direction of a whole congregation of nuns, the work of Apostolic Commissary for Missions and at least two hours a day of intensive mental prayer. Hence its attractiveness. As a child he had asked to be sent to school for fear his mother should turn him into a mollycoddle; and now, as a man, he thought it his duty to accept the burden of political responsibility. A part of him, it is true, rather enjoyed the burden, but there was another part that groaned under its weight. It was because of that groaning that he felt himself justified in enjoying, that he felt finally certain that, in accepting Richelieu's invitation, he was doing God's will.

Richelieu shared the friar's convictions in regard to France, the monarchy, and the disagreeableness of political labour and the obligations which that very disagreeableness imposed. But whereas these convictions were of prime importance to Father Joseph, to Richelieu they were only a secondary consideration. Even if France and the monarchy had meant nothing to him, he would still have found, in his native genius, his inordinate lust for power, his passion for money, amply sufficient reasons for going into politics.

Certain passages in the Cardinal's letters and memoirs throw a very interesting light on the matters we have been discussing; for they reveal to us what Richelieu thought about his political activities, in their relation to God, his fellow men and his own salvation. The Cardinal begins by making a sharp distinction between personal and public morality—between what Niebuhr would call "moral men and immoral society." *"Autre chose est être homme de bien selon Dieu et autre chose être tel selon les hommes."*[1] To take a specific example of this difference, the good man according to God must forgive offences against himself as soon as they are committed; but where offences have been committeed against society, the good man according to men must do everything in his power to take vengeance. "The reason for this difference springs from the same principle as applied to two different kinds

[1] To be a good man according to God is one thing; to be a good man according to men is quite another.

of obligation. The first and greatest obligation of a man is the salvation of his soul, which demands that vengeance should be left to God and not taken by the person offended. The greatest obligation of kings is the repose of their subjects, the preservation in its entirety of their state, and of the reputation of their government; to which end it is necessary to punish all offences against the state so effectively that the severity of the vengeance may remove the very thought of renewing the injury."

Richelieu himself was a representative of the King and an *homme de bien selon les hommes.* This being so, it was not legitimate for him to behave as an *homme de bien selon Dieu,* even though failure so to behave might imperil his chances of eternal bliss. His view of himself was at bottom very similar to that which the more tender-minded of communist sympathizers often take of Lenin—that of a kind of secular saviour, taking upon himself the responsibility for intrinsically evil acts, which he performs, with full knowledge of their consequences for himself, in order to ensure the future happiness of mankind. "Many men," wrote the Cardinal, "would save their souls as private persons who damn themselves as public persons." To benefit the French people, (if not at the moment, at any rate at some future time), to increase the power and glory of France, as personified in her kings, he was prepared to run the appalling risk of going to hell. And his punishment was not reserved exclusively for the next world; like all statesmen, he was called upon, here and now, to accept a frightful burden of fatigues and scruples and anxieties. He was one who, in his own memorable phrase, "lies awake at night that others may sleep fearlessly in the shadow of his watchings"—*"à l'ombre de ses veilles."* In this heroic self-portrait there is, of course, an element of truth; but it is very far from being the whole truth. In describing himself as a Promethean saviour, a voluntary scapegoat suffering for the sake of the people, Richelieu omitted to mention those little items of the five-million-a-year income, the dukedom, the absolute power, the precedence over princes of the blood, the fawnings and flatteries of all who approached him. "Verily, they have their reward."

Father Joseph's rewards were of a more rarefied kind and consisted in the vicarious indulgence of passions suppressed so far as he personally was concerned, in the satisfactions associated with the performance of mainly unpleasant duties, in the strengthening and sustaining sense that he was accomplishing God's will. Unlike Richelieu, he did not consider himself an *homme de bien selon les hommes,* risking his salvation by doing immoral things on behalf of the state. In his own eyes, he was always the *homme de bien selon Dieu*; for he could always (or at least so it seemed to him at the beginning of his political career), "annihilate" the questionable things he did for his country by dedicating them all to God. In this way he believed that he could live and work, even at power politics, in a state of "holy indifference," very similar to the state recommended, in the *Bhagavad-Gita,* to the hero Arjuna, as he prepares to go into battle.

So much for motives and their rationalizations. In temperament, the two men differed profoundly. Father Joseph, as we have seen, was simultaneously Ezéchiely and Tenebroso-Cavernoso. Richelieu exhibited no smallest trace of the Hebrew prophet. He had no enthusiasm, only a fixed intensity of purpose. Inspirations and happy intuitions played little or no part in his life; everything he did was planned and calculated for the sole purpose of bringing, not indeed the greatest happiness to the greatest number, but the greatest advantage to Armand Du Plessis de Richelieu and the greatest glory to France. In a word, he was exclusively Tenebroso-Cavernoso—but a Tenebroso-Cavernoso, we must always remember, strangely mitigated by ill-health and psychological instability. There was madness in the family. Richelieu's elder brother—the Carthusian monk, whom he dragged out of his monastery and made the Cardinal-Archbishop of Lyon—was not merely feeble-minded; he also suffered every now and then from delusions of grandeur, believing himself to be the First Person of the Trinity. Richelieu himself is known to have been a victim to fits of morbid depression and occasional explosions of rage, almost epileptic in their violence. Furthermore, a tradition was preserved in the royal family that, like his brother, he was sometimes subject to delusions. But whereas the poor half-wit thought of himself as God, the arrogant, self-deified genius was doomed by a stroke of beautifully poetic justice, to be convinced that he was less than human. In his spells of mental aberration, the Cardinal imagined himself to be a horse.

These psychological lesions were not, however, so serious that they prevented Richelieu from doing his work. He did it with the efficiency, which is possible only to those who possess, as well as the highest intellectual abilities, an extraordinary strength and fixity of resolution.

Few men will anything very strongly, and out of these few, only a tiny minority are capable of combining strength of will with unwavering continuity. Most human beings are spasmodic and intermittent creatures, who like above everything the pleasures of mental indolence. "It is for this reason," says Bryce, "that a strenuous and unwearying will sometimes becomes so tremendous a power, almost a hypnotic force." Lucifer is the highest mythological incarnation of this intense personal will, and the great men who have embodied it upon the stage of history participate, to some extent, in his satanic strength and magnificence. It is because of this strength and magnificence, so very different from our own weakness and mental squalor, that we continue to hark back nostalgically to the biographies of such men as Alexander, Caesar, Napoleon, and that, as each new imitator of Lucifer arises, we prostrate ourselves before him, begging him to save us. And, of course, many of these Great Men would genuinely like to save their fellows. But since they are what they are, not saints, but petty Lucifers, their well-meant efforts can lead only to the perpetuation, in some temporarily less or more unpleasant form, of those conditions from which humanity is perpetually praying to be saved. Great Men have invariably failed to "deliver the goods"; but because we admire their qualities and envy their success, we continue to believe in them and to submit to their power. At the same time, we know quite well, with a part of our being, that Lucifers cannot possibly do us any good; so we turn for a moment from such incarnations of the personal will to those very different human beings, who incarnate the will of God. The Saints are even more willing to help than the Great Men; but the advice they give is apt to seem depressing to men and women who want to enjoy the pleasures of indolence. "God," say the Saints, "helps those who help themselves"; and they go on to prescribe the methods by which it is possible to help oneself. But we don't want to have to help ourselves; we want to be helped, to have somebody who will do the work on our behalf. So we turn back again to the incarnations of the personal will. These Great Men have not the smallest doubt of their ability to give us exactly what we want—a political system that will make everybody happy and good, a state religion that guarantees God's favours here on earth and a blissful eternity in paradise. We accept their offer; and immediately the other part of our being reverts to the Saints, from whom once again we turn to our disastrous Great Men. And so it goes on, century after century. The pathetic shilly-shallying has left its accumulated traces in our libraries, where the records of Great Men and their activities in history fill about as much shelf-room as the records of the Saints and their dealings with God.

Richelieu was one of the great incarnations of the personal will. It was to his never relaxed inflexibility of purpose that he owed his extraordinary career, and by means of which he was able to stamp his impress so profoundly upon the history of Europe.

Father Joseph gave the appearance of being more dispersed and fluctuating than his political chief. But under the variations of tone and manner, and in spite of those sudden gusts of enthusiasm, by which he seemed periodically to be carried away, he retained a fixity of purpose no less unbending. On more than one occasion, indeed, he proved himself the more determined of the two; when Richelieu showed signs of weakening, the friar revived his courage and, by sheer strength of will, carried him forward, through all difficulties, to the desired goal. "I have lost my support," Richelieu kept repeating after his friend's death, "I have lost my support." That Father

Joseph was able to act as a source of strength to this man, whose genius consisted precisely in being strong, was due, one may guess, to the fact that, for a quarter of a century, he had been following Benet of Canfield's *Rule of Perfection, reduced to the sole point of the Will of God.* In the language of the mystics, "Perfection" is the state of total and continuous self-abnegation in Reality—the state of those who can say, "I live, yet not I, but God lives in me." From their biographies, it is clear that the men and women who have come to such perfection receive, among the other fruits of the spirit, an extraordinary accession of moral strength. It is a strength wholly different in quality from the inflexibility of the tensed, self-centered personal will of the stoic and the petty Lucifer—of the "fiend of righteousness," in Blake's expressive phrase, and the fiend of unrighteousness. The will of the self-abnegated person is relaxed and effortless, because it is not his own will, but a great river of force flowing through him from a sea of subliminal consciousness that lies open in its turn to the ocean of reality. He radiates joy and a beautiful and yet awe-inspiring serenity; he works with irresistible gentleness; being completely humble, he wields the authority of a power infinitely greater than himself, and of which he is merely the instrument.

In his early manhood, Father Joseph displayed this peculiar strength which belongs to the self-abnegated man. That he had completely achieved the perfection of the unitive life may be doubted. If he had, it is hard indeed to believe that anything—even a sense of duty, even a desire for painful self-sacrifice—would have induced him to enter politics. But though he had not gone the whole way, he had certainly gone far—far enough, at any rate, to be able to make a profound impression on the monks whom, as Provincial of Touraine, it was his business to govern and instruct. What struck them as I have already noted, was the gentleness and humility with which he exercised his powers. Vigilant, firm, tolerating no lapse from the Franciscan rule, he knew how to punish without arousing resentment, how to administer rebukes in which he personally was not involved, except as the channel through which a force, recognizably divine, was flowing. When Ange de Joyeuse called him the perfect Capuchin, he was very nearly right. But, alas, not entirely right. Enough of the Old Adam remained in him to succumb to those extremely subtle temptations prepared by his attendant Satan. Without giving up his mystical practices, and in the belief that he could simultaneously serve God and the Cardinal, he became a politician. In spite of the friar's almost superhuman efforts, the attempt to make the best of both worlds failed as completely as his Master had said it would. His policies (as we can now see clearly enough) did not produce the results they were intended to produce; and the quality of his spiritual life (as he himself perceived before he died) progressively deteriorated. Nevertheless, in spite of this deterioration, he carried over into the period of his association with Richelieu something of the more-than-personal strength which had been his in the earlier days. Nor must we forget that, even in cases where the perfection of total self-abnegation in reality is not achieved, the mere practice of spiritual exercises is capable by itself of enhancing the strength of will. Spiritual exercises need not necessarily be associated with God; a man can, if he so chooses, make himself one-pointed for one-pointedness' sake, or for the sake of his nation, his party, his sect, or even the devil. In all these cases he will gain strength, for the simple reason that spiritual exercises are a device for tapping, canalizing and directing the sources of the will below the threshold of awareness. A current flowing from the subliminal sea is in itself a tremendous force, even though this sea may remain cut off from the ocean of reality beyond it. Richelieu seems to have relied entirely on the upper levels of the conscious, personal will. Hence the appalling strain under which he continually lived—a strain that told severely on a constitution never robust at the best of times, and that resulted every now and then in a temporary failure of nerve. It was on these occasions that he turned to the Capuchin for support. From the depths of a nature in which the conscious will had been systematically aligned with the subconscious, and through which, perhaps, a little of the power inherent in reality still flowed, Father Joseph was able to give him the strength he needed.

VII

La Rochelle

RICHELIEU had set himself two great tasks: to unify France under an omnipotent monarchy; to break the power of the Hapsburgs and to exalt the Bourbons in their place. The possibility of defeating Spain and Austria depended, obviously, on the previous accomplishment of the first task. Divided, France was weak. Hampered by his chronically rebellious nobles and by the Protestants, who formed a state within the state, the King was powerless to act against his "hereditary enemies" abroad. The glory of the dynasty and even the safety of the realm (for the Spanish and Austrian Hapsburgs seemed to be aiming at nothing less than the hegemony of Europe) demanded the immediate suppression of feudal privilege and Huguenot power. Only when this had been done would the King be in a position to conduct a foreign war. In the meantime the Hapsburgs would have to be attacked mainly by diplomatic means—by bluff, by endless negotiation, by juggling the balance of power, by subsidizing governments already at war with Spain or Austria.

On matters of domestic policy, Father Joseph had always been in accord with the Cardinal; and by 1624 he was coming reluctantly to accept his foreign policy as well. He saw that, if that great crusade was ever to be undertaken, Spain and Austria must be humbled into submission to French leadership. Within a short time the political conversion was complete; Father Joseph had become as determinedly an enemy of the Hapsburgs as Richelieu himself.

In 1624 the Thirty Years' War was just six years old and had already been the cause of enormous miseries. Bohemia, where the trouble started, was the first to suffer. Then, in 1619, Bethlen Gabor, the Protestant Prince of Transylvania, broke into the imperial domains and pillaged Austria. In 1620 Tilly's Catholics ravaged Bohemia once more and committed many atrocities against the civil population. To such humanitarian protests as were made, Tilly merely replied "that his men were not nuns." In 1621 the Protestants re-entered Bohemia under Mansfeld, and the country suffered as atrociously under its defenders as it had suffered in the previous year under its enemies.

When the Protestant army had devoured everything there was to eat in Bohemia, Mansfeld led his men into the Palatinate. Being without money or supplies, he was compelled to subordinate his policy and strategy to the demands of his soldiers' stomachs. Where there was food there his army must go, regardless of every other consideration. In the Palatinate, Mansfeld was joined by Christian of Brunswick, and between them they succeeded in reducing the people to ruin and despair. Defeated by the imperialists, they were forced to retire into Alsace, and when Alsace had been gnawed to the bone, they occupied Lorraine. From Lorraine, the army was invited in 1623 into Holland. Battles were fought on the way in the Spanish Netherlands, and the forces besieging Berg-op-Zoom were defeated. After which, in 1624, Mansfeld marched his men into East Friesland, which suffered the same fate as Bohemia, the Palatinate, Alsace and Lorraine.

From Paris Richelieu and Father Joseph looked on at what was happening beyond the frontiers and framed a policy expressly intended to prolong the bloody confusion. France had no effective army, and any direct, large-scale attack upon the Hapsburgs was therefore out of the question. But if the war in Germany could be drawn out, Spain and Austria would be so drained of their resources that, by the time France had grown strong, they would be exhausted. To this end it was decided in Paris that the embattled Protestants should receive French support, diplomatic and financial. At the same time new allies were to be sought among the non-belligerents, and determined efforts made to lure the Catholic Electors away from the Emperor (whose triumph, it was pointed out, would necessarily be at their expense, no less than at that of the Protestants) and to group them into a middle party under the tutelage of Louis XIII. These "tenebrous-cavernous" proceedings were supplemented by a small-scale military operation, skilfully directed at one of the vital nerve centers of the Hapsburg system—the Valtelline. Along this valley, which comes down from the Alps to the head of Lake Como, ran the only road by which Spain could communicate with Austria. Spanish troops and bullion from Mexico and Peru could be landed at Genoa, could be moved across Spanish-owned territory to Milan, and from Milan through the Valtelline, which was under the protectorate of the Swiss Confederacy of the Grisons, and across the passes into Austria. If that road were cut, the two branches of the House of Austria could communicate only by sea; and with the rise of Dutch naval power, the

Channel and the Straits of Dover had become to all intents and purposes impassable to Spanish shipping. Intervening nominally on behalf of his Swiss allies, Richelieu swooped down on the strategic valley and, at the end of 1624, garrisoned it with French troops.

It was, among other things, to talk about the Valtelline that Father Joseph went to Rome in the spring of 1625. He remained there for four months and, thanks to the Turciad and his conversational talents, was treated by Urban VIII with signal favour. Twice every week during the whole of his stay the Pope received him in private audience and remained closeted with him for hours at a time. When he trudged home again, it was with the title of Apostolic Commissary of Missions. From this time almost to the day of his death, foreign missions were one of his chief preoccupations. Vicariously, through his organization of devoted Capuchins, he was able to continue the work of evangelization, to which he had been so strongly drawn in his youth. His friars were in every part of the world, from Persia to England, from Abyssinia to Canada. In the midst of his wearisome and questionable political activities, the thought that he was helping to spread the gospel of Christ must often have been a source of strength and consolation. True, his enemies in Spain and Austria and at the Roman Curia accused him of using his missionaries as French agents and anti-Hapsburg fifth columnists. And, alas, the charge was not entirely baseless. Just as Cromwell was, in all sincerity, to identify the interests of England with those of the true Protestant faith, so Father Joseph, with no less conviction, identified the interests of true Catholicism with those of France. He knew that trade follows the cross and that an evangelist can be very useful in representing the interests of the nation to which he belongs. Inevitably, his French Capuchins preached the gospel of the Bourbons as well as that of Christ.

Father Joseph's missions kept him in touch with all kinds of remote, outlandish places; and this awareness of the world overseas, combined with his belief in the providential nature of the French monarchy, made him an imperialist. Dedouvres has convincingly shown that the epoch-making memorandum on colonization and sea power, which in 1626 was presented to the King as the work of another hand, was in fact composed by Father Joseph. The recommendations set forth in this document were followed to the letter first by Richelieu and later by Colbert. "In the name of the greatest colonists and sailors of France," says Dedouvres, "we must salute, in the person of Father Joseph, one of their boldest and most far-sighted precursors on the road of sea power"—a sea power which, as the memorandum insists, must be valuable as an aid, not only to commerce, but also and above all to missionary endeavour.

No less than the overthrow of Hapsburg power, the realization of Father Joseph's dream of sea power and an empire was contingent upon the unification of France; and that work was not to be accomplished easily or very quickly. Richelieu proceeded first against the nobility. An edict was issued in 1626 ordering the destruction of all fortified castles not needed for the defense of the national frontiers. But it was not by tearing down old walls and towers that he could bring the nobles to obedience; they would remain rebellious until such time as he could strike directly at their privileges and persons. His first opportunity for doing this was given to the Cardinal in the spring of 1626 when the King's younger brother, Gaston, was induced to head a conspiracy, in which the most active rôles were played by the Prince of Condé, two bastard sons of Henri IV, and that indefatigably charming and promiscuous lady, the Duchess of Chevreuse. Among the minor conspirators was the Chevreuse's lover of the moment, a gay and brilliant young man called the Marquis de Chalais. Entrusted with the task of murdering Richelieu, Chalais was suddenly overcome by conscientious scruples and, going to the Cardinal, confessed his share in the plot. The Cardinal promised him a reward and went immediately to Gaston; terrified, the heir apparent immediately turned king's evidence. Louis and his minister thereupon acted decisively and swiftly. The two bastards, Vendôme and the Grand Prior, were lured to Paris and there arrested and imprisoned. The prudent Condé forestalled a similar fate by quickly making his peace with the Cardinal. Marie de Médicis, who doted on her worthless Gaston and had been implicated in the conspiracy, was forced to put her signature to a document in which, as usual on these occasions, she solemnly promised loyalty and good behaviour for the future. Nothing was done to Mme de Chevreuse; but for this impunity she had to pay, not long afterwards, by becoming one of the Cardinal's secret agents in England. As the mistress of Lord Holland and the confidant to whom Buckingham had poured out all the secrets of his love for Anne of Austria, she had sources of information not available to any mere masculine ambassador. To Richelieu her reports from London were to be of the utmost value. Meanwhile, however, she was still actively his enemy; for now, when all the trouble seemed to have died down, she stirred it once more into life. Under the influence of her seductions, the infatuated Chalais started to intrigue again. Visiting Gaston in secret, he tried to persuade him to flee the country or head a rising of the Huguenots. But the agents of Richelieu and Tenebroso-Cavernoso were at work. The new plot was discovered; for the second time in three months Gaston turned king's evidence, and put the blame for everything on Chalais. The young man was arrested, tried, not in a regular court of law, but by one of those specially appointed commissions which were to become in the ensuing years the Cardinal's favourite instruments of repression, and after having been induced to incriminate his mistress, was executed. To the other feudal magnates the event seemed incredibly strange and alarming. It was the first time for many years that a rebellious noble had been treated as anything but a candidate for a pension. With the death of Chalais, conspiracy lost a great deal of its old charm. Richelieu had won the first round of his fight against the nobility, and for the time being there was little to fear from that quarter. He was free to devote his whole attention to the Huguenots.

After Luynes' unsuccessful siege of Montauban, in 1621, the King and the Protestants had signed a treaty of peace. But this treaty, as everyone knew very well was only a temporary and provisional agreement—so temporary and provisional that neither side took the trouble to observe its terms. Whenever an opportunity for scoring an advantage arose, it was taken regardless of what might happen to be written on that scrap of paper. Sooner or later, this long-drawn and indecisive conflict between the King and his two million Protestant subjects would have to be settled, once and for all. Neither party believed that it could be settled except by force of arms; both therefore made their preparations.

The first serious breach of the peace was committed in 1625 by a Protestant, the Duke of Soubise. In command of a small squadron of fighting ships, he occupied one of the strategically placed islands off La Rochelle, raided royalist ports and carried off, along with other booty, the five handsome vessels which the last of the Palaeologi had had constructed, at great expense, for the transport of Father Joseph's crusaders. When things became too hot for him in his home waters, Soubise set sail, with his prizes, for England, where the common people immediately took him to their hearts as a Protestant hero. Observing this, Buckingham decided that he would be a Protestant hero too. By leading a combined naval and military expedition to the aid of La Rochelle he hoped to kill two birds with one stone—to recover the popularity which he had lost as the result of the unlucky expedition in aid of the Elector Palatine and of the King's marriage to a Catholic princess; and to take vengeance on Richelieu for having outmanœuvred him in negotiation and, worse still, thwarted his amorous designs on Anne of Austria. In the summer of 1627 he set sail with a great fleet and seven thousand men. After a brisk fight, he made a landing on the island of Rhé, near La Rochelle, and proceeded to lay siege to the strong fort of Saint-Martin. Weeks lengthened into months. The French garrison was starved to the very brink of surrender; then, almost miraculously, supplies were smuggled through from the mainland. The defenders revived, and the siege went on. Direct assaults were tried, and failed. The weather grew worse; the English troops began to sicken. Finally, in November, Buckingham was forced to raise the siege and sail home. He had lost four thousand men and achieved absolutely nothing.

Hostility between the King's forces and the city of La Rochelle broke out in September 1627. A month later, the King arrived with fresh troops from Paris. With him came the Cardinal, dressed in Roman purple, but wearing a breast-plate and a plumed hat, and behind the Cardinal, bare-footed in the mud, trudged Father Joseph.

La Rochelle was too well fortified to be taken by storm, and in the salt marches around the city the royal army sat down for a long siege. Father Joseph was offered quarters in the house occupied by the Cardinal; but he declined this comfortable honour in favour of a deserted summer-house standing beside a broad ditch at the end of the garden. The fabric was old and leaky, and when the wind blew hard from offshore and the tides were high, the ditch overflowed, ankle deep, into the friar's bedroom. But to make up for these slight defects, the building possessed one inestimable advantage; it was private. By going to bed very late and getting up very early, Father Joseph was able to make time each day for at least two hours of mental prayer. In the damp and windy solitude of his gazebo he could meditate in peace.

These periods of recollection, of wordless converse with God and the crucified Saviour, were more than ever necessary to him at this time. Of his life under the walls of La Rochelle, he wrote, in a letter to one of his Calvarian nuns, that it was "worse than hell"; worse, not because of its discomforts and dangers (on the contrary, these must rather have endeared it to a man of Father Joseph's temper), but because the strain and anxiety of his multiple activities made it so peculiarly difficult for him to make the mystical approach to God. In hell, according to the theologians, the principal torment of the damned consists in their being, for ever and totally, deprived of God's presence. When Father Joseph said that public life, particularly public life in war conditions, was worse than hell, he was not using a mere picturesque figure of speech. In terms of the philosophy he had accepted, he was making a precise and sober statement about his psychological condition. In the past he had advanced at least to the outskirts of the kingdom of God, had had at least a partial experience of ultimate reality. Now, the dust and smoke of the Cardinal's kingdom was obscuring his vision. Having known heaven, he now found himself excluded from the light. In affirming that such a state was "worse than hell," he did not exaggerate. Father Joseph could find some slight consolation in the thought that the obstacle between himself and the light of God was his own strenuous performance of God's exterior will, and that, if he tried hard enough, he might one day learn, with God's grace, to "annihilate," in a continuous awareness of the divine presence, even such a life as he was now leading.

Father Joseph's activities during the long months of the siege were varied and enormous. To begin with—and this was certainly the work he found most congenial—he was responsible for the moral, spiritual and, to some extent, also the physical welfare of the army. Under his command he had a whole troop of Capuchins, whom he kept incessantly busy. Services were held for the troops, sermons preached, confessions heard. Collaborating with the surgeons, the friars organized hospitals and attended to the needs of the sick and wounded. When there was any fighting, they were in the thick of it, acting as stretcher bearers, assisting the dying to prepare themselves for eternity. Their courage and devotion were profoundly impressive. To the preaching of such men even soldiers were prepared to listen. Contemporary observers found the results nothing less than astounding. Nobody had ever seen or heard of so well behaved an army.

Unfortunately for Father Joseph, this missionary work among the troops was only the least of his activities. He was still the Cardinal's right-hand man. Foreign affairs—peculiarly ticklish at this time of domestic conflict—had to be discussed, decisions taken, dispatches written. Court intrigues had to be check-mated; quarrelling magnates conciliated. The friar was constantly being called upon to use his infinite dexterity with the nobility. These were the sort of things he had been doing ever since Richelieu came into power. At La Rochelle he was given or took upon himself a number of new responsibilities. Thus, he attended the councils of war, and gave advice on matters of strategy and tactics. Imaginative and ingenious, he was for ever propounding the most brilliant schemes. Some of these were actually tried; but on each occasion, bad staff work resulted in failure. The fault was not the friar's; but his reputation suffered, and he came to be regarded as a rather absurd, clerical White Knight, full of crack-brained notions which were made to seem even more ridiculous than they actually were by his habit of guaranteeing them as divine revelations. These revelations came to Father Joseph at the end of long nights, during which, in his own words, he had "redoubled his prayers that God might give him some light" on the best way of taking the town by surprise. His method was to consider all the available information, work out a number of appropriate plans and then offer the whole in an act of petition, begging for divine guidance in framing a choice. When the guidance came, he took the chosen plan to Richelieu and the council of war.

The information on which the Lord was asked to decide came to Father Joseph mainly from spies in the enemy's camp; for, as in Paris, so here before La Rochelle, the friar acted as chief of Richelieu's secret service. To the Tenebroso-Cavernoso side of him this singularly uninviting rôle seemed to come quite naturally. Years before there was any question of his entering politics, he had gone out of his way to organize a private information service of his own. A host of correspondents kept him in touch with events in all parts of the kingdom. So efficient was this service that, at the time of the expedition into Béarn, he had been able to tell the King and Luynes exactly what was happening in all the Huguenot strongholds. Nor did he confine himself only to France. That unrivalled knowledge of foreign affairs, which made him so useful to the Cardinal, was the fruit of this same private intelligence service. To be well informed, preferably by secret and exclusive channels, had always been a real passion with Father Joseph. Much of his time and energy was spent in elaborately satisfying that passion; and it may even be that the prospect of being able to satisfy it more completely than ever before was one of his inducements for going into politics. In theological language, "idle curiosity" may have been one of the baits employed by Satan to lure him away from God. Against this greed for merely mundane information Father Joseph had been warned, not only by his own master, but by all the great contemplatives of medieval and modern times. News, they had all assured him, is one of the great distractions, separating the mind from reality. For this reason the aspiring contemplative must practise self-denial in regard to curiosity, just as he does in regard to any other craving or intellectual dissipation. That Father Joseph should have disregarded the unanimous advice of all the mystics is strange. How did he justify himself in his own eyes? Partly, no doubt, by the belief that he could "annihilate" his news-gathering activities. Partly, perhaps, by a conviction (born of the consciousness of enormous talents) that he had a vocation for politics comparable to his vocation for preaching and teaching. Even in those early days, when Ezéchiely had gone about the country winning souls to God, Tenebroso-Cavernoso had felt that he too could do God's will, and had prepared himself for his yet undetermined task by a secret and methodical collection of information. Now, through the instrumentality of Richelieu, the task had been assigned to him, and it was worse than hell—worse than hell, even though it was in accord with the divine will; worse than hell, in spite of the fact that he had a real genius, not only for the more avowable forms of politics, but also for the hidden, backstairs business of espionage and the organization of fifth columns. "In Richelieu's enterprises," writes Fagniez, "treason was almost always called in to supplement open force, or to make force unnecessary." And he goes on to give a number of examples of the way in which Father Joseph, acting as head of the secret service, made use of money or honours to buy, now a piece of useful information, now a complaisance, now a downright treachery. Once again, one wonders how he contrived to justify himself in his own eyes. Here he was, a Franciscan friar, vowed to the service of a church which existed for the salvation of souls, but using all his own talents, all the baits of Lucifer, Mammon and Belial, to induce fellow Christians to damn themselves by lying, by breaking their pledged word, by betraying the trust imposed in them. In order to do what he conceived to be his political duty, he had to do the Satanic opposite of what he had promised to do when he entered religion.

Catholic secret agents and Huguenot traitors were received by Father Joseph at his headquarters in the flooded summer house. They came at night, slipping out unobserved through the defenders' lines. The friar would sit with them into the small hours, listening to their reports and giving them instructions. Then, dismissing them with their wages, he would lie down to sleep. Before daybreak he was up again and on his knees for an hour or two of that mental prayer, without which he could not live, but to which, as his political activities were multiplied, he was finding it ever more difficult to bring a spirit that was fit to converse with God.

It was a strenuous life, all the more so as Father Joseph kept four Lents a year and was living, during the greater part of this winter in the salt marshes, on bread and ditch-water, with an occasional feast-day dinner of mouldy stock fish. His body showed the marks of fatigue and undernourishment; but in spite of the Cardinal's protests, he held on his course unswervingly.

The siege settled down to a dismal routine, and by February of 1628 Louis XIII was so desperately bored that he insisted on leaving his army and going back to

Paris. It was the fox hunting at Versailles that lured him away. In the neighbourhood of La Rochelle a sportsman could find only wild fowl and a few hares. The King had done his best to keep himself amused with hawk and arquebus and beagle. On more than one occasion military operations had been suspended that the game might not be disturbed and His Majesty deprived of his favourite, indeed his only recreation. But by February the longing for foxes had become irresistible. Richelieu implored his master to stay. With the King's departure, he insisted, the army would lose heart. Worse, the great nobles who had accompanied the expedition might turn from their wavering loyalty. They were good Catholics, it was true; but the existence of a strong Protestant minority was the guarantee of royal weakness, and royal weakness was the condition of the nobles' power. "We should be fools," Bassompierre had said, "to take La Rochelle." But while the King was actually present it was psychologically difficult for him and his fellows not to behave as fools, not to subordinate long-range interests to the immediate and active expression of traditional loyalty.

There was yet another reason why Richelieu was anxious for the King to stay with his army. The Queen Mother was in Paris; and though Richelieu still made a show of grateful deference towards her, he had done all he could to keep her from interfering in the affairs of state, not merely because she was stupid and incompetent, but also because her pro-Spanish foreign policy was diametrically opposed to his own. Marie's liking for the Cardinal had turned to rancorous hatred, and her palace had become the meeting place of all those who, for whatever reason, desired to see him overthrown. In Paris these malcontents would have free access to the King. What if he were to listen to their whisperings? What if he were to let himself be worn down by the loud incessant hectoring of his mother?

In spite, however, of all his minister could say, Louis set out. The most that Richelieu could get from him was a promise to be back in the spring. Richelieu remained with the forces in an agony of apprehension. From Paris, his agents sent news of intrigues against him—news so alarming, that on several occasions he was on the point of posting back to rejoin the King. It was Father Joseph who kept him at La Rochelle. To desert the army at this juncture would be, he insisted, an act of treason against the church. The Cardinal's place was with the crusaders against heresy. As for the intrigues in Paris, they would come to nothing; for God would not allow them to succeed. Richelieu stayed on.

In April the King moved south again—very slowly, for he had to stop several times on the way to hunt the stag—but in the end he arrived. The siege dragged on. After a number of ineffectual attempts had been made to cut off La Rochelle from the sea, it was decided to build a great dam of stones across the outer harbour, beyond the range of the defenders' cannon. It was a tremendous undertaking, for the channel at this point was more than a mile across. But in spite of all that the pessimists could say, the work was begun. It progressed slowly—so slowly, indeed, that in the summer of 1628 Richelieu lost courage and talked of abandoning the campaign against the Huguenots. The King was growing impatient; the foreign situation was becoming ever more menacing; most of the Cardinal's advisers were convinced that La Rochelle was impregnable; and all the time the expedition was costing money, taxes had had to be increased and the people were murmuring. To raise the siege now, he argued weakly, would be humiliating, indeed, but not fatal; to stay on and be compelled to raise it later would be a catastrophe, from which he could not hope to recover. Once again Father Joseph intervened. To the Cardinal's wavering purpose he brought the reinforcement of a will that no reverses could shake. La Rochelle, he insisted, must be taken, and the King and Cardinal must be present in person when it was surrendered. Sustained by the inflexibility of his friend's purpose, Richelieu recovered his strength; and meanwhile Ezéchiely's eloquence was thundering to good effect in the council chamber and the royal apartments. The siege went on, and the King and his minister remained with the army. Later, when the town was captured, Louis XIII publicly acknowledged the debt that was owing to the Capuchin, affirming that "he was the only man to stand firm in the hope of reducing the town to obedience, and that it was he who had confirmed the others."

In his almost single-handed struggle against the obstinate heroism of the Protestants on the one side and, on the other, against the Cardinal's temporary loss of nerve and the impatience and discouragement of the King and the great nobles, Father Joseph made use of all the resources at his disposal, both human and divine. Among the latter must be listed his Calvarian nuns. These communities of cloistered contemplatives he regarded as (among other things) powerful praying machines, capable, if put into high gear and worked for twenty-four hours a day, seven days a week, of precipitating, so to speak, out of the ether, very considerable quantities of the divine favour. The letters he wrote to the Calvarians at this period contain, along with much exhortation, instruction and advice, accounts of the principal strategic and political problems of the moment, with requests that the nuns should devote all their energies to praying for their auspicious solution. And what a host of things there were to be prayed for! Let them pray, for example, for the success of Father Joseph's pet plan for entering the town by night through an underground sewer and taking the garrison by surprise; (it failed). For the conversion of the Protestant Duke of La Tremoille; (it came off). For an amelioration in the behaviour of the King's brother, Gaston; (his conduct was to remain as base and despicable as it had always been). For the defeat of the second English expedition; (Lord Denbigh's fleet came, tacked about for a few days within sight of the town, then sailed away again). And so on. In common usage, the word "precarious" carries the idea of riskiness and uncertainty; etymologically, it means "contingent upon the answer to prayer."

In view of his mystical training, it seems surprising that Father Joseph should have laid such stress on petitionary prayer. Petitionary prayer is appropriate enough in men and women whose religion is anthropocentric; in the life of those who have learnt, not only to think, but to feel and live, theocentrically, it is obviously out of place. The theocentric position finds its most emphatic statement in the writings of Meister Eckhart. "I tell you by the eternal truth, so long as you have wills to fulfill God's will, and so long as you have any longing for eternal life and God, for just so long you are not truly poor in spirit. For he alone is poor, who wishes nothing, knows nothing, desires nothing." Here is total annihilation, passive in contemplation, active in the affairs of daily life—annihilation such as Benet of Canfield taught and such as Father Joseph himself strenuously tried to practice. But Father Joseph was now in politics, and the nature of politics is such that even the most devout and spiritual politician must constantly be exercising the personal will, either on behalf of himself or of some social organization. But when the personal will is exercised by one who is religious, petitionary prayers for success are felt to be entirely natural and in order. Hence the anomalous nature of Father Joseph's spiritual life, one side of it centered in God, the other in all too human cravings; hence those communities of pure contemplatives, whom he so lovingly instructed in the art of meditation and at the same time treated as praying machines for the materialization of concrete benefits.

Meanwhile, within the city, the people were slowly starving. The horses, the cats, the dogs—all had been killed and devoured; even the supply of rats was running low. From splendid silver dishes the old Duchess of Rohan was eating mice and drinking a bouillon prepared from the harness in her stables. The poor were boiling their old boots and their leather hats. But still, under the leadership of Jean Guiton, its indomitable mayor, the city held out. Through his secret agents, Father Joseph worked away at the morale of the defenders. Broad-sheets were printed, smuggled into the town and distributed. In these, the mayor and his abettors were denounced for their tyranny—a tyranny doubly odious, because it infringed the ancient constitution of La Rochelle, and because it could result only in the exhaustion of the King's clemency and an appalling punishment for all within the city walls, innocent and guilty alike. Other leaflets accused the rich of food hoarding and profiteering. This propaganda had its effects. Several attempts were made on Guiton's life; suspected profiteers were mobbed, many deserters slipped out of the town at night in the hope of obtaining food, pardon and safety. It was a vain hope, for those who were caught, were promptly hanged.

For purposes of negotiation with the city authorities, Father Joseph made use of his cousin, Feuquières, a man of some importance in the royal service, who had been captured in a skirmish outside the walls and was held by the Huguenots as a prisoner of war. (It is worth recording that, during the whole of his captivity, Feuquières' dinner was brought to him every day from the royal table. Roast ducklings, dishes of green peas and strawberries, pastries, copious helpings of beef and lamb and venison were carried through the lines under a flag of truce and delivered to his gaolers, who passed them on unfailingly to the Marquis. All this, at a time when the Rochellois were dying inch-meal of hunger. To us, the whole episode seems almost unthinkably odd; but in the seventeenth century, we must remember, it was axiomatic that a person of quality was different in kind from ordinary people and must be treated accordingly.) Through Feuquières, Father Joseph tried to persuade the rebel leaders to throw themselves on the King's mercy; but faith in their Calvinist God and the hope of English succour made them deaf to all talk of surrender. The siege went on. By the end of the summer, most of the old in La Rochelle and most of the very young were already dead, and the men and women in their prime were dying every day by scores and, as the autumn advanced, hundreds.

Fasting, penances and unremitting labour had lowered Father Joseph's resistance and, in August, he caught a fever and fell very seriously ill. His condition was aggravated by his obstinate refusal to take the rest he needed. From his bed, he continued to write memoranda on policy and to direct the secret service. As it turned out, this last activity was almost the death of him. Coming, as they were forced to do, at night, the spies kept the sick man from sleep. The fever mounted and, in spite of all his desperate efforts to remain lucid and concentrated, external reality slipped away from him and was merged in the phantasmagoria of delirium. For days he fluctuated between life and death; then gradually and painfully re-emerged into the light. When the third and final English expedition came and failed, he was beginning to recover, and three weeks later, when the town at last surrendered, he was well enough to follow the victorious troops and to assist the Cardinal at the solemn mass, now celebrated for the first time for more than fifty years, in the Cathedral. Immediately afterwards, La Rochelle was proclaimed the see of a new Catholic diocese, and to Father Joseph, in recognition of his services during the siege, the King offered the honour of becoming the town's first bishop. The Capuchin declined. Nothing, he said, could induce him to divest the habit of St. Francis or give up his blessed rule of poverty and humility. Nevertheless he was deeply sensible of the King's kindness and, to express his gratitude, he dashed off a pamphlet entitled "The King Victorious, dedicated to the Queen Mother." It was a rousing piece of eloquence that concluded with the reflection that, now that La Rochelle had fallen, His Majesty would be free to turn his arms against another enemy of holy church

—the abominable Turk. In the eleventh year of the Thirty Years' War this was, as of course Father Joseph knew only too well, merely a piece of wishful thinking. But what of that? He loved his crusade, with a love that was

> of a birth as rare
> As 'twas, for object, strange and high;
> It was begotten by Despair
> Upon Impossibility.

Loving thus, he claimed the right to strew an occasional verbal tribute on the grave in which the object of his passion was now so deeply buried.

With the fall of La Rochelle, the political power of the Huguenots in France was at an end. Protestant strongholds, it was true, still held out in Languedoc and the Cevennes; but their reduction would be an easy matter, for they were far from the sea and could hope for no assistance from a foreign enemy. At the beginning of the siege, La Rochelle had counted twenty-five thousand inhabitants; five thousand remained alive, when the city was surrendered. Such, however, was the violence of theological hatred that there were many among the Catholic party who clamoured for further and yet more frightful punishment. To his everlasting credit, the Cardinal would not hear of reprisals. The surviving Rochellois were pardoned, confirmed in the enjoyment of their property and granted freedom of worship. His reward was the Protestants' unswerving loyalty to the crown. Half a century later, Louis XIV, reversed the Cardinal's policy, persecuted the Huguenots and finally revoked the Edict of Nantes. *His* reward was the loss to France by emigration, of a large number of its most productive citizens.

In matters of religious policy, Father Joseph, as I have already had occasion to mention, was completely in accord with the Cardinal. He knew that an orthodoxy accepted under duress will save no souls, and he was therefore opposed to forced conversions. The true faith, he believed, should be propagated by missionaries, not dragoons. On certain occasions, however, he was prepared, in order to obtain a much desired conversion, to use means that were not entirely spiritual. To give an example, in the autumn of 1629, when the King followed up his victory at La Rochelle by an expedition into the Protestant territories of south-central France, Father Joseph accompanied the armies and took charge of the conversion of the heretics. His policy was to concentrate first of all on the nobles and the other leading men of the various communities concerned. If these went over to Rome, he calculated (not quite correctly, as the event was to prove), the common people would follow. To obtain these key conversions, he employed the usual spiritual weapons, exhortation, argument, and the edifying example of a devoted life; but when occasion demanded, he supplemented these with other, more mundane forms of persuasion—the offer of gifts from the royal exchequer, pensions, honours, positions in the administration. Astute Protestant noblemen saw their chance and drove shrewd bargains. No gentleman, they protested, no man of conscience could be expected to change his religious convictions for a paltry six thousand livres a year. But if the Reverend Father would make it ten, well, perhaps. . . . A compromise would be reached at eight, and, with all the traditional pomps and ceremonies, Mother Church would open her arms to yet another erring sheep.

VIII

The Diet of Ratisbon

IN THE years that had elapsed since Richelieu's rise to power, the affairs of Europe had taken no dramatic turn for the worse. The full horrors of the Thirty Years' War were yet to come. For the moment, it seemed as though the devil were content to mark time. In 1625 Denmark entered the war against the Emperor. England had promised the Danes financial help; but the subsidies were never paid, for Parliament, after forcing James to break off his negotiations with Spain and encouraging Charles to support his Protestant brother-in-law, the Elector Palatine, refused to vote any supplies for the carrying on of the war. To disentangle himself from his financial difficulties, Charles had to adopt unconstitutional measures, and these unconstitutional measures resulted at last in the great rebellion. Evil is contagious; the Civil War, Charles's execution and Cromwell's tyranny were due, at least in part, to an infection brought over from war-fevered Germany. Meanwhile, the Danes, disappointed of their money, were unable to make much headway against the enemy. Christian IV collected a considerable army and was joined by Mansfeld and his marauding troops. To the Emperor Ferdinand, the situation seemed threatening—so threatening that, in order to meet it, he was induced to give Wallenstein authority to raise and command a great imperial army. In this way a new instrument of tyranny and oppression was forged, an instrument that was destined to inflict incalculable miseries upon the German people. With a greater air of legality than Mansfeld, but more efficiently and just as ruthlessly, Wallenstein stripped the various provinces through which he marched of all their reserves of coin, food, and any supplies that might be useful for his army. And the pillage went on, year after year, long after Wallenstein's death, to the very end of the war.

In the campaigns of 1625 and 1626, Christian IV and Mansfeld were separated. Wallenstein followed the latter into Silesia, where he had joined forces with Bethlen Gabor, and forced him to accept a truce, shortly after which Mansfeld died. Desperately in need of food for the troops he had raised but (for lack of the English subsidies) could not pay, Christian IV advanced into Brunswick, pillaged the country for a little and was then defeated by Tilly, at Lutter. After that the war died down for a time into a succession of sieges of Danish fortresses. Returning from Silesia in 1627, Wallenstein devoted himself to two tasks: the subjugation of his new duchy of Mecklenburg, forfeited by its rightful owner for his share in the Danish war and presented by Ferdinand to his commander-in-chief; and the conquest, in the Emperor's name, of the whole Baltic coast. Jealous of their liberties, the Hanse towns refused to open their gates to him and, at the beginning of 1628, Wallenstein sat down to the siege of one of them, the second-rate city of Stralsund. At this same moment, hundreds of miles to the south-west, Richelieu and his army were encamped outside the walls of La Rochelle. But whereas, thanks to Father Joseph, the siege of La Rochelle was continued to the bitter end, Wallenstein lost patience and, after six months, abandoned the attempt on Stralsund, cut his losses and marched away. The result, as time was to show, was that Richelieu's position was greatly improved, while that of the Hapsburgs was correspondingly weakened. The victory at La Rochelle united France and closed a breach through which hostile powers might intervene in the country's internal affairs; the defeat at Stralsund left the Baltic coast open to invasion from Scandinavia, but at the same time it had come near enough to victory to frighten the Northern Protestants into a more determined resistance to the centralizing policy of the Hapsburgs. In the following year, 1629, the Emperor did a thing which positively guaranteed the continuance and intensification of Protestant hostility; he issued the Edict of Restitution, which claimed for the Roman church all lands which had been ecclesiastical property before 1552. The prospect of losing more than a hundred and fifty rich bishoprics united the Protestant princes of the North, while the prospect of being persecuted by the Jesuits united their peoples in a stand against what they regarded as naked religious and political aggression.

Meanwhile, trouble had broken out in Italy. At the end of 1627 Vincenzo II of Mantua died without issue, leaving a will by which he bequeathed his duchy to Father Joseph's old friend, Charles Palaeologus Gonzaga, Duke of Nevers. The new sovereign hurried off to Italy and proceeded to install himself among the splendid and long accumulated treasures of the Mantuan palaces. Many of these treasures—among them Mantegna's "Triumph of Caesar" now at Hampton Court—Nevers was forced soon afterwards to sell to Charles I of England; for he was in desperate need of money with which to buy the means for defending his inheritance. Even before Vincenzo's death, the validity of his will had been disputed, and within a very short time of his accession the new duke found himself assailed on all sides by rival Gonzagas—the Duke of Guastalla, the Dowager Duchess of Lorraine and, more menacing then either, the Duke of Savoy, who demanded the Mantuan-owned duchy of Monferrato for his nephew's wife, a daughter of Vincenzo II's elder brother and predecessor on the ducal throne. Lying as it did on the road from Turin to Alessandria and Genoa, Monferrato, with its strong fortress of Casale, was a territory of much strategic importance. Charles Emanuel of Savoy had no wish to see a French prince, backed by French arms and money, installed so close to his capital. The prospect was even more distasteful to the Court of Madrid, for Monferrato lay across the line of communications between the Spanish province of Milan and the sea. Early in 1628 Charles Emanuel and Philip IV's ambassador at Turin signed an agreement stipulating that the two powers should take joint military action against Monferrato, which was then to be partitioned between them. Troops were collected and equipped and, later in the year, Charles Emanuel overran that part of the duchy which lay on the left bank of the Po, while the Spanish governor of Milan addressed himself to the more difficult and laborious task of reducing the fortress of Casale.

So long as La Rochelle held out, it was impossible for Richelieu to do anything to relieve the French outpost which the accidents of heredity had now so conveniently established on the further side of the Alps. The surrender of the Huguenots left him free to act. He moved with as much dispatch as the winter weather, bad organization and court intrigues would permit. In the first days of March 1629, a French army of thirty-five thousand men, with the King and Cardinal at their head, crossed the Alps, defeated the troops of Savoy and captured the stronghold of Susa. A few days later Charles Emanuel signed a dictated peace and, on March 15th, the siege of Casale was raised and the Spanish army marched back to Milan. Richelieu provisioned the town against the renewed attack which he knew would come the moment French forces had been withdrawn, strengthened the fortifications and left a substantial garrison under Thoiras, the commander who had so valiantly resisted Buckingham on the island of Rhé. Meanwhile Father Joseph was in Mantua, telling the duke exactly what was expected of him by the Cardinal and exactly what he might expect in the way of French support. Richelieu was a hard taskmaster, and the duke complained of his severity; but fear of the Hapsburgs and the persuasive eloquence of his old friend and fellow-crusader brought him at last to the acceptance of all the Cardinal's conditions—an acceptance which (though Mantua was sacked by the imperial troops in 1630) permitted him to keep his title and transmit it, at his death in 1637, to an infant grandchild. This grandchild grew up a profligate and left the duchy in due course to an almost imbecile son who finally lost it to the Austrians in 1708. It is a dismal and vaguely cautionary tale—cautionary, like all history, against the consequences of merely behaving like human beings, of existing unregenerately as natural men. We may wish sincerely to avoid the crimes and follies of past generations; but at the same time we wish to live that natural life which (along with its quota of goodness and beauty) produces the very crimes and follies we wish to avoid. That is why, to all but the saints, who anyhow have no need of them, the lessons of history are totally unavailing.

From Italy, Father Joseph followed the royal armies back to France, where they spent the spring and summer of 1629 crushing out the political power of the Huguenots of Provence and Languedoc. It was a savage campaign, with much slaughtering of the inhabitants of captured cities, much hanging of rebels, much condemning of men to slavery in the galleys. Father Joseph did his best to mitigate these horrors; but the King and, above all, Condé, who was in command of part of the forces, were ruthless. By the end of July the royal arms were completely victorious, and the Cardinal was able to ride from city to Protestant city, making triumphal entries, receiving the submission of the magistrates, appointing royal intendants to govern in the King's name, supervising the demolition of walls and towers. Returning to Paris to cope with the ever more menacing intrigues of Marie de Médicis, he left Father Joseph in southern France, with the difficult task of initiating the re-conversion of the people to Catholicism. Of the methods he sometimes used to accomplish this end I have already spoken. They were a bit shady, to say the least of it; but then it was a matter of performing God's exterior will as rapidly and efficiently as possible. . . .

Early in 1630, trouble broke out again in Italy. Disregarding the terms of the peace treaty he had signed the year before, Charles Emanuel once more threw in his lot with the Spaniards. Spanish power was a menace to all the princes of Italy; but for the present at least, Madrid had an interest in preserving Savoy as a buffer state between

France and its own possessions in Lombardy. The French attitude towards Savoy was uncertain and equivocal. Better a known than an unknown evil. Besides, Charles Emanuel wanted his slice of Monferrato.

Once more a Spanish army sat down to the siege of Casale. It was commanded by Ambrose Spinola, the Genoese soldier who survives for us in Velásquez's "Surrender of Breda"—a great master of siege-craft, who had served the Spanish crown not only in the field, but also by the sacrifice (in order to keep his unpaid troops from mutiny) of his entire personal fortune, only to be treated in the last years of his life with the most shameless ingratitude. The injuries and insults heaped upon him by Olivares during this campaign so preyed upon his mind that in September of 1630 he fell sick and died at his post before the walls of Casale.

To relieve Casale was as necessary in 1630 as it had been in 1629; but this time Richelieu found himself paralysed by opposition within the royal family and the ranks of his own cabinet. Mainly because of her personal grudge against the Cardinal, but also because she believed in a specifically Catholic foreign policy, a policy of collaboration with the Hapsburgs in the extermination of heresy, Marie de Médicis was firmly set against the Italian campaign. The young queen, Anne of Austria, had been a Spanish Infanta and, on this point at least, was in accord with her mother-in-law. Their strongest supporter in the Council of State was Marillac, the Keeper of the Great Seal. Another supporter had been Cardinal Bérulle who, until his death in 1629, had used all the authority conferred upon him by his position and the extraordinary sanctity of his life to back up the Queen Mother in her opposition to Richelieu. His talk was of the seamless robe of Christ, of a western world purged of heresy and reunited under the three great Catholic powers, France, Spain and Austria. One wonders if he ever used his fancy to trace out in pictorial terms, the implications of his metaphor. His aim was to transform a seamy robe into a seamless one. To achieve this end, he proposed that Bourbons and Hapsburgs should unite their forces for the purpose of gashing and cauterizing the body within the robe. At some point in the proceedings the seams were automatically to disappear, and all Christendom would find itself united. For Bérulle's own sake, one can only be thankful that he died when he did. Had he lived on, had his policy been adopted, he would have become, like his old schoolfellow, Father Joseph, more and more deeply involved in large-scale iniquity, would have known the bitterness of seeing the disastrous consequences of his good intentions, would at last have realized that between his policy and Richelieu's there was little or nothing to choose; for both had proposed the employment of means, whose consequences could never be the improvement of the existing state of things.

Between his mother and the Cardinal, Louis XIII vacillated in an agony of uncertainty. He disliked Richelieu and felt himself humiliated by the man's superiority; but at the same time he recognized his ability, he was grateful to him for all he had done for the glory of the monarchy, he knew that there was nobody who could take his place. Over against Richelieu stood Marie de Médicis, florid and fairly bulging with female energy, vulgar, loud-voiced, rancorous and obstinately stupid. Ever since his unhappy childhood, the King had hated and feared her, but always with a guilty sense that he ought to love her and listen to what she said. What she said now was that the war must be stopped at once and the Cardinal dismissed. And though he felt sure that Richelieu was right, that he would go on doing great things for the house of Bourbon, Louis listened to his mother's words, and was half persuaded. The spring and summer of 1630 were wasted, from a military point of view, because the King was unable to make up his mind whether to prosecute the war or to make peace, whether to accompany his armies into Italy, or to stay at home. Always sickly and delicate, he had several sharp attacks of illness, which the treatment prescribed by his physicians—daily purgings and weekly bleedings—threatened to make chronic. Away from the court, a soldier among his soldiers, he always felt stronger for a time; but sooner or later his mother's letters would bring back the old neurasthenia, and he would insist on taking the Cardinal back from the frontier to where the two queens were quartered, at Lyons. There, in the council chamber, Richelieu had to set forth, yet once more, his reasons for going on with the war in Italy. The council gave him a vote of confidence, and Louis was reassured. Three times this proceeding was repeated; and meanwhile time was passing, plague had broken out in the army and thousands of soldiers were deserting. At Casale, however, Thoiras still held out.

In this predicament Richelieu did his best to compensate for his enforced inactivity in the field by redoubling his efforts on the diplomatic front. His first system of Protestant alliances had failed him. It was in vain that Louis XIII had given his sister in marriage to Charles I; instead of collaborating with France, England had gone to war on behalf of the Huguenots. Meanwhile Denmark had been decisively defeated by the imperialists. Holland was too weak to do anything effective on land. There remained only Sweden. In the autumn of 1629 Richelieu had sent an agent to Gustavus Adolphus, offering French mediation between the King and his cousin, Sigismund of Poland, with whom he had for years been at war. Peace was quickly restored between the two sovereigns, who agreed to a six-year truce. Having thus secured his flank, Gustavus was now free to invade Germany—a plan which he had long been meditating, partly for religious reasons (for he was an ardent Protestant who regarded the Hapsburgs' Counter-Reformation as diabolic), and partly because he was ambitious to transform the Baltic into a Swedish lake. But Sweden was a poor country and, though Gustavus had the best army in Europe, he lacked the sinews of war. Richelieu now offered him a subsidy of six hundred thousand livres—less than one eighth of his own income—on condition that Gustavus should invade Germany, beat the imperialists, but respect the rights of the Catholic princes. Gustavus, who had no wish to respect Catholics, rejected the offer; and in the summer of 1630 boldly invaded Pomerania, without a subsidy. Richelieu bided his time and continued to dangle the golden bait, knowing very well that the Swedish King would sooner or later be forced by mere poverty to accept his terms.

Meanwhile, at the other end of Germany, Ferdinand had summoned an imperial Diet to meet at Ratisbon. His intention was to persuade the seven Electors of the Empire to appoint his son King of the Romans, a title which would officially consecrate him as his father's successor to the imperial throne. For this favour he expected to have to pay—in what way and precisely how much would be settled by a long-drawn process of haggling at the Diet.

The summoning of the Diet gave Richelieu an excuse for sending a special embassy to Ratisbon—nominally to discuss the question of the Mantuan succession, but in fact to make trouble between the Emperor and the Electors. A professional diplomat, Brulart de Léon, was officially the King's ambassador; but the real representative of France, as everyone knew, was the humble Capuchin who accompanied him on his mission. Father Joseph had no official position, and his credentials to the Emperor attributed to him no powers; he was just an observer, nothing more. As a mere observer, he was able to act and speak with a freedom that would have been impossible in an ambassador; as the right-hand man of Cardinal Richelieu, he was listened to with an attention and a deference which a mere civil servant, like Brulart, could not command.

From the general of the Capuchins Father Joseph had received an "obedience" which permitted him so far to infringe the rules of his order as to ride in a carriage and handle money. Armed with this and his letters of credence, he rejoined Brulart in Switzerland, where the latter had been acting as French ambassador, and together, in the month of July 1630, they set out with all the pomp befitting a King's representatives, for Ratisbon.

There was not much active fighting going on at the moment and, as there was still something to eat in southern Germany, Wallenstein had established his headquarters at Memmingen, about half way between Augsburg and the Swiss frontier. Hearing of the approach of the French envoy and his interesting companion, the commander of the imperial army drove out of the town to meet them, accompanied by "eighteen coaches, filled with princes, dukes and palatines of Hungary and Bohemia." One can imagine the scene on that hot July afternoon: the trains of coaches halted in the dusty road; the coming and going, between ambassador and generalissimo, of emissaries to discuss the delicate and, for seventeenth-century noblemen, infinitely important question of precedence; the happy solution of the problem by a decision that both parties should alight simultaneously and greet one another at a point exactly half way between the two foremost carriages; then the solemn approach and beautifully stylized salutation—the low bow, with the right foot advanced and pointed slightly outwards in the first position of the dance, the elaborate flourish of the plumed hat, followed by the handshake, the few well-chosen words, the enormous compliments. And when the two protagonists have gone through their ritual, there is a similar baroque exchange of courtesies between Brulart's suite and the eighteen carriage-loads of princes, dukes and palatines. In the background, meanwhile, conspicuously grey and tattered in the midst of so much crimson velvet, so much lace and jewelry, stands the Capuchin, his bare horny feet sunk in the dust. To those who salute him, he inclines his head and raises his right hand in benediction. When Wallenstein invites him to join the ambassador and himself in his huge gilded coach, Father Joseph protests that the honour is too great; but the general insists, and in the end he climbs in after the others, and away they roll towards Memmingen and an official banquet, of which it will be impossible for him to partake as he is in the midst of one of his four annual Lents.

Next day, during a lull in the festivities, Wallenstein invited the friar to his quarters for a long confidential talk, the gist of which was communicated to the Cardinal in Father Joseph's next dispatch. It was an interesting conversation and one which any casual eavesdropper would have found extremely odd. For what the two men chiefly discussed was Byzantium and the Holy Places, Turkish power and joint expeditions from the West. Not since those happy days with the Duke of Nevers and Paul V had Father Joseph had the joy of talking crusades with so ardent an enthusiast. Wallenstein was as keen to smash the infidels as St. Louis had been, albeit, as Father Joseph came little by little to discover, not for quite the same reasons. For one who had been sent to school, first with the Moravians, then with the Jesuits, who had exchanged Lutheranism for Romanism out of personal interest, and who believed with conviction only in astrology, the triumph of the Church Militant was not of the smallest interest. Crusading, for Wallenstein, was merely an excuse for the *Drang nach Osten*. That he talked of his vast projects in terms of the Cross and Crescent was merely a historical accident and a matter of convenience. If steam engines had existed in the seventeenth century, he would have talked just as enthusiastically about the Berlin-to-Bagdad railway. His ambition was to create a great federated empire, stretching from the Baltic to the Bosphorus and beyond, into Asia Minor and Syria. Such an empire could be ruled either by the Hapsburgs, with himself, Albrecht von Wallenstein, as their generalissimo and mayor of the palace, or else (and at this point that dark and horribly sinister face of his, the face of a bloated Mephistopheles, the face of a devil who is *not* a gentleman, lit up with inward exultation as he leaned confidentially towards the friar) or else—why not?—by Albrecht von Wallenstein himself, ruling in his own name, by virtue of an irresistible military force. Coming as they did from the Emperor's commander-in-chief, and addressed as they were to the man who was travelling to Ratisbon, among other reasons, for the express purpose of undermining Wallenstein's position with the Emperor, these remarks were, to say the least of it, surprising. But along with his cunning and caution, Wallenstein had the recklessness of one who knows that all things are predestined, that fate is written in the stars and cannot be changed. Let them all know what he planned—Emperor, Cardinal, Pope, King of Spain, the whole lot of them! What did it matter, so long as, from their heavenly houses, the planets looked down on him with favour.

From crusades the conversation shifted, by way of the Palaologi, to Mantua; and with the same astonishing frankness Wallenstein declared himself entirely opposed to the Hapsburg policy in Italy. He knew Nevers and liked him; besides, as the last of the Palaologi, the man might come in useful one day. And anyhow it was senseless for the Emperor to add to his troubles by going to war with France over a piddling little duchy that mattered to nobody except the Spaniards. In these sentiments Father Joseph most heartily concurred and went on to express the hope that His Highness would do all he could to bring His Imperial Majesty to the same opinion. Not that Wallenstein would have much time or opportunity to influence the Emperor, he reflected inwardly; for he felt pretty certain of being able to persuade the Electors to force the general's resignation. Which was a pity in some ways; for

Wallenstein would be a most useful ally in the Mantuan affair. But meanwhile Gustavus Adolphus was already on German soil, and it was essential that, before his campaign started, the imperial armies should be weakened by the loss of their commander. Later on, perhaps, when the King of Sweden had done his work, Wallenstein might be called back to power, might be encouraged in his wild ambitions for personal rule—encouraged just sufficiently to make him a paralysing embarrassment to the Emperor, but not enough, of course, to permit him to become the military dictator of all the Germanies.

Refreshed and considerably enlightened by his stay at Memmingen, Father Joseph drove on with Brulart and their following to Ratisbon, where the Diet was already in session. The Emperor and the five Catholic Electors were present in person; the two Protestant Electors had sent only their representatives. To his surprise—for he persisted in regarding himself as what in fact he was in private life, a humble Capuchin friar—Father Joseph found himself the man most talked about, most in view, most generally notorious in all Ratisbon. Six years of close association with Richelieu had given him already an international reputation. Every well-informed person in Europe had heard of the bare-footed friar who had left his convent to become the collaborator of the most astute, and so far as Hapsburg sympathizers were concerned, the most dangerous politician of his century. Universally known, Father Joseph was almost universally reprobated. This follower of St. Francis who had betrayed the Lady Poverty to live among princes, this dedicated servant of the church who had conspired with the heretics to thwart the Counter-Reformation—what was he but a renegade, an enemy of

God and man? At Ratisbon, Father Joseph discovered for the first time what his contemporaries thought of him.

The first revelation came to him one day, early in the proceedings, when he had gone to pay his respects to Tilly, the old general to whom, in the Turciad, he had devoted two graceful lines of praise:

Tilli, etenim te nostra canet testudo, nec unquam
Egregium nomen gelidi teget umbra sepulcri.[1]

The compliment had been penned at a time when Father Joseph was still an ardent imperialist; now that he had become convinced that Hapsburg power must be destroyed, if true religion, under Bourbon leadership, was to flourish, he would have written rather differently. But whatever his present opinions of Tilly, etiquette demanded that he should call on him. When the interview was over, Tilly accompanied his guest to the door of the reception room, and from there the friar was escorted by a group of the general's aides to the foot of the steps leading into the street. On the way out, one of the gentlemen called de Flamel, turned to the friar, asked him if he was really Father Joseph and, on receiving an affirmative answer, continued: "Then you are a Capuchin; that is to say you are obliged by your profession to do what you can to foster peace in Christendom. And yet you are the man who starts a bloody war between the Catholic sovereigns—between the Emperor, the King of Spain and the King of France. You ought to blush with shame."

Reacting, not to the offence against his personal honour, but to the insult offered a representative of His Most

[1] Tilly! thee too my lyre shall sing, and may the shade of the cold sepulchre ne'er hide thine egregious name!

Christian Majesty, Father Joseph demanded an apology. Tilly tendered excuses and had the offender clapped in irons; but in spite of all this, Father Joseph had reason to believe that the affront was premeditated and that the whole incident on the steps had been carefully staged by Tilly himself. Well, calumny was what the servants of Christ had been taught to expect—yes, and even rejoice in; for to be tried by calumny was a sign, if one were following the way of perfection, that God considered one ripe for the hardest lessons. To suffer slander without resentment or bitterness was possible only to souls that had lost themselves in God. At Ratisbon, Father Joseph redoubled his exercises of passive and active annihilation.

He had need to do so; for what happened at Tilly's headquarters was only the first of a long series of similar trials to his patience. Pamphlets were hawked about the streets of Ratisbon, in which he and his master, the Cardinal, were denounced with that savage intemperance of language characteristic of all controversial writing in the seventeenth century. The pamphlets were in Latin and unsigned. Rumour had it that they were composed by two Spanish ecclesiastics; but the fact that the authors were Father Joseph's political enemies did not prevent them from saying some very just and sensible things about him, things that were being said by men of ordinary intelligence and decent feeling in every part of Europe. People everywhere were wondering, like Flamel, how a Capuchin could reconcile his profession with the framing and execution of policies that resulted, as anyone with eyes in his head could see, in the increase of misery and crime. To them it seemed as though he were deliberately using the reputation of his order to whiten the sepulchre of Richelieu's iniquities. In the epigrammatic Latin of the pamphleteers, *"huic ille tegendo sceleri cucullum praebet."* (He, Joseph, offers him, Richelieu, a friar's hood to hide his crimes in.) Richelieu himself knew very well how important it was for a politician to cover his actions with the prestige of religion and high morality. In his dealings with foreign countries, he always took enormous pains never to seem the aggressor, always to have the appearance of legality and right on his side. Nor was this all; for, in the words of an Italian diplomat of the period, "it is said that when Cardinal Richelieu wishes to play some clever trick, not to say some piece of knavery, he always makes use of men of piety." Bad men could never do the harm they actually accomplish, unless they were able to induce good men to become, first their dupes, and then their more or less willing, more or less conscious accomplices. *"Huic ille tegendo sceleri cucullum praebet."*

What happens when good men go into power politics in the hope of forcibly shoving humanity into the kingdom of God? Echoing the wisdom of common men, the pamphleteers of Ratisbon had their neatly pointed answer in the best Senecan manner. *"Sacrilega sunt arma quae sacra tractantur manu . . . Miles mitrae imperat cum mitra militibus imperat."* (Sacrilegious are the arms wielded by a sacred hand. When the mitre commands the soldier, it is the soldier who commands the mitre.) The whole political history of the church is summed up in those phrases. Again and again ecclesiastics and pious laymen have become statesmen in the hope of raising politics to their own high moral level, and again and again politics have dragged them down to the low moral level upon which statesmen, in their political capacity are compelled to live. That the

Ratisbon pamphleteers should have chosen to wrap up a great moral and political truth in a tissue of lies and scurrility was unfortunate; for by so doing they made it absolutely certain that Father Joseph would pay no attention to what they had to say.

Father Joseph's performance at Ratisbon was a miracle of diplomatic virtuosity. His first task was to allay the suspicions of the Emperor, who had been repeatedly warned by Richelieu's enemies in France—Marillac, the Queen Mother, the great nobles, the extreme Catholic partisans of collaboration with Spain—that the Cardinal was plotting nothing less than the overthrow of Hapsburg power. This happened, of course, to be true; all the more reason, therefore, for persuading Ferdinand that it was false. This Father Joseph accomplished more or less successfully by discrediting the people from whom the Emperor had received these warnings. They were people, he explained, whose personal ambitions had been thwarted by the Cardinal's rise to power, or who objected to the Cardinal's efforts to achieve what His Imperial Majesty was so wisely and benevolently trying to achieve in Germany: the union of a divided country under a single centralized authority. It was true that France had been forced to protect itself against Spanish aggression; but to pretend that the Cardinal or his master had any designs against Austria was a malicious falsehood. . . .

From his interviews with the Emperor, Father Joseph padded away on his bare feet to Maximilian of Bavaria and his fellow Electors. To these he spoke of His Most Christian Majesty's extreme concern for the liberties of his cousins, the German princes. He was shocked to observe the way in which these liberties were now being menaced; his heart bled for the unhappy victims of the Emperor's tyranny. The imperial army, under that arrogant upstart, Wallenstein, had been raised to fight the heretics; but it was being used even more effectively to subjugate the Catholic Electors. With Wallenstein quartered at Memmingen, this solemn Diet was nothing but a farce. Under the threat of overwhelming force the Electors were no longer free agents; it was the end of that grand old German Constitution, to which His Most Christian Majesty and the Cardinal were so deeply and unshakeably attached. Their only hope lay in acting at once, while the Emperor had need of them to nominate his son King of the Romans. Let them refuse even to discuss the question so long as Wallenstein remained in power. If there should be any trouble, Their Highnesses could rely on the Cardinal to come to their aid.

The Electors listened and took heart to do what the Emperor's military successes and his high-handed Edict of Restitution had secretly made them wish to do for some time past. They demanded the dismissal of Wallenstein and a reduction in the size of the imperial army.

Ferdinand had no great love for Wallenstein, whose loyalty he suspected and of whose vast personal ambitions he had been fully informed. At the same time he was loath at this particular juncture to get rid of him. After all, Gustavus was busy up there in the North, consolidating his position and preparing for attack. Father Joseph hastened to reassure him. Gustavus, he cried contemptuously, who was Gustavus? A twopenny-halfpenny little princeling at the head of a troop of starving barbarians. No, Gustavus simply didn't count; pitted against the imperial army, he would be swept off the face of the earth.

And, of course, if by some unlucky chance he should happen to give trouble, the Emperor could always call Wallenstein back to his command and recruit a few more regiments. Meanwhile, with regard to the election, His Imperial Majesty need have no fears. Once Wallenstein was out of the way, the grateful princes would do what they were asked, and the fact that they had voted freely would redound enormously to the glory of the Emperor and enhance his moral authority throughout the Germanies.

All this was sound enough and, feeling that Wallenstein was a moderate price to pay for his son's election, Ferdinand consented to dismiss his general. In September, emissaries were sent to Memmingen ordering Wallenstein to resign. Father Joseph, meanwhile, had sent a letter to the general, reminding him of their delightful conversation about the infidels and advising him to submit without demur to the Emperor's bidding. After all, he pointed out, Gustavus Adolphus was in Pomerania. With his magnificent army he was bound to win some victories, and the moment that happened the Emperor would be forced to come hat in hand to the only soldier in Europe capable of dealing with so formidable an enemy. His Highness would then be able to demand practically anything he liked; to allow himself to be dismissed now would be a stroke of the most consummate policy. Wallenstein accepted the advice, which was in accord with what his horoscopists (Johann Kepler at their head) had discovered in the stars. Obediently and without protest, he resigned his command, and with him were dismissed eighteen thousand cavalry and not less than twice that number of foot soldiers. Merely by talking, Father Joseph had won the equivalent of a major military victory.

Now that Wallenstein had been dismissed and his army cut in half, the Emperor turned to the Electors for his reward. But Tenebroso-Cavernoso had slipped up the back stairs and into their private council chambers before him. Their Highnesses, he whispered, had scored a signal victory; but the fruits of that victory would be wasted unless it were followed up by a second. Now that they had weakened the Emperor, they ought quickly to strike again —strike at the most vulnerable chink in the Hapsburg's armour: the imperial succession. By refusing to nominate Ferdinand's son as his successor by merely hinting at the possibility that they might elect an Emperor from some other royal house, they could put the fear of God into those tyrants at Vienna and Madrid. And if the tyrants should bluster and threaten, the Electors had only to appeal to His Most Christian Majesty; all the resources of France would be at their disposal. This was the moment for Their Highnesses to assert themselves, to remind these Hapsburgs that they were Emperors, not by hereditary right, but only by the grace of the Electors and the grand old German Constitution.

When the Emperor formally asked for the title of King of the Romans for his son, the Electors voted him down, Wallenstein and the army had been sacrificed for nothing. Looking back over the causes of his defeat, Ferdinand perceived, at every turn of the tortuous diplomatic road, a grey cowled figure, hurrying in silence through the shadows. To his ministers, the Emperor ruefully admitted that "a poor Capuchin had beaten them with his rosary, and that, narrow as was the friar's hood, he had contrived to stuff into it six electoral bonnets."

Meanwhile, however, the war of negotiation had been going badly for Father Joseph on some of the other diplomatic fronts, where events in France had placed him in an inextricably difficult and precarious situation. Vacillating between his mother and the Cardinal, Louis XIII had sunk through neurasthenia into physical sickness. On September 22nd, at Lyons, he fell ill of a fever so violent that, a week later, his condition was despaired of and the last rites of the church were administered. Then, on the first of October, the physicians reported that an abscess in the King's body had burst; the fever dropped; it seemed possible that Louis would recover. Richelieu's situation during these last days of September was like that of a man suspended over a precipice by a rope whose fibres, one by one, are snapping under his weight. If the King died, he was infallibly lost. Gaston, who would succeed his childless brother as king, detested the Cardinal; so did the Queen Mother; so did the great magnates whose power he had sought to curb; so did the common people, who knew him only as the ruthless tax gatherer, the instigator of this gratuitous and incomprehensible war, which might at any moment spread from Italy to every corner of Europe and even into France itself. As soon as the King's condition became serious, a group of nobles secretly met and decided, if he died, to deal with Richelieu as Concini had been dealt with thirteen years before. Remembering that eviscerated carcass hanging by the heels from the gibbet of the Pont Neuf, the Cardinal made plans to flee for safety to the papal city of Avignon. It would be a race between the murderers and their victim. Then, at the very moment when the race was timed to start, the King began to recover. For Richelieu it was a respite from his mortal apprehensions—but only a respite, not yet definite and enduring liberation. The King was out of immediate danger, but he was still a sick man, and at his bedside sat the Queen Mother and Anne of Austria. As Louis emerged again into convalescence, the two women prolonged and intensified their persuasions. They were all devotion, all sweetness, all love and forgiveness; but they were determined to badger the unhappy man into doing what they and their political friends desired. Day and night, relaying one another, like a pair of examining magistrates putting a recalcitrant prisoner through the third degree, they pressed the young King to make the decisive move—dismiss his minister, stop the war, reverse his policy. Louis had no strength to argue with them; but he was able at last to summon up enough will power to say, quite definitely, that he would make no decision till he was well again and back in Paris. The Cardinal's respite had been prolonged for a few more weeks.

Receiving word of what was happening at Lyons, Father Joseph found himself in a most painful predicament. His secret mission, which was to drive a wedge between the Emperor and the Electors, had been accomplished; but there was also an ostensible mission, which was to come to terms over the question of Mantua. The Emperor, as had been foreseen, was pressing for a general settlement of all outstanding differences between France and Austria; but as Richelieu's campaign against the Hapsburgs had only just begun, such a general settlement would be premature and must therefore be avoided. Hitherto Father Joseph had succeeded in parrying all the Emperor's attempts to link up Mantua with the European situation as a whole. It was a policy of delay and evasion, deliberately framed to prolong the struggle between the Hapsburgs and France and her allies. Such a policy could be pursued only on condition that Richelieu remained sufficiently powerful at home to override popular and aristocratic opposition to the war. But now Richelieu was in danger of dismissal, even of death; the prime condition of France's anti-Hapsburg policy—the Cardinal's absolute power—was ceasing to exist. To Father Joseph, at Ratisbon, it seemed clear that the only hope for Richelieu lay in regaining popularity and conciliating the great nobles. But there was only one way for the Cardinal to regain popularity and conciliate the great nobles, and that was through an immediate reversal of his foreign policy. To take such a step was a very serious matter, and, before doing so he had written urgently for precise instructions. Owing partly to the Cardinal's procrastination, partly to bad weather which had held up the courier, no answering dispatch had been received; and, on October 13th, acting on his own responsibility, he instructed Brulart to sign a document which provided for a general settlement of Franco-Austrian differences. As a mere observer, he declined at first to append his own signature to the treaty; but the Emperor insisted on it, and in the end he had to give way. As he looked on at the ceremony, Ferdinand gleefully reflected that he had succeeded in pulling out of that grey Franciscan hood political advantages which far outweighed the six electoral bonnets which the friar had so recently stuffed into it. But the Emperor's triumph was short lived. News that an agreement had been signed was brought to Richelieu on October 19th, as he and the convalescent King were returning to Paris. Meanwhile, the full text of the treaty had been sent to the Court at Lyons, where it obtained the approval of all who read it.

The news that the war was over and that there would be no more foreign adventures spread like wild-fire across the country, causing, as Father Joseph had foreseen, universal rejoicing. Next day, a copy of the treaty was brought to Richelieu at Roanne. He read it; then angrily tore it up. The ambassadors had exceeded their instructions, he said; the treaty would not be ratified. It was an act on his part of quite extraordinary courage. By repudiating the treaty, Richelieu invited the hatred of the masses and made more implacable the hostility of the Queen Mother and the nobles. He had been given a chance to save his neck, and he had refused it. If the King were to fail him now—and, at court, the betting was ten to one in favour of the Queen Mother—he was infallibly done for.

Events were to justify Richelieu in taking the risks he did. Three weeks after his refusal to ratify Father Joseph's treaty, there took place that decisive interview between Louis and his mother—the interview from which Marie de Médicis confidently expected to emerge victorious over the Cardinal. Stealing through an unbolted back door, Richelieu broke in upon this interview, and at the sight of him the Queen Mother lost her self-control and began to scream at him, like a fish wife. Her vulgarity was her undoing. The seventeenth-century absolute monarch was a sacred person, in whose presence all, even his closest intimates, were expected to behave with the restraint of a stoic philosopher, a positively Confucian decorum. His mother's proletarian outburst was an insult to the royal dignity. Outraged and revolted, Louis extricated himself from the distasteful situation as quickly as he could, and retired to Versailles. Marie was left in the exultant illusion that she had triumphed. That evening, Louis sent for the Cardinal and confirmed him in his position. Marillac was arrested and, at the news, Gaston of Orleans, who had been closeted with his mother, hastened to Versailles to assure the King of his loyalty and the Cardinal of his henceforth unwavering affection. For Marie, this "Day of Dupes" marked a decisive defeat. After giving trouble for a few months more, she was skilfully manoeuvred by the Cardinal into making an irretrievable mistake: she fled the country. From this voluntary exile Louis never allowed her to return, and the Queen Mother spent the last twelve years of her life wandering from court to court, an ever less welcome guest, chronically short of money, and dependent upon the humiliating charity of the man who had once been her obsequious protégé and was now the master of France and the arbiter of all Europe.

Returning to Paris shortly after the Day of Dupes, Father Joseph was welcomed by his chief with the utmost cordiality. Richelieu bore him no grudge for having exceeded his instructions. Promptly repudiated, the treaty had done no harm. For the rest, Father Joseph's expedition had been entirely successful. Wallenstein had been dismissed and his army weakened; the Electors had asserted their independence of the Emperor and were showing signs of turning towards France, and (hardly less important) time had been gained—time for Gustavus to prepare his next year's campaign, time for the Cardinal himself to overthrow his domestic enemies and consolidate his position. Time in the present juncture was on the side of the Bourbons and against the Hapsburgs, who could only suffer from the prolongation of the German chaos, whereas their rivals to the West of the Rhine stood only to gain by the progressive exhaustion of the imperial resources.

In a memorandum on the affairs of Germany, which he wrote in January 1631, for the instruction of the King, Father Joseph insisted that French policy should be directed to the systematic exploitation of time as the deadliest of all weapons in the Bourbons' armoury. To this end, the negotiations which he had begun at Ratisbon were to be continued, unremittingly. Through his agents the King was to go on offering French protection to the Electors, on condition that all, Protestant and Catholic alike, should band themselves together in a specifically German, anti-Spanish bloc, independent of the Emperor. Such a bloc would be strong enough to negotiate on equal terms with the Hapsburgs, and if the King of France were to act as mediator, the Electors could feel certain of reaching a final settlement favourable to themselves.

If such propositions were not made at once, and made, what was more, with every appearance of sincerity, the Electors would be driven back into the Emperor's camp through fear of Gustavus. Should this happen, Father Joseph went on, the Emperor would find himself in a position to bring about an immediate settlement of all disputes. Which would be disastrous for the Bourbons; for it would leave the Hapsburgs free to turn all their military power against France. Every effort towards an early peace within the Empire and between the Emperor and his foreign enemies must therefore be uncovered and promptly scotched. But how? Father Joseph had his answer. His Most Christian Majesty could avert the catastrophe of an early peace by offering to become a peacemaker. "Assuming the office of mediator and arbitrator, and promising to help the Electors if they have need, the King can spin out matters indefinitely, counterbalance the authority of the Emperor, and retard the coming of peace in Germany until such time as we can be sure of the security of a general pacification"—a general pacification, of course, favourable to Bourbon interests.

While the imperial Diet was in session, there had poured into Ratisbon from every corner of Germany an unending stream of supplicants, seeking redress from the assembled princes for the wrongs inflicted upon them during the campaigns of the preceding years. Nothing, of course, was ever done for them, and they either returned, embittered, to their devastated homes, or else, like Kepler, who had ridden all the way from Silesia to ask for the arrears of his salary as Imperial Mathematician, they quietly died and were stowed away in one of the churchyards of Ratisbon. Among these supplicants was a group of delegates from Pomerania. Humbly, but none the less insistently, they begged the Emperor and the Electors to consider the lamentable state of their province. In the preceding year, Wallenstein's armies had stripped the country so effectively that the people had been starving ever since. Very many had died, and those who survived were eating grass and roots—yes, and young children and the sick and even the newly buried dead.

This seems to have been one of the first occasions, during the Thiry Years' War, when public attention was called to the enforced cannibalism which was to become so horrifyingly common in the Germany of those disastrous years. Emperor and Electors listened sympathetically to the Pomeranians, assured them of their deep concern and left the matter at that. Given the political system within which they lived and performed their functions, given the habits of thought and feeling then current in princely circles, that was all they could be expected to do. Besides, during the whole of the Thirty Years' War, no German ruler ever went hungry. For dukes and prince-bishops there was always more than enough. The common people might be dying of hunger or living obscenely on human carrion; but in the imperial, electoral and episcopal banqueting halls, the grand old German custom of gorging and swilling was never abrogated. Full of beef and wine, the princes were able to bear their subjects' afflictions with the utmost fortitude.

But what about Father Joseph? He had lived among the poor and like the poor. He knew their sufferings, and he was the member of a religious order vowed, among other things, to their service. And yet here he was, pursuing, patiently and with consummate skill, a policy which could only increase the sufferings of the poor he had promised to serve. With full knowledge of what had already happened in Pomerania, he continued to advocate a course of action that must positively guarantee the spread of cannibalism to other provinces.

One wonders what went on in the friar's mind during those daily periods of recollection when, examining his thoughts and actions, he prepared himself for what his master in mysticism called the "passive annihilation" of mental prayer. First, no doubt, and all the time, he reminded himself that, in working for France, he was doing God's external will. *Gesta Dei per Francos* was an axiom, from which it followed that France was divine, that those who worked for French greatness were God's instruments, and that the means they employed could not but be in accord with God's will. When he angled for Father Joseph's soul, Satan baited his hook with the noblest temptations: patriotic duty and self-sacrifice. Father Joseph swallowed the hook, and gave himself to France with as much ardour as he had given himself to God. But a man cannot serve two masters, God is jealous and the consequences of idolatry are disastrous. Because he still persisted in identifying the French monarchy with the ultimate reality apprehended in contemplation, Father Joseph failed to connect the plight of the Pomeranian cannibals with his own and all the other European statesmen's infringement of the first two Commandments.

Sometimes, during his self-examination, it certainly struck him that he had resorted, during his negotiations, to methods of a sometimes rather questionable nature. (It was Father Joseph's contemporary, Sir Henry Wotton, who defined an ambassador as "an honest man sent to lie abroad for the good of his country." In the seventeenth century an envoy was expected not merely to lie, but also to conduct espionage in the country to which he was accredited.) Father Joseph was able to justify his diplomatic activities in two ways: in the first place, it was his patriotic duty to do these things; and in the second, he always tried his hardest to practise "active annihilation" in God, while he was doing them. Tilly and de Flamel and the anonymous Spanish pamphleteers might accuse him of criminal conduct; but what they did not and could not know was that all his actions were performed by one who strenuously cultivated the supreme, all-comprehending virtue which St. François de Sales described as "holy indifference."

The earliest literary reference to "holy indifference" occurs in the *Bhagavad-Gita,* where Krishna assures Arjuna that it is right for him to slaughter his enemies, provided always that he does so in a spirit of non-attachment. When the same doctrine was used by the Illuminés of Picardy to justify unlimited sexual promiscuity, all right-thinking men, including Father Joseph, were properly horrified. But for some strange reason murder has always seemed more respectable than fornication. Few people are shocked when they hear God described as the God of Battles; but what an outcry there would be if anyone spoke of him as the God of Brothels! Father Joseph conducted a small crusade against the Illuminés, who asserted that they could go to bed with one another in a spirit of holy indifference; but there seemed to him nothing in the least improper in his own claim to be a non-attached intriguer, spy and maker of wars.

The truth is, of course, that non-attachment can be practised only in regard to actions intrinsically good or ethically neutral. In spite of anything that Krishna or anyone else may say, bad actions are unannihilatable. They are unannihilatable because, as a matter of brute psychological fact, they enhance the separate, personal ego of those who perform them. But "the more of the creature," as Tauler puts it, "the less of God." Any act which enhances the separate, personal ego automatically diminishes the actor's chance of establishing contact with reality. He may try very hard to annihilate himself in God, to practise God's presence, even while he is acting. But the nature of what he is doing condemns his efforts to frustration. Father Joseph's activities at Ratisbon and as Richelieu's foreign minister were essentially incompatible with the unitive life to which, as a young man, he had dedicated himself and which he was now so desperately struggling to combine with power politics. He could excuse himself for his more questionable acts by the thought that he was doing his best to perform them in a condition of active annihilation in God. The fact that his best efforts were not very successful he attributed, not to the intrinsically un-annihilatable nature of what he was doing, but to his own personal imperfections—imperfections for which the cure was more austerity, severer self-discipline.

Returning to his self-examination, he was able to discover a kind of cosmic and metaphysical justification for his schemes in the thought that what seemed bad from a merely human view-point might really and actually be good. *"Il faut aimer Dieu vengeur,"* he told his nuns, *"aussi bien que Dieu miséricordieux."*[2] God, the avenger, might have his reasons for wishing to destroy large numbers of Central Europeans. Indeed, since history was assumed by Father Joseph to be an expression of the intentions of divine providence, and since, as a matter of historical fact, large numbers of Central Europeans were in process of being starved and slaughtered, it was manifest that God, the avenger, *did* desire their destruction. Therefore, the policy of prolonging the war was not wrong.

Here, his vicarious ambition for France made him forget what had been said in the Gospels to the effect that scandals will always arise, but woe unto those through whom they come. There is an observable correlation be-

[2] We must love God the avenger as much as we love God the merciful.

tween certain undesirable modes of thought and courses of action on the one hand and, on the other, certain catastrophes, such as the Thirty Years' War. But it most certainly does not follow that, because in this sense, a war may be described as the will of God, the individual who labours to prolong it is doing God's will.

Threading the mazes of his own voluntary ignorance, it was thus, explicitly or by implication, that Father Joseph reasoned to himself, as he knelt each night and morning before his crucifix. From justificatory argument, his mind would slip into meditation on the Passion of the Saviour, whose tortured body hung there in image before his eyes. And sometimes, this meditation would give place in its turn to a timeless and ecstatic contemplation of divine suffering—contemplation profound to the verge of trance. Father Joseph had been rapt away to that place which had been, ever since he was a tiny boy, the home of his strange spirit; he was on Calvary, at the foot of the cross, with the beloved disciple and the holy women.

One would imagine, *a priori,* that those whose religious life is centred upon the sufferings of a divine Saviour would be peculiarly compassionate, scrupulous beyond all others in the avoidance of actions calculated to give or prolong pain. "But no *a priori* principles determine or limit the possibilities of experience. Experience is determined only by experience." As a matter of historical fact, those whose religious life is centred upon the sufferings of a divine Saviour have not been pre-eminently compassionate, have not beeen more careful than all others to avoid the infliction of pain. As a matter of historical fact, the record of Buddhism is, in this respect, a good deal better than that of Christianity. Let us examine some of the reasons for the positive cruelty on the one hand and, on the other, the negative indifference to suffering, which have too often characterized the actions of ardent Christians.

Considered merely as an account of the way in which a good man was trapped, tortured and unjustly put to death, the story of the Passion is already sufficiently moving; and, for those who accept them as true, its theological overtones enrich it with a much profounder significance. The good Christian's emotional reactions to this story are always intense, but, unfortunately, not always desirable. Consider, first of all, that common type of reaction so vividly illustrated by the anecdote about Father Joseph's older contemporary, Louis de Crillon, surnamed Le Brave. In his retirement at Avignon, the aged warrior was listening one day to a sermon. The theme was the Passion of Christ, the preacher, full of fire and eloquence. Suddenly, in the middle of a pathetic description of the crucifixion, the old man sprang to his feet, drew the sword he had used so heroically at Lepanto and against the Huguenots, and, brandishing it above his head, with the gesture of one springing to the defence of persecuted innocence, shouted: *"Où étais-tu, Crillon?"*

Movingly told, the story of a cruel injustice has power to drive men forth to commit retaliatory injustices either against the original authors of the crime, or, if these should be dead or distant, upon the men and women who, by means of some fatally common abuse of language, are temporarily identified with the criminals. The motives actuating anti-Semites, crusaders, inquisitors and other Christian persecutors have been many and various; but among them there has almost invariably figured a desire to take vengeance, in some entirely symbolic and Pickwickian way, for the wrong committed on Calvary. Emotional Christianity is two-sided. On the obverse of the medal are stamped the cross and the types of compassionate adoration; all too often in the course of history, its reverse face has displayed the hideous emblems of war and cold-blooded cruelty.

The idea of vicarious suffering is closely associated with the story of the Passion, and in the minds of Christians has produced effects no less ambivalent. Gratitude to a God who assumed humanity and suffered that men might be saved from their merited doom carries with it, as a kind of illegitimate corollary, the thesis that suffering is good in itself and that, because voluntary self-sacrifice is meritorious and ennobling, there must be something splendid even about involuntary self-sacrifice imposed from without. The following lines are taken from a letter addressed to a west-country newspaper by a clergyman of the Church of England, and published in the spring of 1936. "The principle of vicarious suffering pervades history, some suffering and dying for the sake of others. The mother for her sick child, the doctor in his laboratory, the missionary among the heathen, the soldier on the battlefield—these suffer and sometimes die, that others may live and be happy and well. Is it not in accordance with this great principle that animals should play their part by sometimes suffering and dying to help in keeping Britons hardy, healthy and brave?" From which it follows, of course, that fox hunting is something entirely admirable and Christ-like.

That such lines could have been penned in all seriousness by a minister of religion may seem to many almost unbelievable. But the fact that they actually were penned is of the deepest significance; for it shows how dangerous the idea of vicarious suffering can become, what iniquities it can be made, in all good faith, to justify. God took upon himself the sins of humanity and died that men might be saved. Therefore (so runs the implied argument) we can make war, exploit the poor, enslave the coloured races, and all without the smallest qualm of conscience; for our victims are illustrating the great principle of vicarious suffering and, so far from wronging them, we are actually doing them a service by making it possible for them to "suffer and die, that others (by a happy coincidence, ourselves) may live and be happy and well."

Another point: the sufferings of mere humans and, *a fortiori,* of animals are as nothing compared with the sufferings of a God who has assumed human form, taken upon himself the sins of the world and chosen to expiate them all in a single act of self-sacrifice. This being so, the sufferings of human beings and animals are not really of much account. A constant dwelling on the sufferings of Christ and of the martyrs may produce in the emotional Christian an altogether admirable indifference to his own pains; but unless he is very careful to cultivate a compassion commensurate with his courage, he may end by becoming indifferent to the pains of others. The child who had sobbed so bitterly because they had hurt and killed poor Jesus was father of the man who, fifty years later, did everything in his power to prolong a war which had already caused the death of hundreds of thousands of his fellow creatures and was reducing the survivors to cannibalism.

IX

Nothing Fails Like Success

THE Day of Dupes had left Richelieu in a position of undisputed authority. He was now permanently the King's first minister, and Father Joseph, who about this time was given an official place on the Council of State, was his permanent foreign secretary and, from 1634 onwards, his designated successor in the event of the Cardinal's death.

Of the friar's mode of life during these years of his greatest political power, we have the most detailed information. He had his cell at the Capuchin convent of the rue Saint-Honoré, and a room assigned to him at the Louvre. But for the convenience of the Cardinal, who liked to consult with his old friend on all important matters, Father Joseph passed most of his time in the apartments reserved for him at Richelieu's country house of Rueil, six miles west of Paris, or in Paris itself, at the Palais Cardinal now the Palais Royal. Here amid the more than regal splendours of Richelieu's Court, he lived as though in his convent, a life of the austerest simplicity and regularity.

Every morning, summer and winter alike, he rose at four. The first hour of his day was given to mental prayer —acts of intention, self-abasement, adoration, followed by periods, first of discursive meditation on some divine perfection, then of passive annihilation in the suffering Christ and the godhead that he incarnated. Rising from before his crucifix, Father Joseph rejoined his secretary and, since 1619, his constant companion, Father Angelus of Mortagne, and together they read their breviaries. The day's work began at six. Father Angelus would read aloud, decoding when necessary, the day's dispatches from French ambassadors and the less avowable agents of Father Joseph's fifth columns in foreign countries. When the reading was over, Father Joseph dictated suitable replies. This went on for three hours. At nine, the doors of the apartment were thrown open and the friar gave audience to the high officials of the government and the ambassadors of foreign powers. In cases of a particularly thorny and delicate nature, he took his visitors to see the Cardinal, to whose apartments he could descend unseen by means of a private staircase. These interviews were continued till noon or a little later, when he retired to one of the chapels of whatever palace he happened to be living in to say mass. (The Cardinal heard mass at the same hour, but, curiously enough, in a different chapel.) Returning from his devotions, Father Joseph would find his antechamber crowded with visitors of every sort and condition—courtiers who had come to beg a favour, friars bearing reports of their missionary labours among the Huguenots, officials in disgrace, distraught ladies with husbands in the Bastille. None of these was ever sent away uninterviewed, and it was after one o'clock when Father Joseph finally sat down to his first meal of the day, which consisted of soup, followed by "only one dish of butcher's meat, without ragout or roast." Such claustral simplicity of diet profoundly impressed his contemporaries, who were astonished that a man in his position should content himself with so little. (Parenthetically, what an extraordinary fuss our ancestors made about their food! Throughout the Middle Ages and long after, almost to our own day, a man who drank no wine and lived on a vegetarian or low meat diet was regarded as a person of positively heroic virtue. Conditions have changed, and today millions of people go without meat and alcohol and, so far from regarding themselves as martyrs, are perfectly content and would be most reluctant to change their way of life. If our ancestors suffered and felt virtuous under a Lenten regimen, which many now regard as ample and delicious, it was because of the faith that was in them. They believed in meat and alcohol; consequently the lack of meat and alcohol was felt as a dreadful privation.)

Occasionally, Father Joseph dined at the Cardinal's table; but on most days he took his meals in his own apartment, along with his secretary and sometimes one or two intimate friends—ecclesiastics or literary men, of whom (especially of the more edifying and boring ones) the author of the Turciad was a steady patron. When he ate alone, Father Angelus or another friar would read aloud to him from some book of devotion or volume of church history.

Father Joseph had no money of his own and received no salary. His victuals were paid for out of a special allowance granted by the King. This allowance was sufficient to provide him, as well as his food, with a coach, in which he had now been given an "obedience" to ride whenever his business required it, together with horses, a coachman and four lackeys, who were dressed in a distinguishing livery of grey and yellow.

After dinner, if there was a great press of business, he would be sent for by the Cardinal. More often, however, he was free for a couple of hours to give audience. It was at this time that people of the great world were accustomed to pay their respects and ask their favours of him.

At four, he bowed out the last of his visitors and, accompanied by Father Angelus, went into the garden or, if it were raining, into one of the galleries of the palace to recite the remainder of his office, after which he generally found time for another period of mental prayer. At five, he went back to work; the doors were shut and the next three hours were spent in dictating memoranda to the King, political pamphlets or letters to the agents of the crown in foreign parts. At eight he had supper. The bill of fare for this meal has not come down to us. All we can discover about it is that "for dessert he always had gingerbread, either because he liked gingerbread, or else because he wished in this matter to follow the taste of the King, who frequently ate it." When supper was over, the friar slipped down the private staircase into Richelieu's apartments, where the two remained closeted until bedtime, discussing affairs of state. Sometimes, when the business of power politics was slack, a few courtiers might be called in, and there would be general conversation—about the new French Academy, about those three unities which M. Chapelain was so keen on getting into French drama, about the war in Germany, about the latest cases of sorcery and diabolic possession.

The bed to which Father Joseph finally retired was a thin hard mattress, laid on planks. There were no sheets and he slept in the hair shirt he had worn all day beneath his stained and ragged habit. Penitential scourgings kept the broad back and shoulders almost permanently covered with unhealed wounds, and the first contact with the mattress, as he lay down, must always have been acutely painful. But Father Joseph was schooled to such discomforts and had learnt not merely to bear in patience, but actually to rejoice in them; for they were pains imposed and endured for the greater glory of God and the salvation of his soul. Long habit had made his power of endurance so great that, in later life, he chose to add to his religious mortifications a torture prescribed by his physicians. This torture, which consisted in periodically cauterizing the back of the head with a hot iron, was supposed to stimulate his failing sight. Whenever he pushed back his cowl, the scar of that repeated burn could be seen, red and angry, below the tonsure.

Such was the routine of Father Joseph's life as a politician. But this Minister for Foreign Affairs had other duties, which he regarded as no less important than those of his ministry. Once or twice a week he left the Cardinal's palace to spend the day among the Capuchins of the rue Saint-Honoré, or else in the convent of the Calvarian nuns in the Marais. At the rue Saint-Honoré he dealt with the business of that great organization of foreign and domestic missions, of which, since 1625, he had been the head. At the convent in the Marais he preached, he delivered lectures on scholastic philosophy and psychology, he gave instruction in the art of mental prayer, listened to accounts of spiritual progress and advised the nuns in regard to all the problems of the spiritual life.

It is worth remarking that here in Paris, as at Ratisbon, Father Joseph's reputation was very bad—so bad that contemporaries would never accept the true explanation of his weekly absences from court. It was whispered that, during the time when he was supposed to be with the Capuchins or the Calvarians, he was really prowling about the town in disguise, spying for the Cardinal, or giving bribes and instructions to agents so secret and so sinister that they could not be interviewed except by night, at street corners or in the back rooms of disreputable taverns. Romance is always poorer and less strange than the facts it distorts and over-simplifies. This imaginary Father Joseph, who is the prototype of the ridiculously villainous figure bearing his name in Vigny's *Cinq Mars*, is just a bore, whereas the real Father Joseph moves through history as the most fascinating of enigmas.

Those who knew the Capuchin well never, of course, made the mistake that was made by the gossips of the day. Here, for example, is the brief account of him left by Avaux, a reliable witness who was much in contact with the man. After describing Father Joseph's extraordinary power of concentration and capacity for work, Avaux writes as follows: "By nature and by deliberate study, he was a character shut in on himself, one who, except under necessity, took little relaxation in the common life of the senses and who, besides observing the rule of his order, seemed to have prescribed for himself a special rule of his own. Being thus in full enjoyment of all the faculties of his soul, which was never occupied with all those distractions, which make up the half of our lives, and having regularly practised meditation, he could judge in a more orderly fashion of things and affairs." This is Father Joseph, the man of affairs, brought by self-discipline and the habit of mental concentration to a pitch of efficiency surpassing that of other men. For a contemporary account of some of the other facets of the friar's personality, we may turn to Dom Tarisse, an eminent Benedictine, who often saw him and who, like Avaux, was amazed by the way in which a man with so many and such important things to do could concentrate on any given piece of business, however trifling, as though it were the only one he had to deal with. With this capacity for intellectual concentration there went "so great a control over his passions that, if it ever happened that, in the midst of so many thorny interviews, he was surprised into saying something harsh or too emphatic, the words were not out of his mouth before you would hear him moderate the tone of his voice and see him smile." Dom Tarisse then goes on to speak of the austerity of his life, and describes the *"recollection incroyable"* with which he received the sacrament. At the height of his business, we are told, when he was most pressed, if it happened that the conversation turned to spiritual matters, his face would light up and he would discuss the life of prayer for an hour at a stretch, with "so much contentment, feeling and knowledge that you would have imagined him to be a hermit, a man engaged in continual orison." Yet more astonishing to Dom Tarisse was the way in which the friar directed the nuns of his order. This foreign minister, this second-in-command of a great state, instructed them in the spiritual life "with so much fervour and knowledge, such a high mystical doctrine, that the most learned contemplative and spiritual could not have done as much."

This austere and busy life was lived out against a background of ever deepening popular misery, ever increasing governmental ruthlessness. In France, the huge sums required to finance the foreign policy of Father Joseph and his master, the Cardinal, were being extorted, sou by sou, from those least able to pay. "Money," Richelieu remarked in the lordly tone of one who is living sumptuously at other people's expense, "money is nothing, if we accomplish our ends." Caring as he did only for foreign policy, only for the great game of negotiation and war, played between princes for the prize of personal glory and dynastic prestige, he was ready to go to any lengths at home. To the privileged, so long as they did not presume to set themselves up against the central authority, Richelieu was always and on principle very indulgent. Those who felt the full weight of his fiscal tyranny were the poor—artisans and small tradesmen in the towns, and, in the country, the dumb millions of the peasantry. At the end of the reign of Henri IV, the *taille,* a tax levied on commoners as commoners, amounted to about ten million livres annually; at the end of Richelieu's tenure of office, a very slightly increased population was paying the government four and a half times as much. So intense was the hardship inflicted by the Cardinal's fiscal policy that its despairing victims rose repeatedly in revolts, which they knew in advance to be futile, and from which they could expect only the gibbet, the wheel, the branding iron, the galleys and, for those who remained unpunished, a yet more ruthless treatment at the hands of the tax gatherers. In spite of which, rebellion followed rebellion. There were outbreaks in Burgundy in 1630, in Provence in 1631, at Lyons and Paris in 1632, at Bordeaux in 1635, throughout all the provinces of the south-west in 1636, in Normandy in 1639.

Richelieu sent his troops to put down the disorders and continued regularly to decree fresh increases in taxation. He felt sorry for the poor; but, as he wrote philosophically, "only God can make something out of nothing, and extortions which are intolerable in their nature, become excusable from the necessities of war." Whether the war itself was a necessity, he did not pause to inquire. He just took it for granted that it was.

Beyond France's eastern frontiers conditions were, of course, incomparably worse. In 1633 there appeared at Paris, *avec Privilège du Roy,* a series of etchings, preceded by a decorative title page bearing the words: *Les Misères et les Malheurs de la Guerre, Representés par Jacques Callot, Noble Lorrain, et mis en lumière par Israel, son amy.* Like Goya's *Los Desastres de la Guerra,* Callot's *Misères et Malheurs* are pieces of first-hand reporting. Each series is the portrait of a war, taken from the life—but taken in one case by an artist of passionate temperament and possessed of an unrivalled gift for the pictorial expression of his indignations and his pities, in the other by a man whose gift as an illustrator was a gift for complete emotional detachment paradoxically combined with a gift for realistic representation of actuality in all its aspects, the horrible and the pleasant, the tragic and the farcical. Goya was, of course, by far the greater artist of the two; but there are qualities in the art of Callot which make it possible for one to return again and again to his etchings, to pore over them with a fascinated and bewildered, a half-amused and half-horrified admiration. There is nothing quite like these small, crowded, minutely detailed and yet perfectly composed and organized illustrations—illustrations of Florentine masques and festivals, of the figures of the Commedia dell' Arte, of fairs and carnivals, of soldiers on parade, of the intricacies of siege-craft, of the horrors and atrocities of war. There is nothing quite like them, because no other artist has approached his subject in a spirit of such complete neutrality, with so much imperturbability, such a degree of Pyrrhonic *ataraxia*. Callot's art is the aesthetic analogue of the personal conduct of François de Sales, concerning whom it was said that it was a matter of indifference to him whether he was in a state of consolation or of desolation. To infer, however, from his art that Callot himself was emotionally neutral to the scenes he represented is, of course, unjustifiable. Indeed, the fact that he chose to depict the miseries of war is a sufficient indication that he found those miseries distressing. Callot's imperturbability is in his style; and style is by no means always or completely the man. In art, sincerity depends on talent. A man without talent is incapable of "honestly" expressing his feelings and thoughts; for his daubs and doggerel fail utterly to correspond with his mental processes. Similarly, heredity and training may equip a man with a certain kind of talent, which permits him to express one class of ideas, but is not adapted to the expression of other classes. Intrinsically, the dry and elegant precision of Callot's style was most consonant with decorative or topographical subjects. He chose, however, to apply his talent to the delineation of wild merriment and of a wilder horror—to Francatrippa and his companions capering in their carnival masks and fancy dress, to the atrocities of a peculiarly savage war. The result is inexpressibly curious. It is as though the theme of *For Whom the Bell Tolls* had been treated by Jane Austen in the style of *Emma*. Decorously, impassibly, with a meticulous care for detail and a steady preoccupation with formal elegance, he sets before us, first the handsome preliminaries to a campaign—the troops in parade-ground order under their standards—then the campaign itself—battles between opposing armies and, at greater length and in more detail, the sufferings of the civil population at the hands of marauding soldiers, the ferocious attempts of their commanders to enforce discipline. From etching to etching we follow the artist's record of pillage, murder, arson, rape, torture and execution. The little figures in their slouched hats, their baggy pantaloons, their high boots turned back below the knee in a loose, wide cuff of leather stand there frozen in the midst of the most atrocious activity, but always (thanks to Callot's supremely unexpressionistic manner) with the air of dancers holding a pose in a ballet. In one plate it is an inn that is being robbed. In another, the soldiers have turned highwaymen. A third shows the hall of a great house; half a dozen of the ruffians are breaking open the chests and closets, and in the background, another holds down a lady, while his companion, without troubling to remove his hat, prepares to violate her; to the right, a group is standing around a bonfire made of broken furniture, above which the master of the house has been hung head downwards from a hook in the ceiling, while a son, perhaps, or a too faithful servant sits on the floor, tightly bound, his feet roasting in the flames and the swords of his tormenters at his back. It is horrible; but the horror is sterilized by Callot's style into the choreographic symbol of horror. In the next etching we are shown a burning church and soldiers loading the sacred ornaments into a wagon, while from a neighbouring convent, in the words of the rhymed caption which accompanies the plates, others

tirent des saints lieux les vierges desolées,
Qu'ils osent enlever pour estre violées.[1]

[1]. . . drag from the consecrated places the weeping virgins, whom they dare to carry off to be violated.

About twenty of these nuns are being marched off to be raped at leisure round the campfire, in the evening. One—the youngest, no doubt, and the prettiest of the novices—is being hoisted by a couple of privates into the arms of an officer mounted high on his tall charger. A year or two from now, these nuns—such of them as have survived—will have joined the hordes of male and female camp followers, who follow the armies hither and thither across the face of Germany. Half starved, covered only with a few stinking rags, verminous and syphilitic, with burdens on their backs and naked pot-bellied children trailing after them, they will march all summer long behind their masters, they will cower in the rains and frosts of interminable winters, until finally, long before the war is over, the God who has forsaken them once more takes pity and they die, to be eaten by dogs or perhaps by their famished companions. Such, if they had happened to live on the other side of the Rhine, might easily have been the fate of Father Joseph's Calvarians.

From violated nuns, Callot goes on to peasants murdered or led away to slavery, to travellers waylaid in a forest, robbed for profit and butchered for pleasure. Then comes condign punishment at the order of the general. (Callot seems, incidentally, to forget that the generals were often the accomplices of their men, that rapine, arson and murder were not always the consequences of anarchy, but were used deliberately for reasons of strategy and as instruments of policy.) To the punishments meted out to disobedient soldiers, Callot devotes five of his best plates. In the first they are merely being tortured, before a large crowd of interested spectators. But this is only a beginning. Turning to the second, we see at the centre of the plate a noble oak tree, from whose boughs twenty-one corpses are already limply dangling. On a ladder, a twenty-second victim is about to be turned off by the hangman, while, three or four rungs below, a friar holds up the crucifix before his eyes. A second friar gives his benediction to a twenty-third at the foot of the ladder; a twenty-fourth is playing dice on a drum-head against a group of halberdiers, and in the foreground yet another friar is busy with the twenty-fifth. Far off, one can see the tents of the encampment, and in the middle distance the pikes of two regiments of infantry stand up like long bristles against the sky.

In the next etching, two musketeers, with bunches of ribbons hanging from the knees of their baggy knicker-bockers, are taking aim at a malefactor tied to a post. Three or four corpses litter the ground behind the post, and a friar, whom we recognize by his pointed hood as a Capuchin, is talking to another prisoner who will soon be lying with them. Several officers and a large emaciated sporting dog are looking on.

More friars appear in the next plate, preparing more prisoners to rejoin a companion who, this time, is being burnt alive. Their crime is sacrilege; for it is they who have fired the churches which we see blazing in the back-ground. Callot concludes his rhymed caption with two lines that might find their place in one of the Cautionary Stories of Jane and Ann Taylor.

Mais pour punition de les avoir brulez,
Ils sont eux-mesmes enfin aux flammes immolez.[2]

After which we pass on to the most elaborate and the

[2] But as a punishment for having burnt them, they themselves are immolated in the flames.

most impassively frightful of all the executions—that of a *voleur inhumain*, who, on a high scaffold, is being broken on the wheel. The executioner stands over him, his crowbar raised above his head, ready to shatter one of the victim's shins; and at the other end of the wheel's diameter an ecclesiastic in a biretta bends over the naked man, holding a little crucifix close to the upturned face and praying inaudibly through the reiterated screams. At one corner of the scaffold, in a neat little heap, as though left there by a man who has gone for a swim and will be back in a moment, lie the victim's clothes and broad-brimmed hat.

From executions Callot passes to the workings of a providential and poetic justice. In the first of the three plates devoted to this subject, we see a number of mutilated veterans dragging themselves over the ground on the stumps of limbs. The second shows a pleasant suburban walk during a time of truce. The local army has been disbanded and civil law and order temporarily restored. Unemployed and lacking the means to steal their living, the soldiers are reduced to begging for alms. But their *mendicité faict rire le passant*, and some of them have already lain down to die upon the dunghills at the side of the road. More dramatically frightful is the bad end to which the soldiers come in the next etching. Here the enraged peasants have turned against their despoilers, of whom an isolated company has been ambushed by the country people and is in process of being massacred. At the centre of the plate lies the body of an infantryman, half naked; for he has been already stripped of his shirt and doublet. Over him stand two peasants, one of whom is pulling off his boots, while the other, with a great flail, threshes the corpse—again and again in a frenzy of accumulated hatred for all soldiers, in an insane and senseless effort to be revenged, if only symbolically and on dead flesh, for all the outrages suffered through the long years of warfare. That evening, no doubt, the thresher returned in triumph to his family and his pillaged hovel. The burden of loot was heavy on his back—twenty pounds of flour, two or three shirts, ragged, it was true, and much stained with blood, but still very wearable, a whole ham, a pair of boots, two pistols and a flask of distilled liquor. There was a feast after sunset, and everyone was happy and full of hope. Peace, they were all convinced, would come now at almost any moment; the soldiers would vanish and the nightmare be at an end. But the thresher and his neighbours were poor ignorant boors; they knew nothing of those two men, hundreds of miles to the west, in Paris, one dressed in scarlet, the other in tattered grey, and both of them working, working all day long and far into the night, to make quite sure that there should be no peace, that the soldiers should go on marching and the nightmare be prolonged. In 1633, when Callot drew that dry and unimpassioned portrait of the Man with the Flail, the Thirty Years' War had run exactly half its course. There were still fifteen years of *misères et malheurs* to go.

It is necessary now to turn again to the political and military events which were the immediate cause of those miseries and misfortunes of the early 1630's. In the first weeks of 1631, Gustavus Adolphus finally accepted the golden bait, which Richelieu had extorted from the despairing peasants of France, and, along with the bait, accepted the Cardinal's conditions. By the Treaty of Bärwalde the King of Sweden was hired to act, not as the *espada* of the European bull fight, but rather as *banderillero* and *picador*. Richelieu and Father Joseph had no desire to see the Hapsburg monster killed, above all by a Protestant *matador*; Gustavus' function was to wound and exhaust, not only the bull, but himself and all the Protestants as well. After which the French were to step in and occupy the entire bull ring. This policy of playing both ends against the middle had been employed in the previous century by the Papacy, which had encouraged Charles V against those enemies of Catholic unity, the Protestants, and the Protestants against that menace to papal sovereignty, Charles V. It was an ingenious policy, but not of the sort best calculated to make an appeal to French taxpayers or the German victims of military atrocities.

Primed with French money, Gustavus was ready to go into action; but the Protestants, and especially John George, the powerful Elector of Saxony, were still reluctant to join him. With the opening of the campaigning season of 1631, Tilly marched into north-eastern Germany and, in the latter part of March, annihilated a Swedish garrison at New Brandenburg. A fortnight later Gustavus captured Frankfort-on-the-Oder and, by way of retaliation killed exactly as many Catholic prisoners as Tilly had slaughtered Swedes. Meanwhile, Tilly's lieutenant, Pappenheim, was besieging Magdeburg. The city was stormed on May 10th, set on fire and the greater number of its thirty-odd thousand inhabitants massacred. Catholic Germany rang bells, said *Te Deums* and got drunk in honour of its conquering heroes. The Protestants nursed a hatred which their fear of the Emperor and their scepticism in regard to Gustavus' military ability did not allow them to express. Flushed with triumph, Ferdinand now made the mistake of peremptorily refusing Saxony's appeal that he should withdraw the Edict of Restitution, and proceeded to invade the Elector's territories. Thereupon, John George finally made up his mind to join the Swedes. Tilly fought two indecisive engagements with Gustavus, then marched away to fall upon Leipzig. Gustavus followed him and compelled him to give battle at Breitenfeld, where on September 17th, he utterly defeated him. From Leipzig, the Swedes marched south-west to the Rhineland, and there, in a part of the country that had for some years been spared the horrors of war and military occupation, they wintered in luxury, while their leader organized the now triumphant Protestants into an evangelical league under Swedish control.

Meanwhile, from his palaces at Prague and Gitschin, Wallenstein kept sending mysterious emissaries to the conqueror, offering to join with Gustavus in building up a new and greater German empire free from French, Spanish and Hapsburg influences and united by the sword under the dictatorship of the two greatest commanders of the age. That wild, enormous dream of which he had talked a year before with Father Joseph—perhaps the auspicious, star-predicted moment had arrived when it could be made to come true. But Gustavus was not inclined to ally himself with a man to whom the betrayal of old friends and an indulgent master meant so little, and the offers from Bohemia were politely declined. Against his will, Wallenstein was compelled to retain the dubious semblance of loyalty to the Emperor.

In March 1632, Gustavus moved against Bavaria. The imperial armies were once more defeated on the River

Lech, and Tilly received wounds, of which he soon after died. Augsburg and Munich were now occupied by the Swedes, and the peasants who, a few years before, had been driven to ineffectual revolt by the domestic tyranny of their own government, now found themselves at the mercy of a conquering army.

In despair, the Emperor was forced, as Father Joseph and the planets had prophesied that he would be, to turn once more to Wallenstein, who now emerged from retirement and, in a few weeks, by the mere magic of his name, raised a large army of miscellaneous mercenaries—Scotch, Hungarian, German, Irish, Croatian, Polish, Spanish, Italian—all professional soldiers out of a job, and all

> Indifferent what their banner, whether 'twas
> The Double Eagle, Lily or the Lion,

indifferent to everything save the prospect of pay, plunder, women and the chance of serving under a competent and hitherto supremely fortunate commander. The fourteen years of war and, before them the long period of rearmament had created all over Europe a class of military adventurers, landless, homeless, without family, without any of the natural pieties, without religion or scruple, without knowledge of any trade but war and incapable of anything but destruction. To these men the Thirty Years' War seemed deplorably brief. They had worked up a vested interest in it and to any hint of peace they reacted with all the dismay and fury of bishops threatened by disestablishment, or of mill owners at the prospect of a law to regulate child labour. In 1648, when the Peace of Westphalia was finally signed, many of the armies mutinied, and it was with the greatest difficulty that their commanders were able to induce them to accept the *fait accompli*. Demobilization was gradual and had to be drawn out over a period of years; but even so there was much trouble and many of the mercenaries were never reabsorbed into the body politic, but retained, as bandits and pimps and professional assassins, the parasitic character they had acquired during the long years of warfare.

With this motley army Wallenstein drove the Saxons out of Bohemia, then moved against Gustavus. For weeks they faced one another in the neighbourhood of Nuremberg. Then, starved out in a completely devastated country, the Swedes marched off in search of food. Wallenstein thereupon entered Saxony and proceeded to lay waste to the land with a quite extraordinary thoroughness. Gustavus doubled back and, in November, forced him to give battle at Lutzen. The imperialist army was defeated; but Gustavus was killed in the action.

To Richelieu and Father Joseph the news of Gustavus' death came as an immense relief. As a faithful son of the Church Militant, Father Joseph had accepted the Swedish pact with a reluctance, which had been overcome only by the conviction that there was no other way of securing the victory of what he regarded as true Catholic principles. Of Protestant alliances in general he remarked that "one should make use of these things as of a drug, of which a small dose acts as an antidote and a large one kills outright." The trouble with Gustavus was that, being a military genius of the first order, he had been able to force his French allies to swallow doses of Protestantism far longer than is good for a Catholic stomach. Or, to revert to an earlier metaphor, the *picador* had turned *espada* and, when Lutzen happily put an end to him, was on the point of administering the final death blow to Austrian power. But, as we have seen, Richelieu did not desire the death of the Hapsburg monarchy. All he wanted was, in the words of a French historian, "to break the ring of Catholic states united around the House of Austria and to draw them under the patronage and protection of France." His sympathies were not with the Evangelical League, but with "the German Catholic party, and their leader, Maximilian of Bavaria." If he made use of Protestant England, Protestant Holland, Protestant Denmark and, finally, Protestant Sweden, it was because the only persuasions to which the German Catholic princes would listen were those brought to them by Anglican, Lutheran and Calvinist armies. Gustavus had made the grievous mistake of leading these armies all too well and so becoming, within a few months, the master of almost the whole of Germany. His death redressed the balance between Catholics and Protestants, restored the equilibrium of mutually destructive forces. To those who understood the foreign policy of France, the event seemed providential—so very providential, indeed, that there were many who refused to regard it as an accident. It was whispered that Gustavus had been killed, not by Wallenstein's soldiers, but by assassins in the ranks of his own army. And who had hired the assassins? Who had given them their instructions and found them a place near Gustavus' person? Why, naturally, the head of Richelieu's secret service, the ubiquitously sinister Father Joseph.

Such was the friar's reputation that people now connected his name with every strange and questionable occurrence of the time. Thus, not only had he planned the killing of Gustavus Adolphus; he was also deeply implicated in that *cause célèbre,* which for long months was the favourite topic of conversation at court, among the burgesses of Paris and all the provincial towns, in every monastery, convent and vicarage throughout the country—the case of Father Urbain Grandier of Loudun and the nuns he was said to have bewitched. Bogus demoniac possession, artfully faked by a whole convent of hysterical Ursulines, under the coaching of their spiritual directors; monks plotting with lawyers to bear false witness against a hated professional and sexual rival; a fornicating priest, enmeshed in the toils of his own lust and vanity and at last judicially murdered on a false charge and with every refinement of cruelty—it is a story that takes a high place in the annals of human beastliness in general and religious beastliness in particular. Gossip incriminated both the Eminences, the scarlet and the grey. Richelieu was supposed to have engineered the burning of Grandier to revenge himself for a satire of which the latter was reputedly the author. Father Joseph was said to have egged on the protagonists of the iniquitous drama from motives of mere vanity. When exorcised, the Ursulines of Loudon had visions of St. Joseph, and these visitations from his divine namesake were supposed to be taken by the Capuchin as a graceful compliment to himself. Both accusations were unfounded. In the Loudun affair, neither Richelieu nor Father Joseph exhibited anything worse than weakness. Thinking to win a little popularity by getting himself associated with a case that had aroused so much excitement and (in its earlier phases) fanatical enthusiasm, Richelieu gave money to the exorcists, who had been summoned in 1633 to work upon the nuns. It was a regrettable move, which seemed to lend a certain official sanction to the proceedings. As for Father Joseph's intervention, this consisted in a visit paid to Loudun, a brief first-hand examination into what was happening there, and a hasty retreat to Paris. Loudun was a hornets' nest; the case was suffered to take its horrible course. On the 18th of August, 1634, Grandier was duly burned alive.

Meanwhile, in Germany, things were rapidly going from bad to worse. A new Franco-Protestant alliance, the League of Heilbronn, was formed in the spring of 1633, with armies commanded by Bernard of Saxe-Weimar, Horn and Baner. A royal adventurer in search of a country to rule, Bernard now set to work to steal himself a duchy. Reversing the Emperor's policy of re-catholicizing the Protestants, he seized large areas of episcopal territory in the Rhineland, made himself their ruler and started to impose Protestantism on their Catholic population. Upon imperialists the effect of this action was the same as had been the effect upon the Protestants of the Edict of Restitution four years before; it revived their will to war. Bernard's short-lived essay in forcible conversion threw the Emperor into the arms of the Spanish and extreme Catholic party.

Wallenstein, meanwhile, was working for the fulfillment of his old dream of a Germany united under a central authority controlled by himself. Making a private peace with the Elector of Saxony, whom he hoped to use as an ally, he advanced northwards, defeated the Swedes at Steinau, captured a number of towns in which Gustavus had left garrisons, and advancing almost to the Baltic, thoroughly devastated a part of the country which, for more than two years, had enjoyed some measure of freedom from military outrage. While Wallenstein was busy in the North, the Swedes and German Protestants were similarly occupied in Southern Germany.

Bernard's capture of Ratisbon led to the recall of Wallenstein, who abandoned Mecklenburg and Pomerania without achieving any result beyond their devastation. Bad weather now paralysed both armies. The men were billeted out in winter quarters, to eat their way through the meagre stocks accumulated by the civil population. Wallenstein meanwhile, pursued his plans for making peace and unifying Germany under his own sway. At the same time, with the help of Father Joseph's agents and a number of Czech nobles, he was plotting to have himself crowned King of Bohemia. Alarmed, the Emperor dismissed him for a second time. Wallenstein appealed to his officers and openly sought Swedish support. The Swedes were shy, and most of the officers remained faithful to the Emperor. Wallenstein was outlawed, took flight and, on February 25th, 1634, was murdered at Eger by two Scotch Presbyterians and an Irish papist, all three of them officers in his polyglot army.

Wallenstein's place was taken by Gallas, under the nominal command of Ferdinand's son and heir, the King of Hungary. Ratisbon was recaptured, and Augsburg, which had been taken in 1632 by Gustavus was now besieged by the imperialists. It surrendered in the following year, having lost four fifths of its population by hunger and disease. In the summer of 1634, the Cardinal-Infante, at the head of fifteen thousand picked Spanish veterans, came over the Alps from Italy and joined forces with his cousin, the King of Hungary. Rubens has left us a handsome composition representing the dark-haired King and the flaxen Infante saluting one another, with mutually deferential affection, in the midst of their troops and a large number of allegorical eagles, crowns of laurel, river gods and muses—or are they cardinal virtues? Who knows? One pearly masterpiece of flesh painting is singularly like another, and there is never even a birth-mark to distinguish Pasiphae, say, from Temperance, or Bellona from Hélène Fourment. The picture illustrates a fact all too frequently ignored by "philosophic" historians—namely, that art can be almost completely irrelevant to life, and that the study of the masterpieces of painting and poetry and music throws very little light upon the actual character of the age in which they were produced. From a collection of fifteenth-century Italian paintings, who could possibly infer the society described by Machiavelli? More often than not, the work of even the most "representative" artists shows at best what their contemporaries would have liked to be, not what they were. If such creators as Rubens, say, and Corneille are historically significant, it is not because they tell us anything about the concrete facts or real characters of their time; it is because their pictures and dramas so vividly illustrate certain aspects of the bovaristic dreams by which the seventeenth-century mind was haunted—the dream of superhuman splendour and the dream of superhuman nobility, the desire for a more than Persian magnificence impossibly combined with a more than Spartan heroism.

For a little while the King and the Cardinal-Infante almost succeeded in living up to the glories of Peter Paul's imaginary picture of them. On September 6th, at Nördlingen, they met the main Swedish army under Bernard of Saxe-Weimar and overwhelmingly defeated it. Eger put an end to Wallenstein's dream of a Germany united under military dictatorship; Nördlingen put an end to Gustavus' dream of a great Protestant German empire, ruled from Stockholm. Paradoxically enough, Nördlingen also put an end to Ferdinand's dream of a Catholic, Counter-Reformation empire under the authority of the Hapsburgs. Gallas's all too decisive victory precipitated the active intervention of France; and that active intervention was to result in the final ruin of Spain and the permanent exclusion of Austria from western and northern Germany.

In France, the months that followed Nördlingen were spent in preparing the men and munitions for an immense campaign on several fronts—in Italy, in the Valtelline, on the Rhine, in Flanders. Two hundred thousand troops were raised, taxes yet again increased and the oppression of the poor intensified. In his bare, cold rooms at Rueil or in the Palais Cardinal, Father Joseph worked harder than ever at the execution of policies, which it was becoming increasingly difficult for him to "annihilate" in the consciously realized will of God. One in particular must have strained all his powers, not merely as a contemplative, but even as a casuist. This convinced crusader was now trying, through the Prince of Transylvania, to negotiate an agreement with the Turks, who were to be subsidized to attack the Austrian Hapsburgs by land and the Spanish Hapsburgs with galleys and a military expedition across the Mediterranean. To himself and other scrupulous Catholics Father Joseph justified his scheme by arguments similar to those he had used in defence of the Protestant alliances. A small dose of Turks, he claimed, would prove an antidote, not merely to Hapsburg power, but also (surprisingly enough) to the power of Turkey. How did Father Joseph expect to achieve this feat of political homeopathy? The answer is best given in the words used by Louis XIII in a statement made to his confessor, Father Caussin. "I should like the Turk to be in Madrid," said the King, expounding in abbreviated form the ingenious projects of his minister, "so as to force the Spaniards to make peace with me; and afterwards I would join with the Spaniards to make war on the Turk." It is the *reductio ad absurdum* of Machiavellian power politics; Tenebroso-Cavernoso had really excelled himself. Fortunately, perhaps, for the French no less than for the Hapsburgs, the Turks fought shy of the proposed alliance.

The negotiations with the Prince of Transylvania and, through him, with the Porte were continued to the time of Father Joseph's death and were spasmodically renewed for years afterwards. Before they could give any concrete results, the signing of the Peace of Westphalia made the Turkish alliance unnecessary, and the whole plan was quietly dropped.

While Richelieu and Father Joseph were moving towards an open declaration of war against Austria, the Emperor was, for the first time, seriously trying to make peace. Withdrawing from the extreme Counter-Reformation position, he now agreed with John George of Saxony to compromise on the question of the Edict of Restitution. The Elector and any other Protestant prince who so desired might make peace with the Empire on the basis of a return to the *status quo* in 1627. This peace treaty, which was finally concluded at Prague in the middle of May 1635, provided a solid and reasonably just basis for a general pacification. Unfortunately, one week before it was signed, a French herald made his appearance in the

Grand' Place at Brussels and, with elaborate medieval ceremonies, announced that His Most Christian Majesty was now at war with the House of Austria.

A day or two before this declaration of war, Father Joseph wrote to Avaux that "The King's intention is to bring about as soon as he can a general peace with guarantees for the future—a peace which will be a golden age, and, as it were, a new era of Augustus. His means for achieving this are as follows: to back up by the action of several armies every promising negotiation and opening for peace." In other words, war was to be made in order that the world might be delivered from the Hapsburgs and made safe for Bourbon autocracy, with Louis XIII playing the name part, not indeed in a drama (for dramas are dynamic, and Father Joseph cherished the illusion, common to almost all politicians, of a definitive and lasting settlement), but of a magnificent and unchanging *tableau vivant* of the Augustan Age.

Both Richelieu and Father Joseph believed that the war would be short and decisive. The French strategical plan of simultaneous attack on several fronts (a plan, incidentally, conceived on a scale unprecedentedly vast) was nicely designed to shatter the Austro-Spanish power at a single stroke. One summer's campaign was to bring decisive victory. That it failed so lamentably to do so was due to a combination of causes—the undisciplined state of the French armies and the high efficiency of the Spanish infantry, which was still (though its commanders made war in a rather old-fashioned way) incomparably the best in Europe; the difficulty, given the inadequate organizations at Richelieu's disposal, of supplying widely scattered forces; and finally, the chronic shortage of money.

Except in the Valtelline, the anticipated successes were not achieved. The only considerable result of the campaign of 1635 was the reduction of Alsace to a condition almost worse than that of Pomerania in 1630. Father Joseph's policy at Ratisbon bore its fruit in a famine that killed its tens of thousands and transformed many of the survivors into cannibals. Executed malefactors were cut down from the gibbets to serve as butcher's meat and the recently bereaved were forced to guard the cemeteries against the ghoulish activities of body-snatchers. After Nördlingen, many thousands of the defeated Protestants' camp-followers went wandering in great troops, like foraging baboons, desperately looking for something to eat. Unprotected villages were overrun and looted; the larger towns closed their gates and sent out troops of soldiers to drive them away. Strasburg left its gates open, and thirty thousand of the almost sub-human creatures entered the town and, having exhausted the charity of the burghers, began to die by hundreds in the streets. Thereupon the city fathers had the survivors herded out a. the point of the pike to die in the country. To these camp-followers were added the uncounted victims of military outrage—peasants who had been robbed of everything, down to their means of livelihood, ruined artisans, destitute shop keepers and professional men. For a time they managed to subsist on carrion and grass. Then they died; or else, if they met with soldiers from either camp, they were killed—not for what they had, for they possessed nothing; just for fun. "He who had money," wrote a contemporary, "was the soldiers' enemy. He who had none was tortured because he had none"—because, too, the habit of committing atrocities had developed a general taste for atrocities. With cruelty, as with lust, avarice, gluttony and the love of power, *l'appétit vient en mangeant.* Hence the importance of preserving at any cost the unreasoned tradition of civilized conduct, the social convention of ordinary decency. Destroy these, and immediately large numbers of men and women, discovering within themselves no obvious reasons why they should not behave like devils, do behave like devils, and go on doing so until such time as they physically destroy themselves, or grow weary of the strain and uncertainty of diabolic life, or else, for whatever providential reason, discover deep in their own souls the hidden spring of compassion, the potential goodness, latent even in the worst of men and, by the best, fully actualized in the superhuman splendour of saintliness. In 1635 the wartime reaction from common decency was coming to its height, and for several years thereafter the conduct of the armies was even more diabolic than it had been at the time when Callot was collecting his impressions for the *Misères et Malheurs de la Guerre.* As the stock of goods and provisions diminished, owing to previous depredations, the methods of extortion became more savage; and the longer this savagery was drawn out, the more there were, on both sides, who contracted a taste for savagery. Soldiers amused themselves by taking pot shots at passing civilians; by setting their mastiffs, not on bears or bulls, but on human beings; by trying, experimentally, how often and how deeply a man could be cut without dying; by lashing people to trestles and sawing them apart, as though they were logs of wood. Such, then, were the first fruits of Richelieu's entry into the war. In the second year of the campaign the well-laid plans of the Cardinal and the Capuchin re sulted in the invasion of France and, very nearly, the capture of Paris. The failure of an expedition into Belgium by Richelieu's Dutch allies and the arrival of reinforcements from Germany made it possible for the Cardinal-Infante to break through the defences of the north-western frontier. Corbie and La Capelle were taken, the Somme was crossed and the Spaniards advanced as far as Compiègne. Inadequately fortified and practically undefended (for all the French armies were far away on the borders or abroad), Paris seemed to lie at their mercy. There was general panic and, along with terror, a violent uprush of anger against its cause. All the popular hatred of Richelieu, accumulated during eleven years of a rule that had brought hardship to almost everyone in the country suddenly burst out. People remembered the oppressive taxes and the Cardinal's own fabulous wealth, the ostentatious magnificence in which he lived. They remembered too, the senseless war in Italy, the chance to make peace, the refusal to ratify the treaty of Ratisbon—a refusal which public opinion attributed not to its real cause, the patriotic conviction that the French monarchy would be best served by war, but to the Cardinal's personal ambition, to his desire to make himself indispensable by plunging the country into a war which he alone could direct. Well, he had had his war; and what had happened? The Spaniards were at Compiègne and in a few days more would be in Paris. The people remembered what had happened five years before at Magdeburg and, remembering, they hated the Cardinal with yet more passionate fury.

Richelieu had been ill and was suffering under the strain of overwork and unremitting anxiety. Unforeseen disaster, the terrible burden of responsibility and now the openly expressed detestation of the people were too much for him. His nerve failed. He talked of resigning, of going into retirement and leaving others to negotiate a peace with Spain. Once again, as at La Rochelle, Father Joseph stepped in. Eloquently, in the prophetic tones of Ezéchiely, he told the Cardinal that, if he now resigned, he would be shirking the task to which a manifest providence had called him, he would be rejecting his cross, flouting the will of God, surrendering to the powers of evil. Listening, the Cardinal felt himself warmed and strengthened by Father Joseph's words. The deity about whom as a young man, he had written catechisms and theological treatises, whom he had defended against the heretics and daily read about in his breviary, heard about and even, he did not doubt it, substantially perceived at mass, seemed, while Ezéchiely talked, to take on a new reality and saving power. "With God's help"—how often (and how mechanically) he had spoken and written the words! Standing there before him in his dirty old habit, his eyes shining with the light of inspiration, his deep voice vibrant with a passionate zeal, Ezéchiely made him actually feel that the words possessed a meaning. For Richelieu, the friar was a living conduit, through which there flowed into his own soul a power from somewhere beyond the world of time and contingency.

From the general, Father Joseph passed in his exhortations to the particular. It was not enough, he insisted, to resist the temptation of resigning; it was not enough to go back to work in the well-guarded recesses of his palace. He must go out and show himself to the people; by his words and example, he must revive their courage, give them back their confidence in the destinies of France. Let him offer to lead them to the defence of their country, and they would follow enthusiastically. At the thought of the Parisian mob—the mob that had dug Concini from his grave and danced in obscene glee about the mutilated carcass, the mob that now hated him at least as bitterly as it had loathed the Italian favourite twenty years before —Richelieu's sense of the saving power of God began to leave him. He demurred, he started to argue, he suggested alternative and less distressing courses of action. Father Joseph noted the signs of this moral relapse and suddenly dropping the prophetic tone, assumed the almost brutal liberty of an old friend, a fellow soldier, an equal in birth. Curtly, he told the Cardinal that he was behaving *comme une poule mouillée*. It was an insult—for, in popular language, that "wet hen" was an emblem of cowardice—but the insult of a friend, who meant, not to hurt only, but, by hurting, to arouse and tonify. The words had the effect which Father Joseph had hoped for. Richelieu pulled himself together. Ordering his carriage, he drove out, unguarded, into the streets of Paris. Halting where the crowds were thickest, he leaned out of the window of the coach and addressed the people, exhorting them to take heart, to remain calm, to enlist for the defence of the town. The Parisians cheered him to the echo. Admiring the courage of a man who, from being a wet hen had transformed himself into the driest of lions, the people forgot their hatred. For a little while the Cardinal enjoyed something like popularity.

Paris was saved by a combination of the ardour of its civilian defenders and the incompetence of the invading generals. Instead of attacking at once, the Spaniards lingered at Compiègne, giving time for the Parisian militia to be organized and for reinforcements of professional troops to be brought from distant fronts. Then, having missed their opportunity, they turned northward again without a battle, leaving only a garrison to hold the town of Corbie, which finally surrendered in November, after much prophesying on the subject by Father Joseph's inspired Calvarians.

After this the war settled down to a dreary see-saw of indecisive successes and reverses. In Northern Germany, Swedes fought against imperialists and Saxons. Dutch fought against Spaniards in the Netherlands and at sea. French armies fought Spaniards and imperialists and Bavarians in the Rhineland. Bernard of Saxe-Weimar advanced and retreated from his base in Alsace, a province of which (though the Cardinal had other plans) he optimistically hoped to make himself the ruling Duke. In Italy, French troops collaborated with Savoyards to operate rather ineffectively against the Spanish Milanese. And from Bayonne and Perpignan yet other French armies alternately invaded and were pushed out of Spain. The first significant French success did not come until a day or two before Father Joseph's death, when Bernard of Saxe-Weimar captured Breisach, the fortress commanding the Spanish line of communications between Italy and the Netherlands. (A few months later Bernard providentially died of a fever, which settled the inconvenient question of his dukedom and left his hitherto quasi-independent army to be incorporated into the French forces.) But Breisach was only a beginning, and it was not until 1643, when the Cardinal himself was dead, that the war which was to have been so brief and so crushingly decisive really turned in favour of France. At Rocroi, the Duke of Enghien completely annihilated that veteran army of the Netherlands, which was the keystone of Spanish power. From that time, the great arch of Hapsburg empire erected by Charles V and Philip II began to collapse. The Treaty of Westphalia, in 1648, put an end to Austrian pretensions, and that of the Pyrenees, in 1660, marked the final disintegration of Spain and the rise of France to European hegemony. But all this was far away in the future. For the last years of their lives, Father Joseph and the Cardinal were directing a war which, without being disastrous, was also very far from being successful.

During the years that followed his return from Ratisbon, Father Joseph's political power had been steadily growing. Not only was he the Cardinal's right-hand man; he was also in high favour with the King. Louis admired his talents, respected his integrity in all personal relationships, and had for many years been grateful for what the friar had done in trying, sometimes with success, to promote harmony and discipline within the intolerable royal family. Nor was this all. Pious to the point of superstition, Louis XIII felt something akin to awe in the presence of a foreign minister who was also a contemplative, a prophet, and the founder of one of the austerest orders in the whole Catholic church. He admired the effortless serenity of the man who, by incessant meditations, had schooled himself into a perfect self-control. Still more profoundly was he impressed by the sudden vehemences of the Old Testament prophet, the inspirations, sometimes personal, sometimes vouchsafed to one of the Calvarians under his direction, of the ecstatic visionary. Like most uneducated men, the King took the keenest interest in this spiritually shady but spectacular side of the contemplative life. He was deeply impressed by any manifestation of the *siddhis,* as the Indians call them, the psychic powers which may be aroused by meditation and to which the wiser mystics pay as little attention as possible. In this respect, Father Joseph was not so far advanced as some of his younger contemporaries, such as Ollier, whose opinion of visions and prophetic revelations had already been cited. Even in the early and happiest days of his mystical life, Father Joseph had remained intensely orthodox; and orthodox Christianity has always tended to overvalue supernormal occurrences, to identify the unusual with the divine, to confound the merely psychic with the spiritual. This worship of the odd is a phenomenon observable on two levels, the primitive and the highly intellectual—on the level of simple credulous people like Louis XIII and the average peasant, and on the level of scientists impressed by the evidence of things that cannot be explained in terms of the current hypotheses, of a Pascal, for example, arguing from miracles to the truth of Christian theology, of a Descartes, dallying in his youth with Rosicrucianism, of an Oliver Lodge, building a religion on the foundation of evidence suggesting the survival after death of a certain psychic factor, of a Carrel impressed by supernormal healing and the power of prayer. Trained as they are to concentrate upon the events of the world of space and time, men of science are peculiarly liable, when they turn religious, to revert to that primitive kind of religion in which "miracles" play an important part. They are concerned less with the "kingdom of heaven within" than with external "signs," less with the knowledge of eternity than with power in space-time. Their religion, in a word, is not mystical, but a kind of occultism. Occultism and mysticism are present in all historical religions—a great deal of the first, a very little of the second. As a matter of biographical fact, many men and women of great spiritual insight have begun their religious career as occultists, much interested in signs, and have ended as pure mystics, mainly or exclusively interested in the kingdom of heaven, the beatific vision, the knowledge of eternal reality. Many more have started out upon the mystical road, but have never completely rid themselves of the occultism in which they were brought up. Of these Father Joseph was one. He undertook passive and active annihilation, that his soul might be fit to be united with the imageless, eternal godhead; but he also attached great importance to *siddhis* and, indeed, to any unusual psychic phenomena which might turn up in the course of his meditations. What he practised himself, he taught his nuns. The Calvarians were minutely instructed in the art of mental prayer, but were also encouraged to cultivate their *siddhis* and pay close attention to the workings of their sub-conscious. As we have already seen, Father Joseph used the convents under his charge, not only as praying machines for the materialization of divine favours, but also as prophesying machines for sharpening political and military foresight. Nor was this all. In response to the letters he wrote regarding the generally very unsatisfactory situation at court, his nuns would receive from on high admonishments addressed to the exalted personage who happened at the moment to be giving most trouble.

Reports of these revelations were written out and forwarded to Father Joseph, who passed them on, with suitable comments from Ezéchiely, to the party concerned. Here, for example, is a message for Louis XIII, transmitted by Christ, picked up by one of the Calvarians and, by Father Joseph, read aloud to his royal master. "At this time," (these are the very words of the Second Person of the Trinity), "it is essential that the King should apply his whole mind to the war, taking care to let his servants know that he will reward and punish them according to their achievements." And so on, with much useful advice on the conduct of monarchs in war time. The revelation concludes with the admonition that Louis must work harder and cease to indulge in his black moods of depression and self-pity. To communications such as this and to the commentaries, with which the friar accompanied them, Louis listened humbly and with the awed sense of being very near the source of all goodness, power and knowledge. Resolving to amend his ways, he would record his good intentions in a formal document, signed, sealed and witnessed. It was a contract entered into with his better self, an IOU made out to heaven. Fully determined to meet his obligations, he would address himself with all his might to obeying the divine commands. But, alas, in a few days his poor neurotic temperament had proved too much for his resolutions. The old indecision paralysed his efforts at hard work; the old pathological boredom prevented him from taking an interest even in the war; the old sense of guilt and personal inferiority darkened his world again and made it horrible and utterly wearisome. Ezéchiely would have to come to the rescue with another revelation, another burst of prophetic eloquence.

As early as 1632 it had been unofficially decided that, if Richelieu died, Father Joseph should succeed him as

President of the Council of State. That he might speak with the necessary authority, it was necessary for him to be made a Prince of the Church. Through his ambassador at Rome, Louis requested that, at the next promotion of cardinals, a hat might be reserved for his Capuchin. In the course of the next six years the request was repeated several times and with growing insistence. But, in spite of his admiration for the Turciad and a personal liking for its author, Urban VIII was not inclined to do what the King desired. There were several reasons why he did not want to make Father Joseph a cardinal. To begin with, there was already one Capuchin cardinal and this gentleman was strongly opposed to any move that would give him a rival and competitor within the Sacred College. Then there was the Emperor Ferdinand, who remembered his encounter with Father Joseph at Ratisbon and had no wish to see so powerful an enemy promoted to a position, in which he could be even more dangerous to Austrian interests. Similar objections were raised in Madrid. And finally there was the fact, which no Counter-Reformation Pope could safely ignore, that Father Joseph enjoyed the worst possible reputation among the rank and file of the Catholic laity and clergy. Notorious even before the Diet of Ratisbon, he had climbed since 1630 to even higher eminences of ill fame. All things considered, it was not at all surprising that the Pope should have so long refused to grant His Most Christian Majesty's petition. The surprising thing is that, in the end, he finally gave way. In 1638 the hat was definitely promised—too late; for the friar died before he could receive it. The man whom Father Joseph was to have succeeded, survived him by four years, a sick man, it is true, but to the very end in fullest possession of the intelligence and that inflexible will which had brought him to power and for eighteen years had kept him in the saddle. In Richelieu's life, as in that of all chronic invalids, there were periodical ups and downs, alternations of better and worse. In 1632, the year in which the first request for Father Joseph's hat was made, Richelieu suffered severely from the aggravation of a disorder which had first begun to afflict him ten years before. Piles—for it was from piles that the Cardinal suffered—can be a very painful, exhausting and mentally depressing complaint. Combined with his other ailments, they brought the Cardinal to a very low ebb.

In the seventeenth and eighteenth centuries no event in the life of an eminent personage was entirely private. Even the act of excretion was often performed in public, and for those whose rank entitled them to this privilege, kings and princesses were at home and made conversation while seated on the *chaise percée*. Diseases and the most intimate forms of medical treatment were no less public. Louis XIV's enemas were discussed by the whole court, and his fistula, or fissure of the fundament, was a matter of national concern. A generation earlier, it had been the same with the Cardinal's piles. There was not a corner of the kingdom to which the news of them had not penetrated. Sympathizers expressed their condolences and many reputedly infallible remedies were sent in—among others a powder invented by a Capuchin monk and guaranteed to cure, not only the Cardinal's hemorrhoids, but also the King's childlessness. When all of these had failed; a deputation of clergy proceeded to the Cathedral of Meaux and returned with the relics of that seventh-century Irish hermit, who is the patron saint of Brie and has left his name to the hackney cab, St. Fiacre. The relics were applied; but, in spite of his high reputation as a healer, St. Fiacre was no more successful than anyone else. One regrets the fact, not only for the sake of poor Richelieu, but also because St. Fiacre's failure has lost us some curious literature and perhaps some splendid works of art. One can imagine, if the miracle had occurred, the volume of odes, by several hands, in honour of the event. These would have been more odd than good. Not so the enormous composition by Rubens, *that* would have been a thing of unqualified beauty and magnificence. Robed in great cataracts of red silk, Richelieu kneels in the right foreground and rolls up his dark impassive eyes towards a heaven in which, in the top left-hand corner and at an altitude of about two hundred and fifty feet, the Holy Trinity and the Virgin look down from their soft cloud, considerably foreshortened, but with an expression of the liveliest benevolence. Poised only a foot or two above the Cardinal's head, St. Fiacre descends, much bearded and in the ragged homespun appropriate to anchorites. One hand is raised in benediction and in the crook of his other arm, he carries his emblems—a slice of Brie cheese, a shillelagh and a miniature four-wheeler. From aloft, he is followed by a squadron of cherubs, nose-diving and banking above a delightful landscape where, in the distance, the siege of La Rochelle is in full swing. Immediately above and behind the Cardinal, Louis XIII stands at the head of a flight of steps, his left hand on his hip, his right supported by a long malacca cane. Trailing pink draperies, Victory hovers over him, while the livid form of Heresy grovels in the middle distance. At the bottom of the canvas, immediately below the Trinity and a plane or two behind the nearest foreground, we see a group consisting of Father Joseph at prayer, Sacred Theology in blue and white satin and, representing Literae Humaniores, a young woman from Antwerp, with no clothes on, pointing at a marble slab, upon which we read a Latin inscription alluding to the foundation of the Académie Française. . . . But, alas, this splendid work was never painted; the bones of St. Fiacre were taken back to Meaux and the unhappy Cardinal continued to suffer the tortures of the damned.

The lowering effects of this and his other diseases were responsible in part for Richelieu's failure of nerve in 1636. Father Joseph's intervention helped the Cardinal to overcome the psychological symptom, but did nothing, of course, to remove its physical cause. After as before the crisis, Richelieu remained a sick man, much depressed by his ailments and in constant need of moral support, no less than of medical care. For the former he turned to Father Joseph, who combatted his friend's discouragement by frequent talks about religion and exhortations to a better way of life. Under the influence of these talks, Richelieu began to display an unwonted piety. He gave much money to religious institutions. He confessed often and regularly, and received communion every week. Yet more surprisingly, he composed between 1636 and 1639, a *Treatise of Christian Perfection,* in which he advocated what Father Joseph and his master, Benet Fitch, called "active annihilation" and what Brother Lawrence and most other mystics have described as "the practice of the presence of God." "It is enough," wrote Richelieu, "to establish oneself several times a day in the divine presence and to perform no action which can destroy it; for it is certain that the divine presence is held to persist until we perform an action contrary to it." It is to be presumed that, to some extent at least, he practised what he preached. The effects were evidently consoling; for, though the Cardinal had always been afraid of hell, he faced his death without a qualm and in the evident conviction that he had done nothing that merited damnation. The priest who attended him during his last hours admonished him to prepare his soul to meet its creator by forgiving all his enemies. From his death-bed, the Cardinal serenely answered that "he had never had any enemies, save only those of the State." There is something almost awe-inspiring about a self-complacency so enormous and expressed at such a moment. When the news of his passing was brought to Urban VIII, the old Pope sat for a moment in pensive silence. "Well," he said at last, "if there is a God, Cardinal Richelieu will have much to answer for. If not, he has done very well."

Meanwhile the man to whom Richelieu had turned for moral support ("où est mon appui?" he cried when he was told of Father Joseph's death; "j'ai perdu mon appui") was himself in need of consolation. The effort to make the best of both worlds—to be simultaneously a power politician concerned to forward the interests of the Bourbons and a contemplative concerned to worship God "in spirit and in truth"—had failed, and he was becoming ever more acutely conscious of the failure. Because he was quite unaware of the true nature of God, Richelieu could blandly say that "it was enough to establish oneself several times a day in the divine presence and to perform no action that can destroy it." Father Joseph knew something about God and therefore that this was *not* enough, and that actions which might not destroy what a man like Richelieu fondly imagined to be the divine presence were absolutely fatal to the presence of reality as it is in itself. He had tried to "annihilate" his activities as foreign minister, negotiator, master of spies, political pamphleteer; but these activities had been too many and intrinsically of too bad a nature to suffer such annihilation. "In all the conditions of life," he had written twenty years before, "it is necessary that every individual should be able, at the height of the tempest, to cast his eyes, when the need arises, towards the sovereign good, as towards a flaming torch that beckons to him from afar and to which he strives to come by this act of union, not indeed as one of the perfect and not in their eminent degree—not with all sails set and on the open sea of a total denudation, a complete abandonment of all the ordinary means, in the manner of the great ocean-going ships, but hugging the well-known shore, without giving up meditation and the other aids described in this Method, which lead to union." Well, he had been a beginner, hugging the shores of vocal prayer and discursive meditation; then, growing more proficient in pure contemplation, he had launched out further and further into the boundless sea of divine reality. And then Richelieu had appeared, and it had seemed his duty to do the exterior will of God by serving that instrument of providence called the French monarchy. At the beginning he had not doubted his capacity to do his political duties and still remain at sea, in the presence of God. But as time went on he had found himself forced back towards the coast, and his glimpses of that bright torch of the sovereign good became more and more infrequent. As a young man, he had described the experience of union with an eloquence, whose passionate ardour seems to prove two things; first, that he had himself experienced union and, second, that that experience of union was not of the highest order; for mystical experiences of the highest order do not lend themselves to expression in terms of the violently emotional language employed by Father Joseph. "God deigns," he had written, "to enter unto us and grants us the favour of entering into him by a mutual immersion and reciprocal flowing together, which is expressed in Holy Scripture, when God bids us open our mouth and promises to fill it. This dilatation means that the soul should enlarge the whole capacity of her free will, that is to say, should produce acts of the greatest and most whole-hearted love she can conceive. And it is not enough to open one's mouth in an ordinary way, as one does for eating, speaking and breathing; one must be like a man who, after having run long and violently after something he desperately longs to catch, stands breathless, opens his mouth and feels his heart beating, as though he were ready to die. Some open their will to God as if to eat, that is to say, as if they were to receive some inward sweetness; others as though to talk and make discourses of God; others again as if to breathe, in order to give refreshment to a spirit suffocated by this world's cares. To do this is not to love God perfectly. One must expel the life of self-will in every panting breath, one must hunt down one's nature in an implacable course towards perfection, to the end that one may exhale and infuse one's whole being, open mouthed, into the mouth of God. . . . Thus the Scripture says, according to the Hebrew, that Moses died upon the mouth of God. . . . Oh, sacred resting place of happy lassitudes! Oh, treasure of eternal repose, of which our soul bears within it all the depths and breadths, since God opens himself unto her to exactly the same extent as she is willing to open herself unto him."

Only Father Joseph's worldly side, only Tenebroso-Cavernoso was calm. Ezéchiely, the religious side of him, lived in a kind of chronic passion, almost a frenzy of zeal. To Ezéchiely it was the most natural thing in the world to talk violently about the prayer of quiet, to compare the contemplative to a frantically panting runner. All the practical mystics, including Benet of Canfield, have warned would-be contemplatives against an excess of zeal. Uncontrolled, the hunger and thirst after God may become an obstacle, cutting off the soul from what it desires. If a man would travel far along the mystic road, he must learn to desire God intensely but in stillness, passively and yet with all his heart and mind and strength. Father Joseph himself speaks of the state of inner confusion awaiting the soul "that has not been taught to control its inclinations by the virtue of Grace, which one receives in large measure during the act of union, when one is given the sceptre of the spirit to dominate one's feelings." It may be doubted, however, whether he himself was ever granted this sceptre of the spirit. That he had a very complete control of all his lower passions is certain; but we have the evidence of his passionate and explosive writings, as well as of his recorded taste for sudden revelations, visions and raptures, to show that he never succeeded in overcoming his all too natural desire to take the kingdom of heaven by violence. It is permissible to believe that, if he had overcome it, if his experience of union had been more tranquil, freer of his own intense feelings about God and fuller of God himself, he would never have consented to imperil this genuine awareness of reality for the sake of political duties hardly compatible even with his monastic vows and certainly incompatible with the life of contemplation.

Father Joseph's experience of union may have been incomplete and not of the highest order; but on its own level, it was undoubtedly authentic. With the passage of the years, however, even this experience became rarer. Given over to unannihilatable activities, he came to be possessed, in spite of his daily practice of mental prayer, by a sense of bitterness and frustration. Visions, it was true, and prophetic revelations were still vouchsafed to him; but the unitive life of his early manhood was at an end; he had the dreadful certainty that God had moved away from him. It was a dark night of the soul—but not that salutary dark night described by St. John of the Cross, not the dark night of those who are undergoing the final and excruciating purgation from self-will; no, it was that much more terrible, because fruitless and degrading, dark night, which is the experience of those who have seen God and then, by their own fault, lost him again. That Father Joseph knew what had happened to him is proved by the following passage from a letter written in this latest period of his life to one of the Calvarian Abbesses. "I know," he says, "by personal experience—I who, in punishment for my faults and for having misused the time God gave me, have now so little leisure to think of my inward being and am for ever distracted by a host of different occupations—I know how bad it is not to be united to God, not to give one's soul into the possession of the spirit of Jesus, to be led according to his will;

and I know too how necessary it is for this to keep good company, in which the faithful can help and strengthen one another. When I think thus and then look and see how I and the most part of creatures live our lives, I come to believe that this world is but a fable, and that we have all lost our senses—for I make no difference, except for a few externals, between ourselves, the pagans and the Turks."

These are despairing words, words that make one wonder whether the unhappy man had come to doubt of his salvation. And having penned them, back he had to go to the hideous work to which his duty to the Bourbons had harnessed him, the work of spreading famine and cannibalism and unspeakable atrocities across the face of Europe. Back he had to go to the distracting cares which cut him off from the vision of reality; to the bad company of King and Cardinal, ambassadors and spies; back finally to all the criminal follies of high statesmanship; to the Satanic struggle for power in a world, which he knew to be a fable, a mere nightmarish illusion, to the orgies of violence and cunning; to the dreary battles of force and fraud, waged by two parties of madmen, between whom, as he had now come to perceive, there was nothing whatever to choose. And as a reward for turning his back upon God, they had promised to give him a red hat.

X

Politics and Religion

THE nature of Father Joseph's life is such that the record of it can hardly fail to raise, in an inquiring mind, a number of questions not directly related to that biography. These questions are all more or less puzzling, but so intrinsically important that the historian of this strange career would be doing less than his duty if he failed at least to try to answer them.

The first question concerns facts. What were the historical consequences of the policy which Father Joseph assisted Richelieu to carry out? The others are of a more speculative nature and involve problems in morals. What ought to have been the attitude of a man in Father Joseph's position towards politics? What, if anything, can a contemplative do for his fellow men outside the field of politics? And, conversely, what can politicians do for their fellow men within that field, and with no assistance from the contemplative? Let us consider these questions in order.

Of the immediate results of Richelieu's foreign policy, as measured in terms of human misery, I have already spoken. Statistically speaking, what was the total sum of this misery? Popular tradition in Germany has tended to exaggerate the figures. In the later seventeenth and during the eighteenth century there grew up a myth of the Thirty Years' War—a myth more dramatically frightful even than the reality, and for that very reason more potent in its effects upon the minds of those who believed it. Recent research has shown that the old mythical statistics must be considerably scaled down. But even when all the necessary discounts have been made, the figures are sufficiently appalling. In 1618, the population of Germany was about twenty-one millions. In 1648 it had shrunk to about thirteen millions. At a period of history when the population curve for Europe in general was turning upwards, these lands east of the Rhine lost above one third of their inhabitants by massacre, famine, exposure and disease. More than any other war in recent European history, the Thirty Years' War was a people's war, in the sense that it involved non-combatants equally with professional soldiers.

Material destruction was relatively less than the destruction of human life. In the seventeenth century explosives were not manufactured in bulk and were relatively inefficient. But, without a plentiful supply of explosives, it is difficult to destroy solidly built structures of stone. What perished, therefore, was only what could be readily burned —that is to say, dwelling houses, especially the flimsy hovels of the poor. Town and country suffered almost equally. The burghers were stripped of their money and lost their trade. The peasants were stripped of their produce and lost their homes, implements, seed, and animals. The loss of cattle, sheep and swine was particularly serious. As we have seen in the case of revolutionary Russia, a depleted stock of animals can only be replaced over a long period of time. Two or three generations passed before the natural rate of increase had made up for the depredations of Wallenstein and Mansfeld, Tilly and Gustavus, the Spanish and the French.

On the structure of German society the Thirty Years War produced certain undesirable effects, which have proved to be of great historical significance. Here again the myth which has helped to mould the modern German mind fails at many points to correspond to reality. It has been customary in Germany to attribute all the country's ills to the Thirty Years' War. But the truth is that even before the war began, Germany was in a bad way. German prosperity was based on commerce and had been bound up with that of Venice. During the sixteenth century, the trade routes had changed their course. The Mediterranean lost its commercial significance, and the economic basis, upon which the urban life of Germany had been built, began to crumble away. Meanwhile the production of agricultural wealth declined owing to the Peasants' War, which left the defeated party an oppressed majority implacably hostile to its masters. Agriculture does not flourish, when a state of latent civil war exists between owners and workers. Confusion was worse confounded by religious and political division. Two thousand sovereign states, most of them surrounded by tariff walls and many with independent currencies more or less seriously debased, created so much internal friction that the exchange of goods and services between one part of the country and another became a matter of the greatest difficulty. At the same time the Reformation had divided the people, first into two, and then, with the advent of Calvinism, into three mutually hostile camps. Into this dismal Germany of the late sixteenth and early seventeenth centuries no outstanding figures were born. The intellectual life of the country was stagnant and the prevailing standards of morals and manners were brutishly low. Foreign travellers in Germany were struck by only one thing—the revolting gluttony and intemperance of the inhabitants. The Germans, or at any rate the more prosperous of them, ate and drank more than any other people in Europe, and were extremely proud of the fact. At this particular moment of history, they had nothing else to be proud of.

The Thirty Years' War completed the ruin of which the discovery of America, the Reformation and the Peasants' War had begun. Commerce and industry came to a standstill, with the result that a large proportion of the burghers lost their economic independence and became petty civil servants in the pay of one or other of the two hundred independent sovereigns, who ruled the country after the Peace of Westphalia. That great instrument of governmental tyranny, the German bureaucracy, was forged in the seventeenth century.

A ruling bureaucracy cannot function efficiently without its proper complement, a docile population resigned to being ruled. This docile German population was also a product of the Thirty Years' War. The Peasants' War had ended in a victory for the landowners; but in spite of this, the later sixteenth century had witnessed a certain relaxation in the old feudal restraints. During and immediately after the Thirty Years' War, those peasants who survived the massacres and the famines found themselves, owing to the extreme shortage of labour, in a position to demand better social and economic conditions. It looked for a moment as though the catastrophe might have at least one good result, the liberation of the German peasantry. Actually, it had a precisely contrary effect. The Peace of Westphalia strengthened the independent princes and their nobility—strengthened them so much that they were able to reverse the trend towards the modernization of German society and to reimpose the old feudal servitudes with a strictness and effectiveness unknown for generations. So far as the agricultural population of Germany was concerned, the most important consequence of French foreign policy was the creation of a new, monstrous kind of artificial Middle Age. When the time came for the rise of a new German power, the Prussians found an elaborate bureaucracy and a cowed and regimented population all ripe and ready to their hands.

Within Germany itself, the political consequences of the Thirty Years' War were almost entirely bad. Modelling themselves on Louis XIV, the post-Westphalian princes either stultified or abolished outright the local diets by means of which their fathers' tyranny had to some extent been mitigated. Autocracy became the tradition of the country.

Meanwhile, Austrian power had been finally and forever excluded from western and northern Germany. The states which still nominally formed part of the Empire were in fact independent of the Hapsburgs—independent enough to be, as Richelieu and Father Joseph had intended them to be, under the influence of the Bourbons. So far as France was concerned, this was an admirable arrangement; but it was an arrangement that could persist only on two conditions: first, that the French monarchy should remain stable, neither unduly declining nor unduly expanding its power, and second, that the Germans themselves should not be reunited, either voluntarily or under compulsion. By the beginning of the nineteenth century both these conditions had ceased to be fulfilled. The French monarchy had declined and collapsed, to be replaced by an aggressive military dictatorship that scared all Europe into opposition; and the Prussian monarchy had arisen and was in a position to create a new unified German state. By breaking the power of Austria, Richelieu and Father Joseph had made sure that, when Germany came to be united, it should not be united as a federated, non-national and not wholly German empire, but as a highly centralized, purely Teutonic nation. The final blow to the federal idea—the only political philosophy with any chance of working, under modern conditions, in central and eastern Europe—was delivered in 1919 when, instead of reforming and strengthening the Hapsburg empire, the allied politicians broke it up into half a dozen independent, but entirely non-viable, national states.

Richelieu's policy had been directed to the weakening of Spain and Austria, the disintegration of Germany and the substitution of Bourbon for Hapsburg predominance in Europe. That policy was successful—so successful, indeed, that when Louis XIV carried it to its insanely logical conclusion, perpetual aggressive warfare against everybody, all Europe united against the Bourbons, just as on earlier occasions all Europe, including France, had united against the Hapsburgs. By the end of the long reign France was bankrupt, her trade and industry almost ruined, her oppressed peasantry in a state of latent rebellion, and large stretches of her territory almost depopulated. In the economic field, private enterprise had been discouraged; in the religious and political, freedom of worship and all the traditional autonomies and checks on tyranny had been abolished. The ground had been prepared for the Revolution; and out of the Revolution was to come, along with the "progress through catastrophe" of which political optimists are fond of speaking, Napoleonic imperialism and, by reaction, German nationalism, the Prussian empire and the disasters of the twentieth century.

About politics one can make only one completely unquestionable generalization, which is that it is quite impossible for statesmen to foresee, for more than a very short time, the results of any course of large-scale political action. Many of them, it is true, justify their actions by pretending to themselves and others that they can see a long way ahead; but the fact remains that they can't. If they were completely honest they would say, with Father Joseph,

J'ignore où mon dessein, qui surpasse ma vue,
Si vite me conduit;
Mais comme un astre ardent qui brille dans la nue,
Il me guide en la nuit.

If hell is paved with good intentions, it is, among other reasons, because of the impossibility of calculating consequences. Bishop Stubbs therefore condemns those historians who amuse themselves by fixing on individuals or groups of men responsibility for the remoter consequences of their actions. "It strikes me," he writes, "as not merely unjust, but as showing an ignorance of the plainest aphorisms of common sense, . . . to make an historical character responsible for evils and crimes, which have resulted from his actions by processes which he could not foresee." This is sound so far as it goes; but it does not go very far. Besides being a moralist, the historian is one who attempts to formulate generalizations about human events. It is only by tracing the relations between acts and their consequences that such generalizations can be made. When they have been made, they are available to politicians in framing plans of action. In this way past records of the relation between acts and consequences enter the field of ethics as relevant factors in a situation of choice. And here it may be pointed out that, though it is impossible to foresee the remoter consequences of any given course of action, it is by no means impossible to foresee, in the light of past historical experience, the sort of consequences that are likely, in a general way, to follow certain sorts of acts. Thus, from the records of past experience, it seems sufficiently clear that the consequences attendant on a course of action involving such things as large-scale war, violent revolution, unrestrained tyranny and persecution are likely to be bad. Consequently, any politician who embarks on such courses of action cannot plead ignorance as an excuse. Father Joseph, for example, had read enough history to know that policies like that which Richelieu and he were pursuing are seldom, even when nominally successful, productive of lasting good to the parties by whom they were framed. But his passionate ambition for the Bourbons made him cling to a voluntary ignorance, which he proceeded to justify by speculations about the will of God.

Here it seems worth while to comment briefly on the curious time sense of those who think in political terms. Courses of action are recommended on the ground that, if carried out, they cannot fail to result in a solution to all outstanding problems—a solution either definitive and everlasting, like that which Marx foresaw as the result of the setting up of a classless society, or else of very long duration, like the thousand-year futures foretold for their regimes by Mussolini and Hitler, or like the more modest five-hundred-year Pax Americana of which Miss Dorothy Thompson has spoken. Richelieu's admirers envisaged a Bourbon golden age longer than the hypothetical Nazi or Fascist era, but shorter (since it had a limit) than the final, classless stage of Communism. In a contemporary defence of the Cardinal's policy against the Huguenots, Voiture justifies the great expenditures involved by saying that "the capture of La Rochelle alone has economized millions; for La Rochelle would have raised rebellion at every royal minority, every revolt of the nobles during the next two thousand years." Such are the illusions cherished by the politically minded when they reflect on the consequences of a policy immediately before or immediately after it has been put in action. But when the policy has begun to show its fruits, their time sense undergoes a radical change. Gone are the calculations in terms of centuries or millennia. A single victory is now held to justify a *Te Deum*, and if the policy yields apparently successful results for only a few years, the statesman feels satisfied and his sycophants are lavish in their praise of his genius. Even sober historians writing long after the event tend to express themselves in the same vein. Thus, Richelieu is praised by modern writers as a very great and far-sighted statesman, even though it is perfectly clear that the actions he undertook for the aggrandizement of the Bourbon dynasty created the social and economic and political conditions, which led to the downfall of that dynasty, the rise of Prussia and the catastrophes of the nineteenth and twentieth centuries. His policy is praised as if it had been eminently successful, and those who objected to it are blamed for their short-sighted views. Here, for example, is what Gustave Fagniez has to say of the French peasants and burgesses who opposed the Cardinal's war policy—a policy for which they had to pay with their money, their privations and their blood. "Always selfish and unintelligent, the masses cannot be expected to put up for a long time with hardships, of which future generations are destined to reap the fruits." And this immediately after a pasage setting forth the nature of these particular fruits—the union of all Europe against Louis XIV and the ruin of the French people. Such extraordinary inconsistency can only be explained by the fact that, when people come to talk of their nation's successes, they think in terms of the very briefest periods of time. A triumph is to be hymned and gloated over, even if it lasts no more than a day. Retrospectively, men like Richelieu and Louis XIV and Napoleon are more admired for the brief glory they achieved than hated for the long-drawn miseries which were the price of that glory.

Among the sixteen hundred-odd ladies whose names were set down in the catalogue of Don Giovanni's conquests, there were doubtless not a few whose favours made it necessary for the hero to consult his physician. But pox or no pox, the mere fact that the favours had been given was a thing to feel proud of, a victory worth recording in Leporello's chronicle of successes. The history of the nations is written in the same spirit.

So much for our first question, regarding the consequences of the policy which Father Joseph helped to frame and execute. Now for the questions of ethics. Ethically, Father Joseph's position was not the same as that of an ordinary politician. It was not the same because, unlike ordinary politicians, he was an aspirant to sanctity, a contemplative with a considerable working knowledge of mysticism, one who knew the nature of spiritual religion and had actually made some advance along the "way of perfection" towards union with God. Theologians agree that all Christians are called to union with God, but that few are willing to make the choice which qualifies them to be chosen. Father Joseph was one of those few. But having made the choice, he went on, some years later, to make another; he chose to go into politics, as Richelieu's collaborator. As we have seen, Father Joseph's intention was to combine the life of political activity with that of contemplation, to do what power politics demanded and to annihilate it in God's will even while it was being done. In practice, the things which had to be done proved unannihilatable, and with one part of his being Father Joseph came to be bitterly sorry that he had ever entered politics. But there was also another part of him, a part that craved for action, that yearned to do something heroic for the greater glory of God. Looking back over his life, Father Joseph, the contemplative, felt that he had done wrong, or at any rate been very unwise, to enter politics. But if he had not done so, if he had remained the evangelist, teacher and religious reformer, he would probably have felt to the end of his days that he had done wrong to neglect the opportunity of doing God's will in the great world of international politics—*gesta Dei per Francos.*

Father Joseph's dilemma is one which confronts all

spirituals and contemplatives, all who aspire to worship God theocentrically and for his own sake, all who attempt to obey the commandment to be perfect as their Father in heaven is perfect. In order to think clearly about this dilemma, we must learn first of all to think clearly about certain matters of more general import. Catholic theologians had done a great deal of this necessary clear thinking, and, if he had cared to make use of them, Father Joseph could have found in the teachings of his predecessors and contemporaries most of the materials for a sound philosophy of action and a sound sociology of contemplation. That he did not make use of them was due to the peculiar nature of his temperament and talents and, above all, to his intense vicarious ambition for the French monarchy. He was lured away from the path of perfection by the most refined of all temptations—the baits of loyalty and self-sacrifice, but of a loyalty to a cause inferior to the supreme good, a sacrifice of self undertaken in the name of something less than God.

Let us begin by a consideration of the theory of action which was current in the speculative writings available to Father Joseph. The first thing we have to remember is that, when theologians speak of the active life as contrasted with that of contemplation, they do not refer to what contemporary, non-theological writers call by the same name. To us, "life of action" means the sort of life led by movie heroes, business executives, war correspondents, cabinet ministers and the like. To the theologians, all these are merely worldly lives, lived more or less unregenerately by people who have done little or nothing to get rid of their Old Adams. What *they* call active life, is the life of good works. To be active is to follow the way of Martha, who spent her time ministering to the material needs of the master, while Mary (who in all mystical literature stands for the contemplative) sat and listened to his words. When Father Joseph chose the life of politics, he knew very well that it was not the life of action in the theological sense, that the way of Richelieu was not identical with the way of Martha. True, France was, *ex hypothesi* and almost by definition, the instrument of divine providence. Therefore any policy tending to the aggrandizement of France must be good in its essence. But though its essence might be good and entirely accordant with God's will, its accidents were often questionable. This was where the practice of active annihilation came in. By means of it, Father Joseph hoped to be able to sterilize the rather dirty things he did and to make them harmless, at any rate to himself.

Most people at the present time probably take for granted the validity of the pragmatists' contention, that the end of thought is action. In the philosophy which Father Joseph had studied and made his own, this position is reversed. Here contemplation is the end and action (in which is included discursive thought) is valuable only as a means to the beatific vision of God. In the words of St. Thomas Aquinas, "action should be something added to the life of prayer, not something taken away from it." To the man of the world, this statement is almost totally devoid of meaning. To the contemplative, whose concern is with spiritual religion, with the kingdom of God rather than the kingdom of selves, it seems axiomatic. Starting from this fundamental principle of theocentric religion, the practical mystics have critically examined the whole idea of action and have laid down, in regard to it, a set of rules for the guidance of those desiring to follow the mystical path towards the beatific vision. One of the best formulations of the traditional mystical doctrine in regard to action was made by Father Joseph's contemporary, Louis Lallemant. Lallemant was a Jesuit, who, in spite of the prevailing anti-mystical tendencies of his order, was permitted to teach a very advanced (but entirely orthodox) kind of spirituality to the men entrusted to his care.

Whenever we undertake any action, Father Lallemant insists, we must model ourselves upon God himself, who creates and sustains the world without in any way modifying his essential existence. But we cannot do this unless we learn to practise formal contemplation and a constant awareness of God's presence. Both are difficult, especially the latter which is possible only to those very far advanced along the way of perfection. So far as beginners are concerned, even the doing of good works may distract the soul from God. Action is not safe, except for proficients in the art of mental prayer. "If we have gone far in orison," says Lallemant, "we shall give much to action; if we are but middlingly advanced in the inward life, we shall give ourselves only moderately to outward life; if we have only a very little inwardness, we shall give nothing at all to what is external, unless our vow of obedience commands the contrary." To the reasons already given for this injunction we may add others of a strictly utilitarian nature. It is a matter of experience and observation that actions undertaken by ordinary unregenerate people, sunk in their selfhood and without spiritual insight, seldom do much good. A generation before Lallemant, St. John of the Cross had put the whole matter in a single question and answer. Those who rush headlong into good works without having acquired through contemplation the power to act well—what do they accomplish? *"Poco mas que nada, y a veces nada, y aun a veces dano."* (Little more than nothing, and sometimes nothing at all, and sometimes even harm.) One reason for hell being paved with good intentions has already been mentioned, and to this, the impossibility of foreseeing the consequences of actions, we must now add another, the intrinsically unsatisfactory nature of actions performed by the ordinary run of average unregenerate men and women. This being so, Lallemant recommends the least possible external activity until such time as, by contemplation and the unremitting practice of the presence, the soul has been trained to give itself completely to God. Those who have travelled only a little way along the road to union, "should not go out of themselves for the service of their neighbours, except by way of trial and experiment. We must be like those hunting dogs that are still half held upon the leash. When we shall have come by contemplation to possess God, we shall be able to give greater freedom to our zeal." External activity causes no interruption in the orison of the proficient; on the contrary it is a means for bringing them nearer to reality. Those for whom it is not such a means should as far as possible refrain from action. Once again Father Lallemant justifies himself by the appeal to experience and a purely utilitarian consideration of consequences. In all that concerns the saving of souls and the improving of the quality of people's thoughts and feelings and behaviour, "a man of orison will accomplish more in one year than another man in all his life."

What is true of good works is true, *a fortiori,* of merely worldly activity, particularly when it is activity on a large scale, involving the collaboration of great numbers of individuals in every stage of unenlightenment. Good is a product of the ethical and spiritual artistry of individuals; it cannot be mass-produced. All Catholic theologians were well aware of this truth, and the church has acted upon it since its earliest days. The monastic orders—and pre-eminently that to which Father Joseph himself belonged—were living demonstrations of the traditional doctrine of action. This doctrine affirmed that goodness of more than average quantity and quality could be practically realized only on a small scale, by self-dedicated and specially trained individuals. In his own work of religious reform and spiritual instruction, Father Joseph always acted on this same principle. The art of mental prayer was taught by him only to individuals or small groups; the Calvarian rule was given as a way of life to only a very few of the nuns of Fontevrault, the order as a whole being much too large to be capable of realizing that peculiar spiritual good which the reform was intended to produce. And yet, in spite of his theoretical and experimental knowledge that good cannot be mass-produced in an unregenerate society, Father Joseph went into power politics, convinced not only that by so doing he was fulfilling the will of God, but also that great and lasting material and spiritual benefits would result from the war which he did his best to prolong and exacerbate. He knew that it was useless to try to compel the good ladies of Fontevrault to be more virtuous and spiritual than they wanted to be; and yet he believed that active French intervention in the Thirty Years' War would result in "a new golden age." This strange inconsistency was, as we have often insisted, mainly a product of the will—that will which Father Joseph thought he had succeeded in subordinating to the will of God, but which remained, in certain important respects, unregenerately that of the natural man. In part, however, it was also due to intellectual causes, specifically to his acceptance of a certain theory of providence, widely held in the church and itself inconsistent with the theories of action and the good outlined above. According to this theory, all history is providential and its interminable catalogue of crimes and insanities is an expression of the divine will. As the most spectacular crimes and insanities of history are perpetrated at the orders of governments, it follows that these and the states they rule are also embodiments of God's will. Granted the truth of this providential theory of history and the state, Father Joseph was justified in believing that the Thirty Years' War was a good thing and that a policy which disseminated cannibalism, and universalized the practice of torture and murder, might be wholly accordant with God's will, provided only that it was advantageous to France. This condition was essential; for as a politician, one was justified by the providential theory of history in believing that God performs his *gesta per Francos,* even though, as a practical reformer and spiritual director one knew very well that the deeds of God get done, not by the Franks at large, but by one Frank here and another there, even by occasional Britons, such as Benet Fitch, and occasional Spaniards, such as St. Teresa.

Mystical philosophy can be summed up in a single phrase: "The more of the creature, the less of God." The large-scale activities of unregenerate men and women are almost wholly creaturely; therefore they almost wholly exclude God. If history is an expression of the divine will, it is so mainly in a negative sense. The crimes and insanities of large-scale human societies are related to God's will only in so far as they are acts of disobedience to that will, and it is only in this sense that they and the miseries resulting from them can properly be regarded as providential. Father Joseph justified the campaigns he planned by an appeal to the God of Battles. But there is no God of Battles; there is only an ultimate reality, expressing itself in a certain nature of things, whose harmony is violated by such events as battles, with consequences more or less disastrous for all directly or indirectly concerned in the violation.

This brings us to the heart of that great paradox of politics—the fact that political action is necessary and at the same time incapable of satisfying the needs which called it into existence.

Only static and isolated societies, whose way of life is determined by an unquestioned tradition, can dispense with politics. In unstable, unisolated, technologically progressive societies, such as ours, large-scale political action is unavoidable. But even when it is well-intentioned (which it very often is not) political action is always foredoomed to a partial, sometimes even a complete, self-stultification. The intrinsic nature of the human instruments with which, and the human materials upon which, political action must be carried out, is a positive guarantee against the possibility that such action shall yield the results that were expected from it. This generalization could be illustrated by an indefinite number of instances drawn from history. Consider, for example, the results actually achieved by two reforms upon which well-intentioned people have placed the most enormous hopes—universal education and public ownership of the means of production. Universal education has proved to be the state's most effective instrument of universal regimentation and militarization, and has exposed millions, hitherto immune, to the influence of organized lying and the allurements of incessant, imbecile and debasing distractions. Public ownership of the means of production has been put into effect on a large scale only in Russia, where the results of the reform have been, not the elimination of oppression, but the replacement of one kind of oppression by another—of money power by political and bureaucratic power, of the tyranny of rich men by a tyranny of the police and the party.

For several thousands of years now men have been experimenting with different methods for improving the quality of human instruments and human material. It has been found that a good deal can be done by such strictly humanistic methods as the improvement of the social and economic environment, and the various techniques of character training. Among men and women of a certain type, startling results can be obtained by means of conversion and catharsis. But though these methods are somewhat more effective than those of the purely humanistic variety, they work only erratically and they do not produce the radical and permanent transformation of personality, which must take place, and take place on a very large scale, if political action is ever to produce the beneficial results expected from it. For the radical and permanent transformation of personality only one effective method has been discovered—that of the mystics. It is a difficult method, demanding from those who undertake it a great deal more patience, resolution, self-abnegation and awareness than most people are prepared to give, except perhaps in times of crisis, when they are ready for a short while to make the most enormous sacrifices. But unfortunately the amelioration of the world cannot be achieved by sacrifices in moments of crisis; it depends on the efforts made and constantly repeated during the humdrum, uninspiring periods, which separate one crisis from another, and of which normal lives mainly consist. Because of the general reluctance to make such efforts during uncritical times, very few people are prepared, at any given moment of history, to undertake the method of the mystics. This being so, we shall be foolish if we expect any political action, however well-intentioned and however nicely planned, to produce more than a fraction of the general betterment anticipated.

The history of any nation follows an undulatory course. In the trough of the wave we find more or less complete anarchy; but the crest is not more or less complete Utopia, but only, at best, a tolerably humane, partially free and fairly just society that invariably carries within itself the seeds of its own decadence. Large-scale organizations are capable, it would seem, of going down a good deal further than they can go up. We may reasonably expect to reach the upper limit once again; but unless a great many more people than in the past are ready to undertake the only method capable of transforming personality, we may not expect to rise appreciably above it. At the beginning of this chapter we asked ourselves what the politicians could do for their fellows by actions within the political field, and without the assistance of the contemplatives. The answer would seem to be: not very much. Political reforms cannot be expected to produce much general betterment, unless large numbers of individuals undertake the transformation of their personality by the only known method which really works—that of the contemplatives. Moreover, should the amount of mystical, theocentric leaven in the lump of humanity suffer a significant decrease, politicians may find it impossible to raise the societies they rule even to the very moderate heights realized in the past.

Meanwhile, politicians can do something to create a social environment favourable to contemplatives. Or perhaps it is better to put the matter negatively and say that they can refrain from doing certain things and making certain arrangements which are specially unfavourable.

The political activity that seems to be least compatible with theocentric religion is that which aims at increasing a certain special type of social efficiency—the efficiency required for waging or threatening large-scale war. To achieve this kind of efficiency, politicians always aim at some kind of totalitarianism. Acting like the man of science who can only deal with the complex problems of real life by arbitrarily simplifying them for experimental purposes, the politician in search of military efficiency arbitrarily simplifies the society with which he has to deal. But whereas the scientist simplifies by a process of analysis and isolation, the politician can only simplify by compulsion, by a Procrustean process of chopping and stretching designed to make the living social organism conform to a certain easily understood and readily manipulated mechanical pattern. Planning a new kind of national, military efficiency, Richelieu set himself to simplify the complexity of French society. That complexity was largely chaotic, and a policy of simplification, judiciously carried out by desirable means would have been fully justified. But Richelieu's policy was not judicious and, when continued after his death, resulted in the totalitarianism of Louis XIV—a totalitarianism which was intended to be as complete as anything we see in the modern world, and which only failed to be so by reason of the wretched systems of communication and organization available to the Grand Monarque's secret police. The tyrannical spirit was very willing, but, fortunately for the French, the technological flesh was weak. In an era of telephones, finger printing, tanks and machine guns, the task of a totalitarian government is easier than it was.

Totalitarian politicians demand obedience and conformity in every sphere of life, including, of course, the religious. Here, their aim is to use religion as an instrument of social consolidation, an increaser of the country's military efficiency. For this reason, the only kind of religion they favour is strictly anthropocentric, exclusive and nationalistic. Theocentric religion, involving the worship of God for his own sake, is inadmissible in a totalitarian state. All the contemporary dictators, Russian, Turkish, Italian and German, have either discouraged or actively persecuted any religious organization whose members advocated the worship of God, rather than the worship of the deified state or the local political boss. Louis XIV was what is called "a good Catholic"; but his attitude towards religion was characteristically totalitarian. He wanted religious unity, therefore he revoked the Edict of Nantes and persecuted the Huguenots. He wanted an exclusive, nationalistic religion; therefore he quarrelled with the Pope and insisted on his own spiritual supremacy in France. He wanted state-worship and king-worship;

therefore he sternly discouraged those who taught theocentric religion, who advocated the worship of God alone and for his own sake. The decline of mysticism at the end of the seventeenth century was due in part, as has been pointed out in an earlier chapter, to the fatal over-orthodoxy of Bérulle and his school, but partly also to a deliberate persecution of mystics at the hands of ecclesiastics, who could say, with Bossuet, that they worshipped God under the forms of the King, Jesus Christ and the Church. The attack on quietism was only partly the thing it professed to be—a punitive expedition against certain rather silly heretical views and certain rather undesirable practices. It was also and more significantly a veiled assault upon mysticism itself. The controversial writings of Nicole, who worked in close collaboration with Bossuet, make it quite clear that the real enemy was spiritual religion as such. Unfortunately for Nicole, the church had given its approval to the doctrines and practices of earlier mystics, and it was therefore necessary to proceed with caution; but this caution was not incompatible with a good deal of anti-mystical violence. Consciously, or unconsciously, Nicole and the other enemies of contemplation and theocentric religion were playing the game of totalitarianism.

The efficiency of a pre-industrial totalitarian state, such as that which Richelieu planned and Louis XIV actually realized, can never be so high as that of an industrial state, possessed of modern weapons, communications and organizing methods. Conversely, it does not need to be so high. A national industrial system is something so complicated that, if it is to function properly and compete with other national systems, it must be controlled in all its details by a centralized state authority. Even if the intentions of the various centralized state authorities were pacific, which they are not, industrialism would tend of its very nature to transform them into totalitarian governments. When the need for military efficiency is added to the need for industrial efficiency, totalitarianism becomes inevitable. Technological progress, nationalism and war seem to guarantee that the immediate future of the world shall belong to various forms of totalitarianism. But a world made safe for totalitarianism is a world, in all probability, made very unsafe for mysticism and theocentric religion. And a world made unsafe for mysticism and theocentric religion is a world where the only proved method of transforming personality will be less and less practised, and where fewer and fewer people will possess any direct, experimental knowledge of reality to set up against the false doctrine of totalitarian anthropocentrism and the pernicious ideas and practices of nationalistic pseudo-mysticism. In such a world there seems little prospect that any political reform, however well intentioned, will produce the results expected of it.

The quality of moral behaviour varies in inverse ratio to the number of human beings involved. Individuals and small groups do not always and automatically behave well. But at least they *can* be moral and rational to a degree unattainable by large groups. For, as numbers increase, personal relations between members of the group, and between its members and those of other groups, become more difficult and finally, for the vast majority of the individuals concerned, impossible. Imagination has to take the place of direct acquaintance, behaviour motivated by a reasoned and impersonal benevolence, the place of behaviour motivated by personal affection and a spontaneous and unreflecting compassion. But in most men and women reason, sympathetic imagination and the impersonal view of things are very slightly developed. That is why, among other reasons, the ethical standards prevailing within large groups, between large groups, and between the rulers and the ruled in a large group, are generally lower than those prevailing within and among small groups. The art of what may be called "goodness politics," as opposed to power politics, is the art of organizing on a large scale without sacrificing the ethical values which emerge only among individuals and small groups. More specifically, it is the art of combining decentralization of government and industry, local and functional autonomy and smallness of administrative units with enough over-all efficiency to guarantee the smooth running of the federated whole. Goodness politics have never been attempted in any large society, and it may be doubted whether such an attempt, if made, could achieve more than a partial success, so long as the majority of individuals concerned remain unable or unwilling to transform their personalities by the only method known to be effective. But though the attempt to substitute goodness politics for power politics may never be completely successful, it still remains true that the methods of goodness politics combined with individual training in theocentric theory and contemplative practice alone provide the means whereby human societies can become a little less unsatisfactory than they have been up to the present. So long as they are not adopted, we must expect to see an indefinite continuance of the dismally familiar alternations between extreme evil and a very imperfect, self-stultifying good, alternations which constitute the history of all civilized societies. In a world inhabited by what the theologians call unregenerate, or natural men, church and state can probably never become appreciably better than the best of the states and churches, of which the past has left us the record. Society can never be greatly improved, until such time as most of its members choose to become theocentric saints. Meanwhile, the few theocentric saints who exist at any given moment are able in some slight measure to qualify and mitigate the poisons which society generates within itself by its political and economic activities. In the gospel phrase, theocentric saints are the salt which preserves the social world from breaking down into irremediable decay.

This antiseptic and antidotal function of the theocentric is performed in a variety of ways. First of all, the mere fact that he exists is profoundly salutary and important. The potentiality of knowledge of, and union with, God is present in all men and women. In most of them, however, it is covered, as Eckhart puts it, "by thirty or forty skins or hides, like an ox's or a bear's, so thick and hard." But beneath all this leather, and in spite of its toughness, the divine more-than-self, which is the quick and principle of our being, remains alive, and can and does respond to the shining manifestation of the same principle in the theocentric saint. The "old man dressed all in leather" meets the new man, who has succeeded in stripping off the carapace of his thirty or forty ox-hides, and walks through the world, a naked soul, no longer opaque to the radiance immanent within him. From this meeting, the old man is likely to come away profoundly impressed by the strangeness of what he has seen, and with the nostalgic sense that the world would be a better place if there were less leather in it. Again and again in the course of history, the meeting with a naked and translucent spirit, even the reading about such spirits, has sufficed to restrain the leather men who rule over their fellows from using their power to excess. It is respect for theocentric saints that prompts the curious hypocrisy which accompanies and seeks to veil the brutal facts of political action. The preambles of treaties are always drawn up in the choicest Pecksniffian style, and the more sinister the designs of a politician, the more high-flown, as a rule, becomes the nobility of his language. Cant is always rather nauseating; but before we condemn political hypocrisy, let us remember that it is the tribute paid by men of leather to men of God, and that the acting of the part of someone better than oneself may actually commit one to a course of behaviour perceptibly less evil than what would be normal and natural in an avowed cynic.

The theocentric saint is impressive, not only for what he is, but also for what he does and says. His actions and all his dealings with the world are marked by disinterestedness and serenity, invariable truthfulness and a total absence of fear. These qualities are the fruits of the doctrine he preaches, and their manifestation in his life enormously reinforces that doctrine and gives him a certain strange kind of uncoercive but none the less compelling authority over his fellow men. The essence of this authority is that it is purely spiritual and moral, and is associated with none of the ordinary social sanctions of power, position or wealth. It was here, of course, that Father Joseph made his gravest and most fatal mistake. Even if his mysticism had proved to be compatible with his power politics, which it did not, he would still have been wrong to accept the position of Richelieu's collaborator; for by accepting it he automatically deprived himself of the power to exercise a truly spiritual authority, he cut himself off from the very possibility of being the apostle of mysticism.

True, he could still be of use to his Calvarian nuns, as a teacher of contemplation; but this was because he entered their convent, not as the foreign minister of France, but as a simple director. Outside the convent, he was always the Grey Eminence. People could not speak to him without remembering that he was a man from whom there was much to hope or fear; between themselves and this friar turned politician, there could no longer be the direct contact of soul with naked soul. For them, his authority was temporal, not spiritual. Moreover, they remembered that this was the man who had organized the secret service, who gave instructions to spies, who had outwitted the Emperor at Ratisbon, who had worked his hardest to prolong the war; and remembering these things, they could be excused for having their doubts about Father Joseph's brand of religion. The tree is known by its fruits, and if *these* were the fruits of mental prayer and the unitive life—why, then they saw no reason why they shouldn't stick to wine and women, tempered by church on Sundays, confession once a quarter and communion at Christmas and Easter.

It is a fatal thing, say the Indians, for the members of one caste to usurp the functions that properly belong to another. Thus when the merchants trespass upon the ground of the *kshatriyas* and undertake the business of ruling, society is afflicted by all the evils of capitalism; and when the *kshatriyas* do what only the theocentric *brahmin* has a right to do, when they presume to lay down the law on spiritual matters, there is totalitarianism, with its idolatrous religions, its deifications of the nation, the party, the local political boss. Effects no less disastrous occur when the *brahmins* go into politics or business; for then they lose their spiritual insight and authority, and the society which it was their business to enlighten remains wholly dark, deprived of all communication with divine reality, and consequently an easy victim to preachers of false doctrines. Father Joseph is an eminent example of this last confusion of the castes. Abandoning seership for rulership, he gradually, despite his most strenuous efforts to retain it, lost the mystical vision which had given him his spiritual authority—but not, unfortunately, before he had covered with that authority many acts and policies of the most questionable nature. (Richelieu was a good psychologist, and it will be rembered that "whenever he wanted to perform some piece of knavery, he always made use of men of piety.") In a very little while, the last vestiges of Father Joseph's spiritual authority disappeared, and he came, as we have seen, to be regarded with general horror, as a man capable of every crime and treachery.

The politically minded Jesuits, who practised the same disastrous confusion of castes, came to have a reputation as bad as Father Joseph's. The public was wrong in thinking of these generally virtuous and well-intentioned men as fairy-tale monsters; but in condemning the fundamental principle of their work in the world, it was profoundly right. The business of a seer is to see; and if he involves himself in the kind of God-eclipsing activities which make seeing impossible, he betrays the trust which his fellows have tacitly placed in him. Mystics and theocentrics are not always loved or invariably listened to; far from it. Prejudice and the dislike of what is unusual, may blind their contemporaries to the virtues of these men and women of the margin, may cause them to be persecuted as enemies of society. But should they leave their margin, should they take to competing for place and power within the main body of society, they are certain to be generally hated and despised as traitors to their seership.

To be a seer is not the same thing as to be a mere spectator. Once the contemplative has fitted himself to become, in Lallemant's phrase, "a man of much orison," he can undertake work in the world with no risk of being thereby distracted from his vision of reality, and with fair hope of achieving an appreciable amount of good. As a matter of historical fact, many of the great theocentrics have been men and women of enormous and beneficent activity.

The work of the theocentrics is always marginal, is always started on the smallest scale and, when it expands, the resulting organization is always subdivided into units sufficiently small to be capable of a shared spiritual experience and of moral and rational conduct.

The first aim of the theocentrics is to make it possible for any one who desires it to share their own experience of ultimate reality. The groups they create are organized primarily for the worship of God for God's sake. They exist in order to disseminate various methods (not all of equal value) for transforming the "natural man," and for learning to know the more-than-personal reality immanent within the leathery casing of selfhood. At this point, many theocentrics are content to stop. They have their experience of reality and they proceed to impart the secret to a few immediate disciples, or commit it to writing in a book that will be read by a wider circle removed from them by great stretches of space and time. Or else, more systematically, they establish small organized groups, a self-perpetuating order of contemplatives living under a rule. In so far as they may be expected to maintain or possibly increase the number of seers and theocentrics in a given community, these proceedings have a considerable social importance. Many theocentrics, however, are not content with this, but go on to employ their organizations to make a direct attack upon the thorniest social problems. Such attacks are always launched from the margin, not the centre, always (at any rate in their earlier phases) with the sanction of a purely spiritual authority, not with the coercive power of the state. Sometimes the attack is directed against economic evils, as when the Benedictines addressed themselves to the revival of agriculture and the draining of swamps. Sometimes, the evils are those of ignorance and the attack is through various kinds of education. Here again the Benedictines were pioneers. (It is worth remarking that the Benedictine order owed its existence to the apparent folly of a young man who, instead of doing the proper, sensible thing, which was to go through the Roman schools and become an administrator under the Gothic emperors, went away and, for three years, lived alone in a hole in the mountains. When he had become "a man of much orison," he emerged, founded monasteries and composed a rule to fit the needs to a self-perpetuating order of hard-working contemplatives. In the succeeding centuries, the order civilized northwestern Europe, introduced or re-established the best agricultural practice of the time, provided the only educational facilities then available, and preserved and disseminated the treasures of ancient literature. For generations Benedictinism was the principal antidote to barbarism. Europe owes an incalculable debt to the young man who, because he was more interested in knowing God than in getting on, or even "doing good," in the world, left Rome for that burrow in the hillside above Subiaco.)

Work in the educational field has been undertaken by many theocentric organizations other than the Benedictine order—all too often, unhappily, under the restrictive influence of the political, state-supported and state-supporting church. More recently the state has everywhere assumed the rôle of universal educator—a position that exposes governments to peculiar temptations, to which sooner or later they all succumb, as we see at the present time, when the school system is used in almost every country as an instrument of regimentation, militarization and nationalistic propaganda. In any state that pursued goodness politics rather than power politics, education would remain a public charge, paid for out of the taxes, but would be returned, subject to the fulfillment of certain conditions, to private hands. Under such an arrangement, most schools would probably be little or no better than they are at present; but at least their badness would be variegated, while educators of exceptional originality or possessed of the gift of seership would be given opportunities for teaching at present denied them.

Philanthropy is a field in which many men and women of the margin have laboured to the great advantage of their fellows. We may mention the truly astounding work accomplished by Father Joseph's contemporary, St. Vincent de Paul, a great theocentric, and a great benefactor to the people of seventeenth-century France. Small and insignificant in its beginnings, and carried on, as it expanded, under spiritual authority alone and upon the margin of society, Vincent's work among the poor did something to mitigate the sufferings imposed by the war and by the ruinous fiscal policy which the war made necessary. Having at their disposal all the powers and resources of the state, Richelieu and Father Joseph were able, of course, to do much more harm than St. Vincent and his little band of theocentrics could do good. The antidote was sufficient to offset only a part of the poison.

It was the same with another great seventeenth-century figure, George Fox. Born at the very moment when Richelieu was made president of the council and Father Joseph finally committed himself to the political life, Fox began his ministry the year before the Peace of Westphalia was signed. In the course of the next twenty years the Society of Friends gradually crystallized into its definitive form. Fanatically marginal—for when invited, he refused even to dine at Cromwell's table, for fear of being compromised—Fox was never corrupted by success, but remained to the end the apostle of the inner light. The society he founded has had its ups and downs, its long seasons of spiritual torpor and stagnation, as well as its times of spiritual life; but always the Quakers have clung to Fox's intransigent theocentrism and, along with it, to his conviction that, if it is to remain at all pure and unmixed, good must be worked for upon the margin of society, by individuals and by organizations small enough to be capable of moral, rational and spiritual life. That is why, in the two hundred and seventy-five years of its existence, the Society of Friends has been able to accomplish a sum of useful and beneficent work entirely out of proportion to its numbers. Here again the antidote has always been insufficient to offset more than a part of the poison injected into the body politic by the statesmen, financiers, industrialists, ecclesiastics and all the undistinguished millions who fill the lower ranks of the social hierarchy. But though not enough to counteract more than some of the effects of the poison, the leaven of theocentrism is the one thing which, hitherto, has saved the civilized world from total self-destruction. Father Joseph's hope of leading a whole national community along a political short cut into the kingdom of heaven on earth is illusory, so long as the human instruments and material of political action remain untransformed. His place was with the antidote-makers, not with those who brew the poisons.

XI

The Final Scene

In May, 1638, Father Joseph had a stroke, and for a time he lay partly paralysed and unable to speak. Rest, however, soon restored him to health—the somewhat precarious health of an ageing man, incessantly under strain, burdened with responsibilities and enormously overworked. During the summer, he returned to his ministerial duties; but, knowing that the end could not be very far away, he arranged to delegate a good deal of his work to others, so that he might have more time to "keep good company." During these last months of his life he was much with his spiritual daughters, the Calvarians, at their convent in the Marais. Here he worked incessantly, preaching, giving lectures on religious and philosophical subjects, instructing in the art of mental prayer, offering spiritual direction to those who needed it. At this period he was often heard to say that "he thought more of contributing to the perfection of the humblest Calvarian nun than of all the kingdoms of the world." One can only wish that he had always been of this opinion.

In this last year of Father Joseph's life things had not gone too well for the French armies. Condé had failed ignominiously in northern Spain. In Italy, the forces of France and Savoy had had to retreat before the Spaniards. An offensive in the Low Countries had been halted by the imperialists. The only good news came from Alsace.

Here, in a starving and half depopulated country, Bernard of Saxe-Weimar had defeated successively the armies of De Weert, Goetz and Charles of Lorraine, and was now, in the autumn of 1638, besieging Breisach, the fortress which dominated the Spanish lines of communication between Italy and the Netherlands. Moving between the convent in the Marais and Rueil or the Palais Cardinal, Father Joseph followed the fluctuations of the distant campaign with an interest that, for all his words about the kingdoms of the earth, was at least as eager and anxious as his concern for the perfection of his nuns. In spite of his stroke and the imminence of death, he was still the foreign minister of France, the designated successor of Richelieu, and co-author with the Cardinal of the policy for which Bernard and his savage adventurers were fighting at Breisach.

On Saturday, December 11th, Father Joseph left the cell that was his office and moved into the cell reserved for him, as spiritual director of the Calvarians, in the Marais. Over the week-end he intended to deliver three long lectures on the proper use of that modified version of Benet Fitch's spiritual exercises, in which the nuns were being trained. The Saturday and Sunday lectures were given without mishap or undue fatigue. But in the middle of the third lecture, which began at six o'clock on the morning of Monday, December 13th, he was interrupted by a sudden paroxysm of retching and vomiting. He retired for a little, but would not allow the nuns to be dismissed, and when the attack was over, went on with his discourse, which lasted in all for two hours and a half. His sense of physical weakness was extreme, and he kept imagining that his voice would not carry to the back of the hall.

When this happened, he would interrupt himself to ask if all could hear him. The nuns replied that they could, and replied quite truthfully; for Father Joseph was making such prodigious effort of will to overcome his weakness that his voice was actually louder than usual.

When the lecture was over, Father Joseph retired to his quarters and spent the rest of the day in prayer, which he interrupted only to receive the priest who acted as confessor to the convent. Feeling his end to be near, he made a general confession.

In the evening he emerged from his cell and had an interview with the Abbess and the senior nuns, who acted as her assistants. The conversation turned on what had once been Father Joseph's favourite subject—crusades. One of the nuns remarked that it was certain that the Holy Places would be recovered very soon; for Father Joseph had had revelations to that effect. To this the friar answered that she was mistaken. It had never been revealed to him that the Holy Places would soon be recovered. All he had received in his visions and raptures was a divine command "to do all I could to rescue Jesus from captivity."

The next morning Father Joseph said mass at seven in the convent chapel, and afterwards had his final interview with the Abbess and her assistants. He spoke to them of their duties and of that spiritual perfection, that condition of continual union with God, to the attainment of which they had dedicated their lives. When he finally took his leave, the words of farewell were pronounced on either side with a special solemnity, a more than ordinary emotion.

From the Marais Father Joseph travelled in a horse

litter to Rueil, where he had an appointment with the Cardinal. He talked with Richelieu that night and, again on the following day. On Thursday, December 16th, he rose, as usual, before dawn and after making his devotions, addressed himself to the day's business. A long letter had just come in from the Capuchin missionaries in Abyssinia. Father Joseph listened to the reading of it with the keenest interest and at once dictated a reply. At ten he left his room, said mass and, after giving a few interviews, sat down to dinner. He ate with appetite and seemed in better health than he had been for some time. When dinner was over, he was visited by the papal nuncio, Cardinal Bichi, with whom he had a long conversation on matters of ecclesiastical policy—perhaps, too, on the subject of his red hat, which had now been so definitely promised that the announcement of his promotion was expected any day. When the interview was over, Father Joseph respectfully accompanied the nuncio as far as the main entrance of the palace. On the way back he had to cross the great hall, which was being got ready for the performance of a play. Here he found Richelieu, who had come out of his apartments to see how the work was going forward. The Cardinal was in good spirits and banteringly invited his old friend to come that evening and see the show, assuring him that he could do so with a clear conscience; for the play was written on a most serious theme, and was highly edifying. In the same vein, Father Joseph replied that unfortunately he had a prior engagement to "do some play-acting with his breviary"; and taking leave of the Cardinal, he returned to his room. Here he said his office, passed some time in prayer, then sat down to supper. While he was eating, his secretary, Father Angelus of Mortagne, read aloud to him from a chronicle of the crusades.

These strange tales of heroism and brutality, of devotion and greed, of single-mindedness and the most cynical double-dealing, were the last messages which came through to Father Joseph from the world of politics. As he rose from the table, he was suddenly struck down by another attack of apoplexy. Speechless and almost completely paralysed, he was laid on his bed. Messengers ran to summon a priest and the Cardinal's physicians.

On the stage in the great hall, the actors were mouthing their alexandrines into the darkness, where sat the Cardinal and his courtiers. Suddenly there was a little stir in the audience. The captain of the guard was bringing a friar, who had something urgently important to say to His Eminence. Richelieu frowned angrily at the interruption, began a sharp phrase of rebuke; then, hearing what the friar was whispering, uttered what was almost a cry of pain and sprang to his feet. The actors were silenced in mid-harangue. Staring open-mouthed into the auditorium, now suddenly alive with lights, they saw the Cardinal hurrying out between two lines of obsequiously bowing and curtsying ladies and gentlemen.

Greatly distressed, Richelieu went up to the friar's room and, sitting down beside the narrow bed, took the sick man's hand and felt it lifeless and unresponding in his own. *"Mon appui,"* he was thinking, *"où est mon appui?"* The doctors came and bled their patient. Then it was the turn of the priest. All knelt; extreme unction was administered.

Father Joseph lived through the night and next morning seemed slightly better. The news of his second stroke had been carried to Paris, where a prudent secretary immediately drew up, for the King's signature, a letter to the Pope, in which His Holiness was informed of the sad event and begged not to proceed with the announcement of Father Joseph's promotion. His Most Christian Majesty had the right to ask for only a limited number of promotions to the Sacred College; for this reason, a hat inadvertently presented to a dying man would be a total loss to the French monarchy.

Meanwhile, from the Capuchin convent of the rue Saint-Honoré, three of the friar's colleagues had posted down to Rueil—Pascal of Abbeville, the Warden of the convent, the Provincial of Paris, and the General of the Capuchin order, an Italian, who happened at the moment to be in France. They were shown into the friar's room and the General asked in Italian: "Do you know me?" Father Joseph was able to press his hand to signify that he did. The General then went on to explain that, if the sick man were to be given absolution and a plenary indulgence according to the rules of the order, he must make some sign of repentance. With an immense effort of will, Father Joseph lifted his right hand and feebly struck it several times against his breast. Then, pausing a long time to rest, he made the sign of the cross. His eyes filled with tears. Absolution was given, and the General and Provincial retired, leaving Father Pascal, who remained with the sick man to the last.

Later in the day an even more eminent and wholly unexpected visitor presented himself, no less a person than Gaston of Orleans. For the last fifteen years Gaston had been leading and betraying conspiracies against the royal authority, and on several of these occasions Father Joseph had played the part of an intermediary between the King and his despicable young brother. In the course of these encounters, Gaston had conceived a great liking and respect for the friar. This death-bed visit was motivated by a genuine affection.

Towards evening came the priest who had received Father Joseph's general confession at the Marais, four days before. Taking his place at the bedside, he told his penitent that the time had now come for him to put aside all thought of creatures and to set his mind solely upon God —the God to whom he would so soon be required to render an account of all his acts. As he spoke of repentance, the friar's eyes filled once again with tears and suddenly, to the amazement of the physicians, who thought for a moment that this might be a sign of recovery, he found his voice. "Render an account," he whispered, echoing the confessor's final phrase.

"Yes," the priest insisted, "you will have to render an account; for God is your judge, and will weigh you in the balance."

Still weeping, Father Joseph continued to repeat the same three words. "Render an account," he said again and again, "render an account."

Hopeful now of saving their patient, the doctors redoubled their efforts. Opening a vein, they let a great quantity of blood; but the effect was contrary to what they had expected. The ability to move his limbs, which in some slight measure he had recovered during the day, began, as night advanced, to leave him.

Father Angelus, whom, as a youth, Father Joseph had converted and who, for almost twenty years, had been his constant companion, knelt beside the bed and, with the

BREAKING ON THE WHEEL

Etching by Jacques Callot

SOLDIERS WAYLAID BY PEASANTS

Etching by Jacques Callot

patience of one who teaches a child, helped the dying man to make a few last little gestures of contrition, little signs of love for God and confidence in the divine mercy. A crucifix was placed in Father Joseph's hands, and he was able once or twice to bring it to his lips. In spite of the creeping advance of paralysis, the power of speech still remained—just enough power to permit of the continued repetition of the same single phrase: "Render an account, render an account."

Towards midnight the hands lost their ability to hold the crucifix. Seeing that the end was very near, Father Angelus asked his old friend to give him his blessing. For a time there was no movement in the stiffening body; then, slowly, one finger of the right hand was lifted a little way from the sheet and after a few seconds dropped back, never to move again. The death agony lasted through the night, and it was not till the early morning of Saturday, December 18th, that the heart finally stopped beating.

In the interval between the friar's death and his interment, Charles de Condren, the man who had succeeded Bérulle as General of the Oratory and one of the most beautifully saintly figures of his age, was asked if he would preach the funeral sermon. To the highly placed personage who brought the invitation Condren answered that he could not, with a good conscience, praise a man who had been the instrument of the Cardinal's passions, and who was hated by the whole of France.

Father Joseph's body was buried in the church of the Capuchins, in a grave near the steps of the altar next to that of the great gentleman friar who had received him into the order, Ange de Joyeuse. A few days after the funeral, all Paris was chuckling over the exploit of an anonymous practical joker. On the slab which covered what remained of the man who had once been called the perfect Capuchin, an unknown hand had chalked this distich:

Passant, n'est-ce pas chose étrange
Qu'un démon soit près d'un ange?[1]

It is always easier to make an epigram about a man than to understand him.

[1] Passer-by, is it not a strange thing that a demon should be next to an angel?

Appendix

THE posthumous history of Father Joseph is so odd and improbable that it deserves to be made the subject of a full-length study. Within ten years of his death a long and detailed biography of the Grey Eminence was written by a certain Lepré-Balin, who was a friend of Father Angelus of Mortagne and had access to all the relevant documents in the possession of the Capuchins, as well as to the entire collection of Father Joseph's state papers. These last he put together and edited under the title of "Supplement to the History of France." For some unexplained reason, neither the biography nor the Supplement was ever published. The manuscript of the first remained in the archives of the Calvarian nuns, whence it passed into the keeping of the Capuchins of Paris. That of the second disappeared for two hundred and fifty years and was discovered, about 1890, by Gustave Fagniez in the library of the British Museum. How it originally found its way to England is not clear; all that is known for certain is that, early in the nineteenth century it belonged to the Earl of Bridgewater and that from his collection it passed to that of Tom Moore.

Meanwhile the only biographies of Father Joseph to be published were the three put out in the first years of the eighteenth century by a singular personage called the Abbé Richard. An unbeneficed priest in sore straits for money, Richard had his eye on a certain canonry of Notre-Dame of Paris, which was in the gift of a M. du Tremblay, who was the grandson of Father Joseph's younger brother, Charles. To ingratiate himself with the nephew, Richard conceived the plan of writing a flattering biography of the great-uncle. Obtaining access to the manuscript of Lepré-Balin's Life, he quickly turned out a little book which, so far as it goes, is tolerably accurate. It was duly published, and the Abbé waited for his reward. It did not come. Furious, Richard decided to take his revenge. Into the text of his first eulogistic biography he interpolated a number of new paragraphs, in which Father Joseph was accused of every crime from murder to simony. The new version was published anonymously under the alluring title of *Le Véritable Père Joseph.* Needless to say, this "true" Father Joseph sold a great deal better than Father Joseph *tout court.* But the sums which could be picked up from the booksellers were paltry in comparison with the income from that delicious canonry. The Abbé had an idea of genius. Rushing to his desk he penned an impassioned refutation of his own calumnies. This refutation was duly printed, and excited a certain interest in the public, but left the du Tremblay family unmoved. The Reverend Richard died in penury.

For more than a century and a half historians were content to take Richard's flattery, calumny and refutation, add them together and divide by three. The result of this operation was supposed to be a true picture of the Grey Eminence.

In the middle of the nineteenth century, a learned archivist, called M. Pelletier, became interested in Father Joseph and spent years collecting the materials for a new and adequate biography. This huge preliminary labour was practically completed when Napoleon III went to war with Prussia. During the Commune of 1871, the building in which M. Pelletier had stored the vast accumulations of his notes was burnt to the ground. It began to look as though some higher power were concerned to keep the world in ignorance of Father Joseph.

This impression, it must be confessed, was not dispelled even in 1894, when Gustave Fagniez published his huge work, *Le Père Joseph et Richelieu.* For though Fagniez had made extensive researches, though he had been the happy discoverer of Lepré-Balin's "Supplement," his book cannot be said to do much to illuminate its subject. Not light, but darkness visible, is what it sheds on the scene. *Le Père Joseph et Richelieu* consists of twelve hundred pages of miscellaneous historical documents, very badly arranged and published without an index. The book is not a biography (for Fagniez's concern was with political history, and he was hardly even aware of Father Joseph as a living man); it is a collection of raw materials for a biography and as such it must, unfortunately, be read by anyone who is interested in the Grey Eminince.

At the time when Fagniez published his book, a learned young ecclesiastic, the Abbé (afterwards Canon) Dedouvres, had just begun what was to be a lifetime of research on Father Joseph. Dedouvres, who died about 1929, was professor of Latin at a Catholic university in the west of France, a post which he combined with the duties of almoner to the Congregation of Our Lady of Calvary, in whose archives are preserved its founder's unpublished papers—three or four million words of diversified documentation, at which, from 1638 to the present day, no scholar, with the exception of Dedouvres, has ever so much as glanced.

The relations between the two historians of Father Joseph were anything but cordial. Fagniez felt that he had a right to an absolute monopoly of Grey Eminences, a corner in political Capuchins. So acute was his sense of proprietorship that for years he absolutely refused to divulge the whereabouts of Lepré-Balin's precious "Supplement," which he had had the luck to discover in the British Museum. The cream of Lepré-Balin went into his *Le Père Joseph et Richelieu*; but he was determined that no other historian should get a drop even of the milk. To all requests for information he returned a blank refusal. What, then, was his rage when young Dedouvres rediscovered the "Supplement" on his own account and published the fact to the whole learned world! A few years later the Abbé added insult to injury. Fagniez had declared that the Turciad was irretrievably lost. Dedouvres, by a process of pure inductive ratiocination, came to the conclusion that the poem must be extant and in the Barberini library at Rome. A post-card to the librarian brought back the answer that there, in effect, it was. The rules of the game demanded that Fagniez should congratulate his rival on this triumph; but his real feelings found vent in the ferocious review he wrote of the Abbé's next brochure.

Up to this time the story is like something out of Balzac—the Balzac of *Le Curé de Tours*. But from now on it becomes pure Anatole France. For about forty years the Abbé worked away at Father Joseph, and in the course of those years he published fully twenty articles and pamphlets about his hero. But the articles appeared in parish magazines and provincial Catholic quarterlies; the pamphlets were issued in editions of two or three hundred by country printers in obscure sub-prefectures. At the time of their author's death only four of these twenty items had found their way even into the Bibliothèque Nationale. Lord Acton himself hardly provides a finer example of learning for learning's sake and not for the public's.

In the later years of his life Canon Dedouvres decided to work up his notes and articles into a continuous biography of Father Joseph. I need hardly add that death interrupted him long before his task was finished. Here, if one were writing a novel, one would conclude with a delightful little chapter describing the gradual annihilation of the old scholar's life-work—Father Joseph's childhood gnawed up by mice to line their nests, his spiritual directions to the Calvarians serving as toilet paper, the Diet of Ratisbon used by the cat's meat man to wrap his wares. And so on. But history is rarely so definitive as fiction. In 1932 the two volumes which Dedouvres had actually completed were published. In them, the biography of Father Joseph was brought down, in great detail, to the siege of La Rochelle. But the powers which for so long had been so careful to preserve a darkness round the memory of the Capuchin, saw to it that even this partial lifting of the veil should enlighten only the smallest possible number of readers. Like the pamphlets and articles, the unfinished book was published in the provinces and in a very small edition. Even among professional historians few have read or even heard of it. And yet the book deserves to be known; for though it is by no means what one would call a great biography, it succeeds in giving the reader some impression of the enigmatic figure, about whom it is written. Which is more than can be said of Fagniez's *Le Père Joseph et Richelieu.*

The present volume is based, in the main, upon the materials contained in the two thousand pages of Fagniez and Dedouvres. Many things have been omitted as intrinsically without much interest and, above all, as irrelevant to the dominant theme of this book, which is the history of a man who tried to reconcile politics with spiritual religion. Thus, I have made no mention of Father Joseph's dealings with the extreme Gallicans of his day; nor of his collision with Saint-Cyran, the fascinating, pathetic and absurd pseudo-saint of Port-Royal; nor of his campaigns against those precursors of the Quietists, the Illuminés. Nor has it seemed to me necessary to reproduce the details, still extant, of Father Joseph's negotiations or the minutes of his despatches. In themselves, these accounts of diplomatic haggling and chicanery are about as interesting as would be the shorthand record of the discussion between two peasants over the merits and price of a broken-winded horse. In such dismal transactions there is nothing historically significant except their outcome and its generally disastrous consequences.

For the religious history of Father Joseph's time I have relied on the first five volumes of Brémond's *Histoire du Sentiment Religieux en France.* This book, which is at once an historical narrative, a critical commentary and an anthology culled from a practically inaccessible literature, ranks as one of the most valuable works of scholarship produced in the present century. To anyone who is interested in the psychology of human beings as they normally are and as they might be if they chose, Brémond's volumes constitute an indispensable source book. They are no less indispensable to those who, more modestly, take an interest in French seventeenth-century history.

Only a few of the significant religious writings of our period have been reprinted and, of most of them, the early editions are hard to find even in important libraries. I count myself very fortunate in having been able to lay my hands on a copy of the seventeenth-century Italian translation of Benet Fitch's *Rule of Perfection*. Extremely interesting in itself, this book is also of great historical significance; for from it, as I have tried to show, Bérulle and his followers derived the principles of their personalistic pseudo-mysticism, and Father Joseph learned that technique of "active annihilation," by means of which he hoped to be able to disinfect his politics.

No attempt has been made in this book to depict in any detail the political and social background to Father Joseph's career. Historical events and conditions have been described as briefly as possible and only in so far as they were strictly relevant to the main theme.

In conclusion, I would like to express my gratitude for much valuable assistance rendered by the Librarian and staff of the library of the University of California at Los Angeles.

Index